THE DOC SCHNEIDER SONGBOOK

MUP-P546

Published by Mercer University Press
1501 Mercer University Drive
Macon, Georgia 31207

Special First Edition

9 8 7 6 5 4 3 2 1

Books published by Mercer University Press are printed
on acid-free paper that meets the requirements of the American
National Standard for Information Sciences—Permanence
of Paper for Printed Library Materials.

Book design by Burt&Burt

ISBN 978-088146-620-1

Cataloging-in-Publication Data
is available from the Library of Congress

Printed in Canada

THE DOC SCHNEIDER SONGBOOK

HOMEMADE SONGS: 1974-2016

RICHARD A. SCHNEIDER

Includes Poems in the Cupboard and Other Stuff

MERCER UNIVERSITY PRESS
MACON, GEORGIA
2016

TABLE OF CONTENTS

for Helen

we're still laughing and telling our stories

a, b, c, d, and e

PREFACE

"—and here's no great matter," T. S. Eliot wrote in *The Love Song of J. Alfred Prufrock.* Although that poem was published 101 years ago, I feel certain Eliot had in mind this volume that you now hold in your hands.

I waited a long time for someone to ask for a book of my songs. I could not wait any longer. I was having trouble remembering the words and chords and I needed a songbook. So I went ahead and bit the bullet and asked for it myself. Mercer Press assured me that no one else had any interest but I told them you never know. They said yes we do. Oh, well.

My love of music comes from my mother—who still loves everything from the crooners to show tunes to the newest of the new. My first guitar came from my father who brought it home in a brown paper bag when I was 14. There was more in that paper bag than I ever dreamed of.

I feel like I have been out forever trick or treating and I have finally gotten home to pour out my treasures and look them over. You can come look at them too. Take anything you want.

I have enjoyed writing these songs—and performing them—over the last 40 odd years. They have become my cool companions and they have been the bridges to all the loves of my life and all the friends who have filled up my heart. These are my homemade songs—written by a musically illiterate and inept musician—but somehow they sing just fine just the same.

Anyway, here they are. Only thing I got to show. If it turns out that you secretly enjoy this book, rest assured that your secret is safe with me. After all, I am a lawyer by day and night and a songwriter in between. I know how to keep things confidential.

Doc Schneider
August 2016
Atlanta, Georgia

PS: Let me offer a word about the organization of this songbook.

*First, there are three sections of sheet music corresponding to my three officially released CDs—**Choices & Chances**, **Second Chances**, and **Songs & Stories Live**.*

*After the first three sections, there is a section called **Songs in the Garden**—which is a selection of sheet music and lead sheets for songs that have not yet made it to an official album release. I have not included all of the songs I have written and recorded but, for goodness sake, we needed to draw a line somewhere. At least that is what my editor said. You can find recordings of some of these bootleg songs on my website at www.legalguitarist.com.*

*After Songs in the Garden is a section called **Behind the Curtain** where I include scraps of this and that to illustrate the process of songwriting.*

*Finally, in the deep end of the book, I go off the deep end and include **Poems in the Cupboard** and **Little Tall Tales**—a handful of poems and a couple of stories that I came across while gathering the songs included here and decided to let them come along for the ride.*

DOC
Schneider
choices & chances
If I had my choices...might have missed

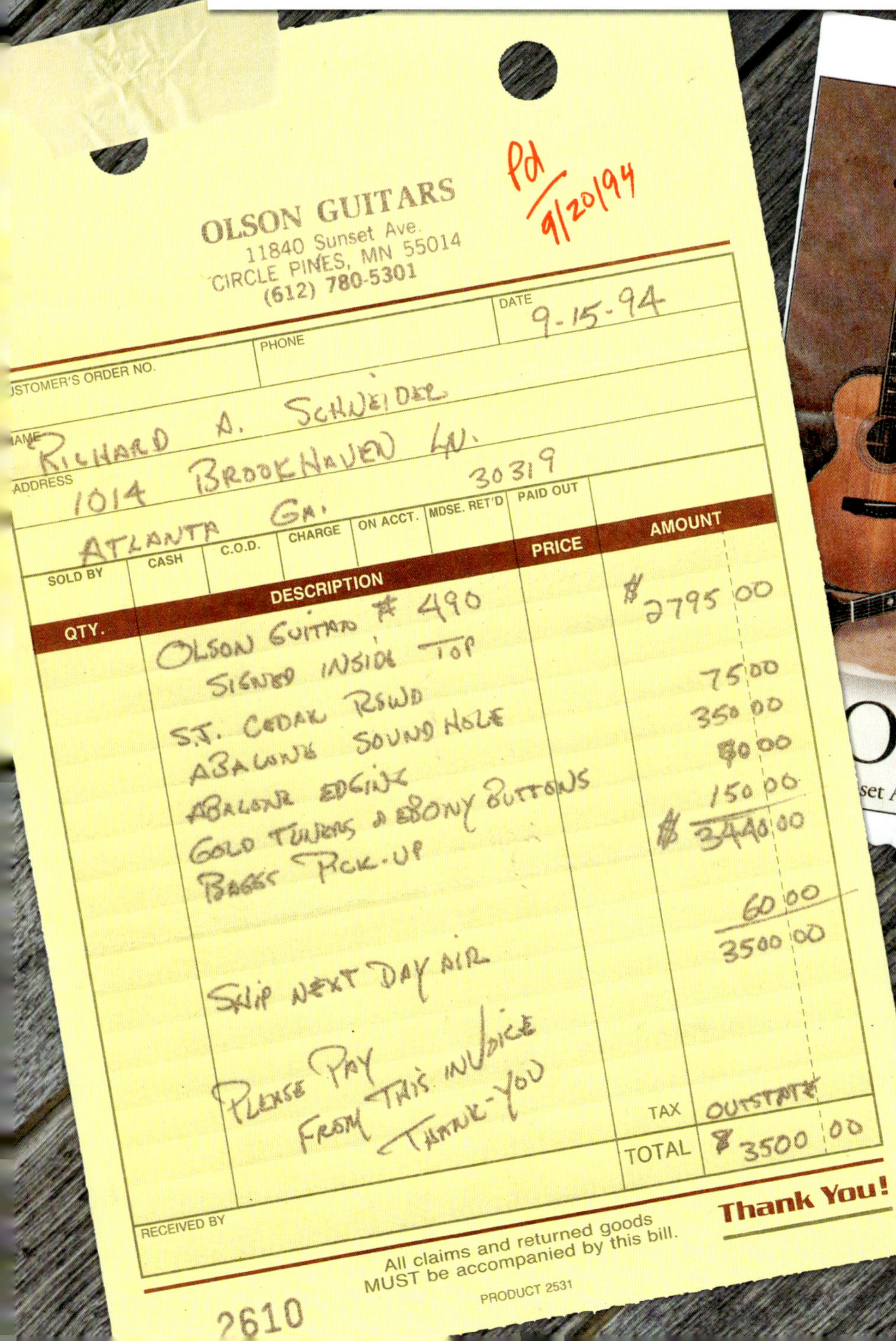

OLSON GUITARS
11840 Sunset Ave.
CIRCLE PINES, MN 55014
(612) 780-5301

Pd 9/20/94

CUSTOMER'S ORDER NO.	PHONE	DATE 9-15-94

NAME Richard A. Schneider
ADDRESS 1014 Brookhaven Ln.
Atlanta Ga. 30319

SOLD BY	CASH	C.O.D.	CHARGE	ON ACCT.	MDSE. RET'D	PAID OUT

QTY.	DESCRIPTION	PRICE	AMOUNT
	Olson Guitar # 490		$2795 00
	Signed inside top		
	S.J. Cedar Rswd		75 00
	Abalone Sound Hole		350 00
	Abalone edging		80 00
	Gold Tuners & Ebony Buttons		150 00
	Baggs Pick-up		$3440 00
			60 00
	Ship next day air		3500 00
	Please pay from this invoice Thank-you		
		TAX	Outstate
		TOTAL	$3500 00

RECEIVED BY

Thank You!

All claims and returned goods MUST be accompanied by this bill.

PRODUCT 2531

2610

Look What This Brings

Words and Music by Doc Schneider

Tuning: D A D G A D

2

Bm7♭13 A7sus4 Gsus2 Dsus4
Look what this brings flying all the way from Minnesota

Dmaj11/F♯ Gsus2 Em11 A7sus4
Straight to my heart, all the way home

C6(9) Gadd9/B Gsus2 A7sus4 Dsus2(4)
Just like a ray of light shot through the sky at night

D/A Gsus2 D/A Gsus2
Light up the room, light me up too

D/A A7sus4 D Gsus2 D Gsus2
Fly me away with you

D/A A7sus4 D Gsus2 D
Fly me away with you

Wherever You Are

Words and Music by Doc Schneider

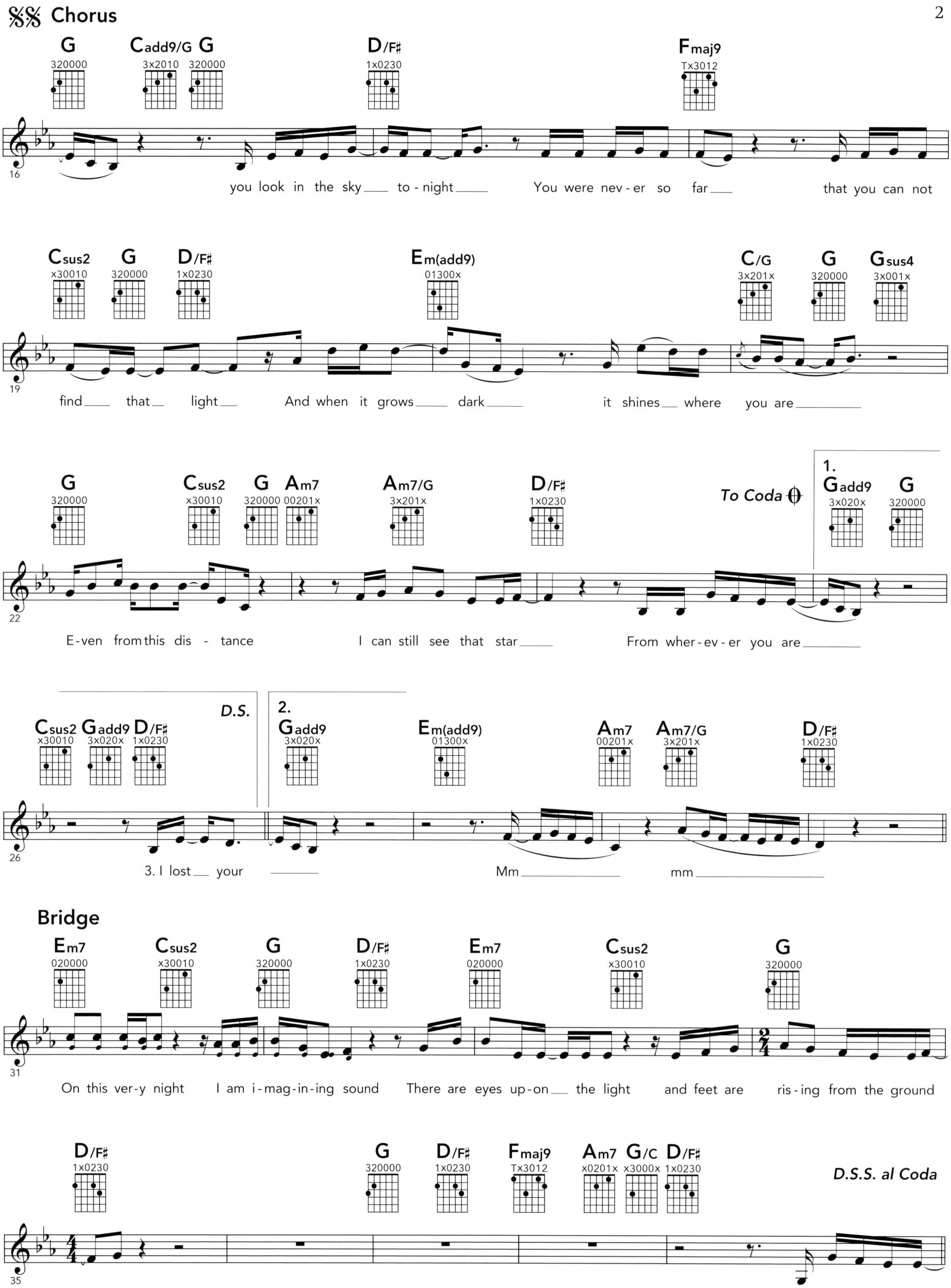
%% Chorus
G Cadd9/G G D/F♯ Fmaj9
you look in the sky to-night You were nev-er so far that you can not
Csus2 G D/F♯ Em(add9) C/G G Gsus4
find that light And when it grows dark it shines where you are
G Csus2 G Am7 Am7/G D/F♯
To Coda
1. Gadd9 G
E-ven from this dis - tance I can still see that star From wher-ev-er you are
Csus2 Gadd9 D/F♯
D.S.
2. Gadd9 Em(add9) Am7 Am7/G D/F♯
3. I lost your
Mm
mm
Bridge
Em7 Csus2 G D/F♯ Em7 Csus2 G
On this ver-y night I am i-mag-in-ing sound There are eyes up-on the light and feet are ris-ing from the ground
D/F♯ G D/F♯ Fmaj9 Am7 G/C D/F♯
D.S.S. al Coda

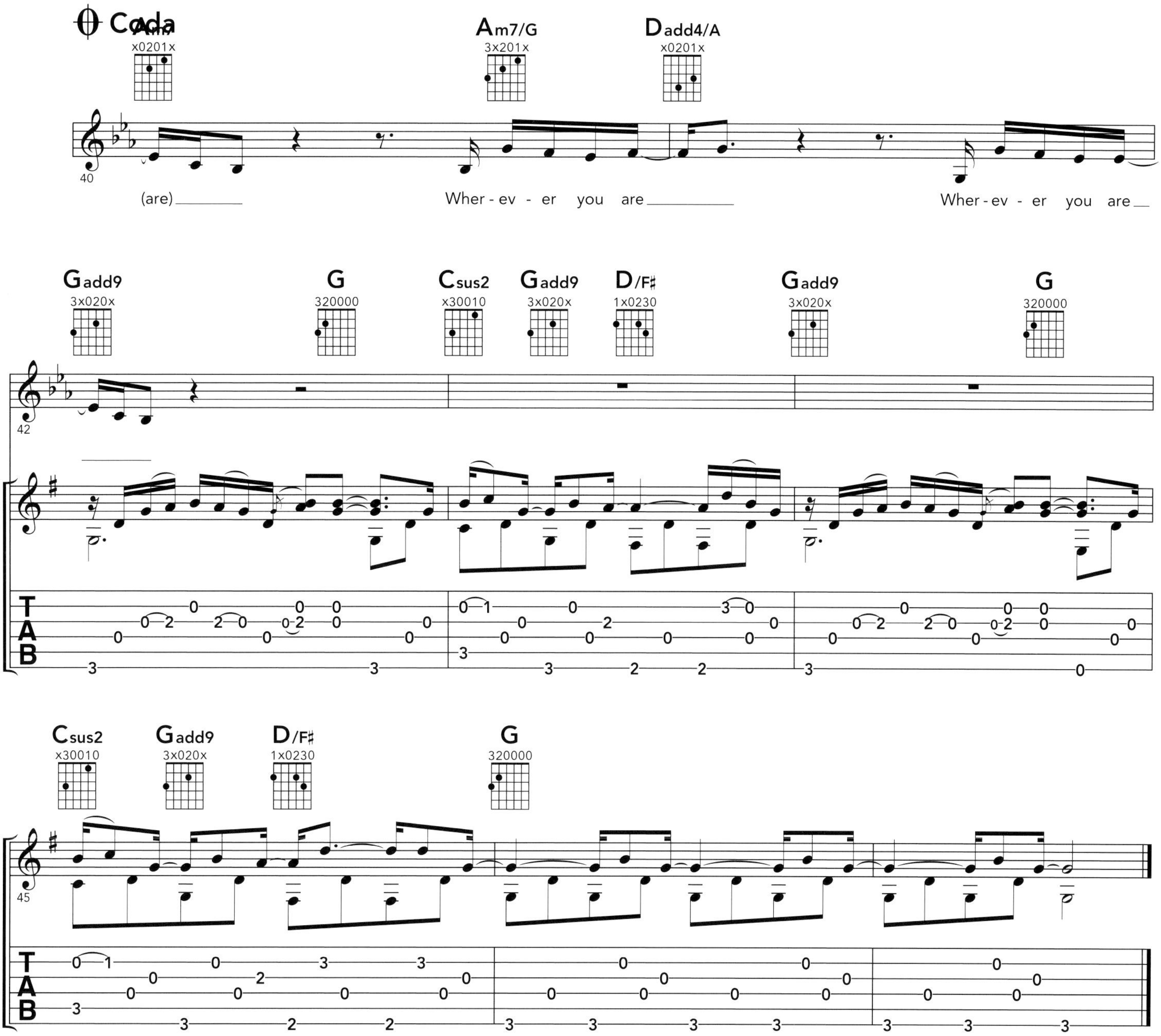

Intro

Gadd9 G Csus2 Gadd9 D/F♯
Gadd9 G Csus2 Gadd9 D/F♯ G

1\.
G Em(add9)
I close my eyes to this December night
Am7 Am7/G D/F♯
In this cold air I turn my face up to the light
G Em(add9)
I feel your lips floating down from years ago
Csus2 G Csus2 D/F♯
I feel my pain____ melting like the falling snow

2\.
G Em(add9)
I feel my feet rising from the ground
Am7 Am7/G D/F♯
This busy street, it hardly makes a sound
G Em(add9)
I hear my voice promising forever
Csus2 G Csus2 D/F♯
And though we left, this moment left me never…

Chorus

G Cadd9/G G D/F♯
Wherever you are,_______ you look in the sky tonight

Fmaj9 Csus2 G D/F♯
You were never so far that you cannot find that light

Em(add9) C/G G Gsus4
And when it grows dark, it shines where you are

G Csus2 G Am7 Am7/G D/F♯
Even from this distance,_ I can still see that star

Gadd9 G Csus2 Gadd9 D/F♯
From wherever you are

G Em(add9)
3. I lost your face somewhere long ago

Am7 Am7/G D/F♯
And of your eyes, the color now is all I know

G Em(add9)
But on this night, this falling snow can bring you back

C D/F♯
And in this light, all the rest just fades to black

G Em(add9)
4. It is the hope that I remember here

Am7 Am7/G D/F♯
It is the life that I remember breaking clear

G Em(add9)
It was your hand I felt within my hand

C G C D/F♯
A burning warm burning down this frozen land

Repeat Chorus

Gadd9
…From wherever you are

Bridge

Em7 Csus2 G D/F♯
On this very night I am imagining sound

Em7 Csus2 G D/F♯
There are eyes upon the light and feet are rising from the ground

G D/F♯ Fmaj9 Am7 G/C D/F♯

Repeat Chorus

Gadd9 G Csus2 Gadd9 D/F♯ G

Original Chords (standard tuning, no capo)

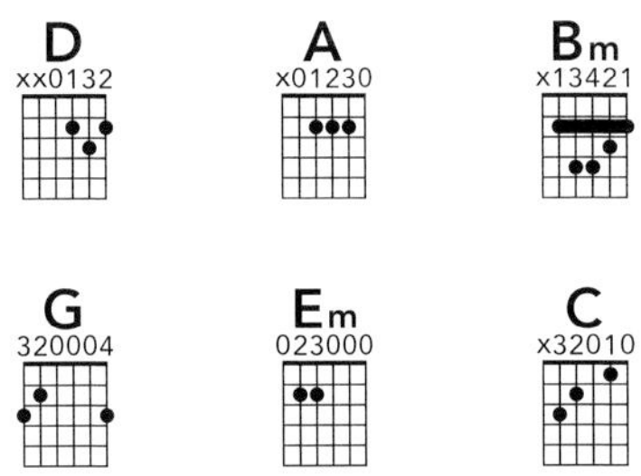

Intro

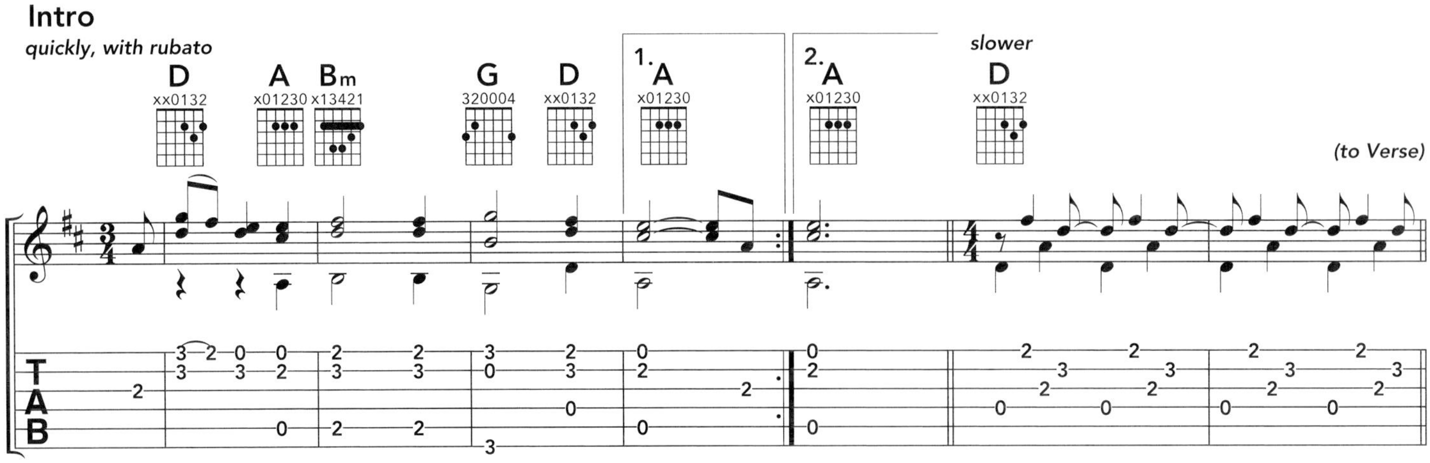

5

Intro

D A Bm G D A
D A Bm G D A D

D
1. I close my eyes to this December night

Em A
In this cold air I turn my face up to the light

D Bm
I feel your lips floating down from years ago

G A
I feel my pain melting like the falling snow

D
2. I feel my feet rising from the ground

Em A
This busy street hardly makes a sound

D Bm
I hear my voice promising forever

G A
And though we left, this moment left me never…

Chorus

D A
Wherever you are, look in the sky tonight

C G A
You were never so far that you cannot find that light

Bm G
And when it grows dark, it shines where you are

D G Em G A
Even from this distance, I can still see that star

D
From wherever you are

D
3. I lost your face somewhere long ago

Em A
And of your eyes, the color now is all I know

D Bm
But on this night, this falling snow can bring you back

G A
And in this light, all the rest just fades to black

D
4. It is the hope that I remember here

Em A
It is the life that I remember breaking clear

D Bm
It was your hand I felt within my hand

G A
A burning warm burning down this frozen land

Repeat Chorus

Bridge

Bm B D A
On this very night I am imagining sound

D G D A
There are eyes upon the light and feet are rising from the ground

Repeat Chorus

Em A
...Wherever you are, wherever you are

D
Wherever you are

D A Bm G D A
D A Bm G D A D

These Were My Friends

Words and Music by Doc Schneider

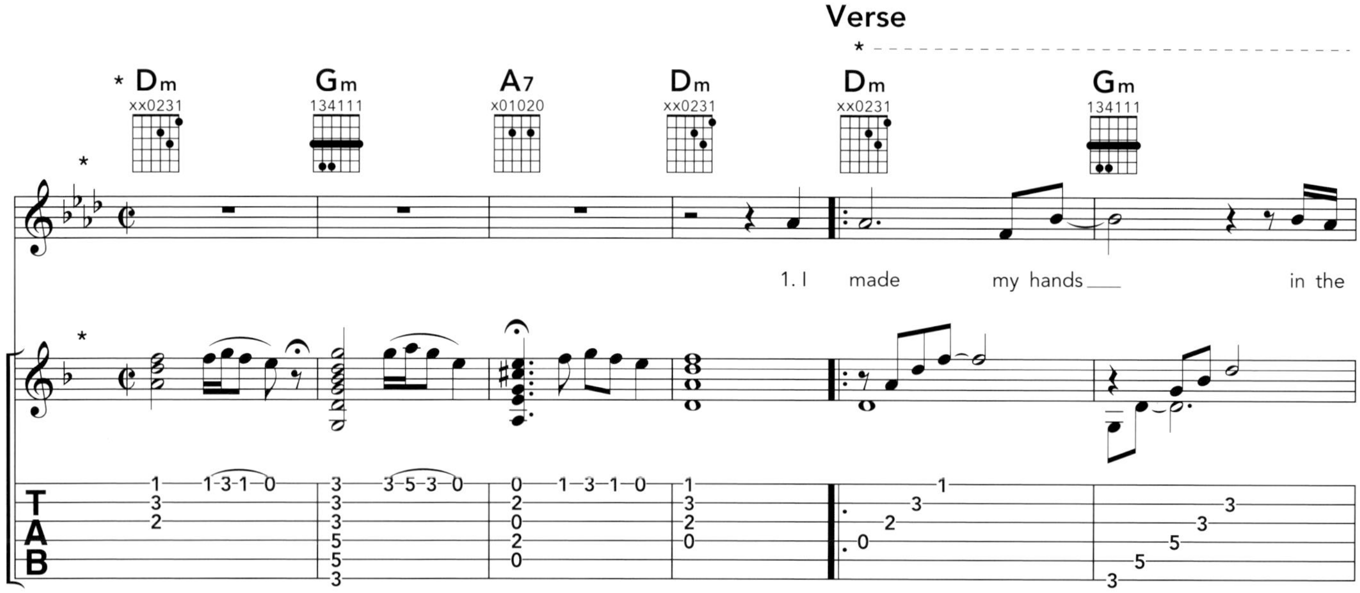

* Vocal written at concert pitch (key of Fm). Guitar notation, tab, and chords written respective to capoed guitar (key of Dm).

** Halftime feel for first six measures of second verse.

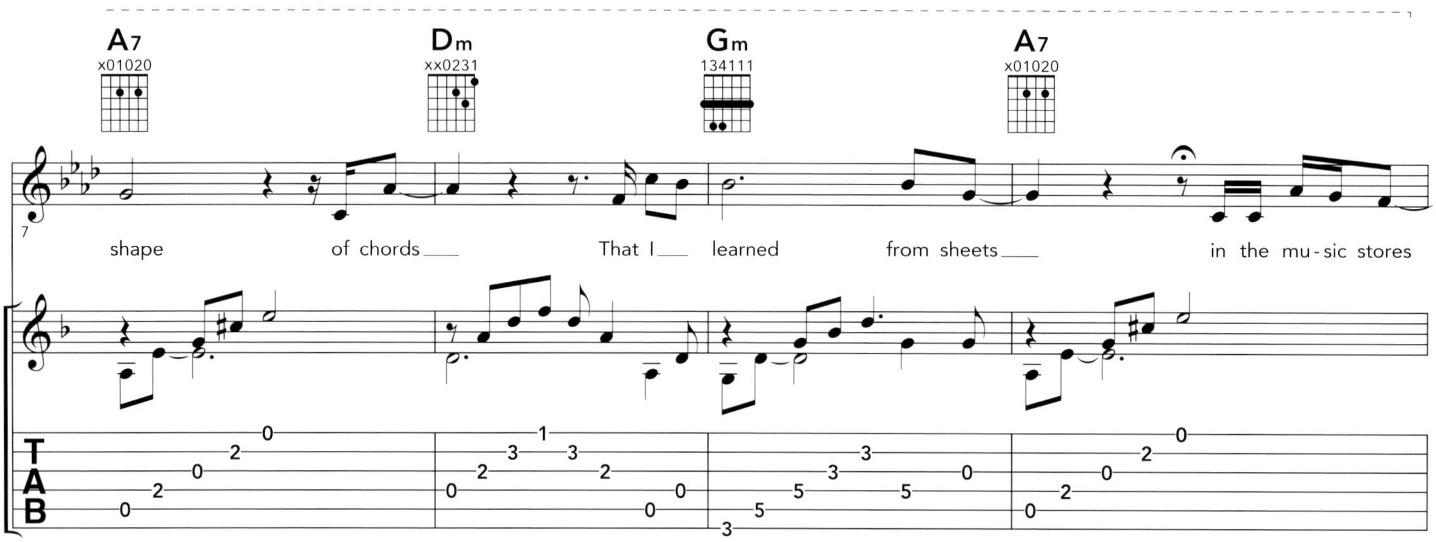

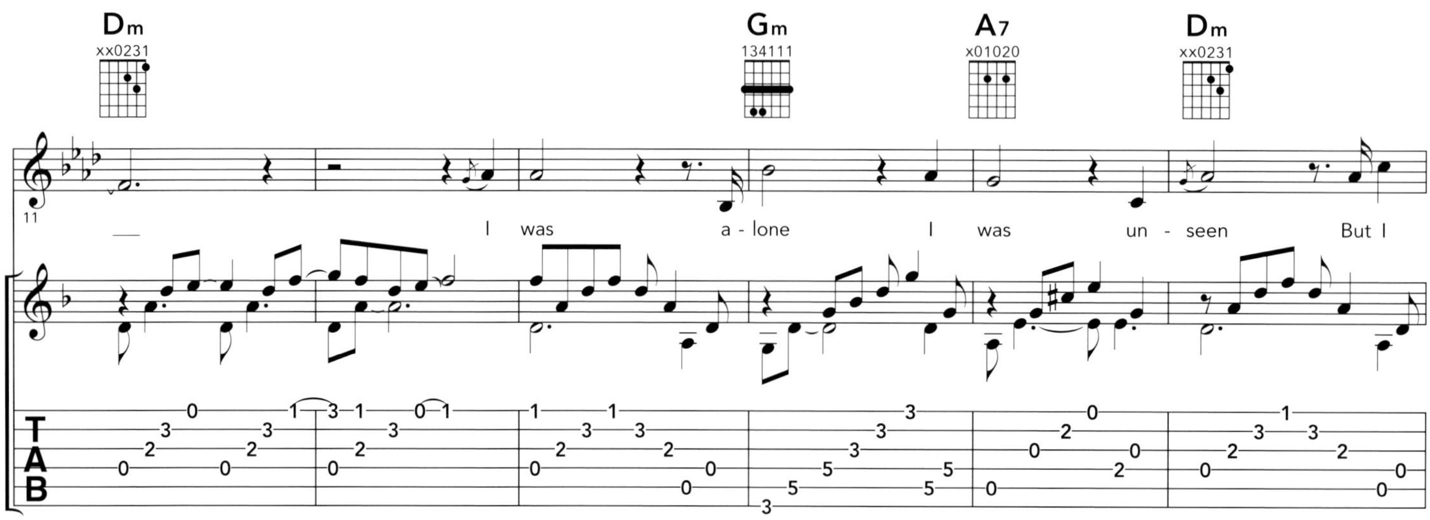

Gm A7 Dm Dm
sang a-long and it set me free
Sweet one sing-ing 'bout the
G C Em F Dm G
mud-slide The song could make you close your eyes
Rain and fire burn-ing in the
C Em F Em Am F C Dm
Car-o-li-na skies
Pink car-na-tion po-et paints a sad and star-ry night
G F G C
And near the win-dow a young girl's sing-ing She's so far a-way to-night
These were my
Chorus
C G F
friends in the dark days These were my friends on a dark Long Is-land night
To Coda
G C G Dm G
These were my friends sing-ing some-day
You may bring this ray of bright-ness
F G C
to some-one else-'s life
Bridge
Am Em
And I al-most lost the feel-ing

134211 134211 Am x02310 Em 023000
with-out mean-ing or in - tent But my songs were slow-ly drown-ing
Dm xx0231 G 320004 Dm xx0231 G 320004
in my le-gal ar - gu-ment But the muse she is a ma - gi
C x32010 Em 023000 F 134211 Dm xx0231 G 320004
and it's mag-ic that she brings Takes me back sits me
Am x02310 G/B x2004x C x32010 Am x02310 Em 023000
down hands me these six strings So I lim-ber up my fin-gers
F 134211 G 134211 Am x02310 Em 023000
and I call back all my friends And we have a grand re-un - ion
Dm xx0231 G 320004
D.S. al Coda
and the mu - sic nev-ver ends These were my
Coda
Am x02310 G/B x2004x C x32010 F 134211 G 134211
to some-one else - 's life Oh you may bring this ray of bright - ness to

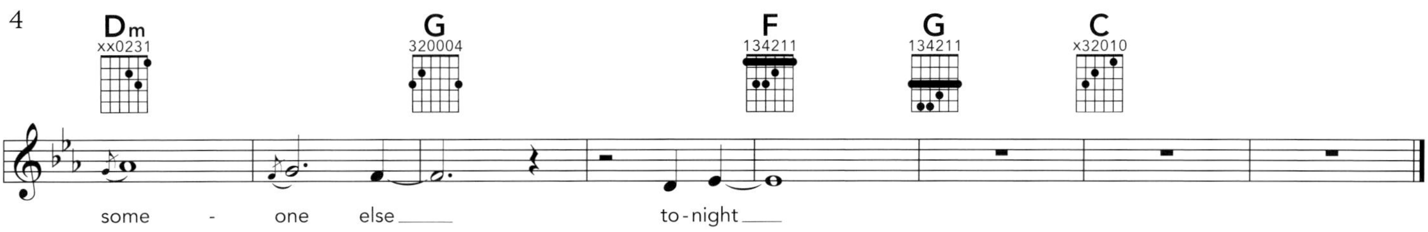

Intro
Dm Gm A7 Dm

1\. Dm Gm A7 Dm
I made my hands in the shape of chords
Gm A7 Dm
That I learned from sheets in the music stores
Dm Gm A7 Dm
I was alone, I was unseen
Gm A7 Dm
But I sang along and it set me free
Dm Gm
Sweet one singing 'bout the mudslide
C Em F
The song could make you close your eyes
Dm Gm C Em F
Rain and fire burning in the Carolina skies
Em Am F C Dm
Pink carnation poet paints a sad and starry night
Dm Gm
And near the window a young girl's singing
F G C
She's so far away tonight

Chorus
C G
These were my friends in the dark days
F G
These were my friends on a dark Long Island night
C G
These were my friends singing someday
Dm G F G C
You may bring this ray of brightness to someone else's life

2\. Dm Gm A7 Dm
On Newport's shore I wrote a song
Gm A7 Dm
About coming home again and love gone wrong
Dm Gm A7 Dm
I traveled South, sang songs at night
Gm A7 Dm
And found a girl, and saved my life
Dm Gm C Em F
Souvenirs and love songs and stars that fall at night
Dm Gm
Like the captain and the cowboy
C Em F
We all fall in love sometimes
Em Am F C Dm
Cold Spring Harbour outlaw sings a song from Oyster Bay
Dm Gm
Pours his heart into his baby grand
F G C
And we want to hear him play

Repeat Chorus

Bridge
Am Em F G
And I almost lost the feeling without meaning or intent
Am Em Dm G
But my songs were slowly drowning in my legal argument
Dm G C Em F
But the muse, she is a magi, and it's magic that she brings
Dm G Am G/B C
Takes me back, sits me down, hands me these six strings
Am Em F G
So I limber up my fingers and I call back all my friends
Am Em Dm G
And we have a grand reunion and the music never ends

Repeat Chorus
Dm G Am G/B C
…You may bring this ray of brightness to someone else's life
F G Dm G F G C
Oh, you may bring this ray of brightness to someone else tonight

BANKRUPTCY

The Legal Guitarist

Words and Music by Doc Schneider

Verse
D G A
1. I am not young I am not old I am a middle creature I can be warm I can be cold I am a
2. See additional lyrics.
D G A
double-feature I was the kid who was so bold to talk back to the teacher And now the law has got my soul and I'm a le-
Pre-Chorus
D D A G A D
gal preacher Hey say A - men say A - men There's no need to run and hide when a law - yer's on your
G A D
side Say A - men say A - men
1.
2.
D.S. al D.S.S.

3

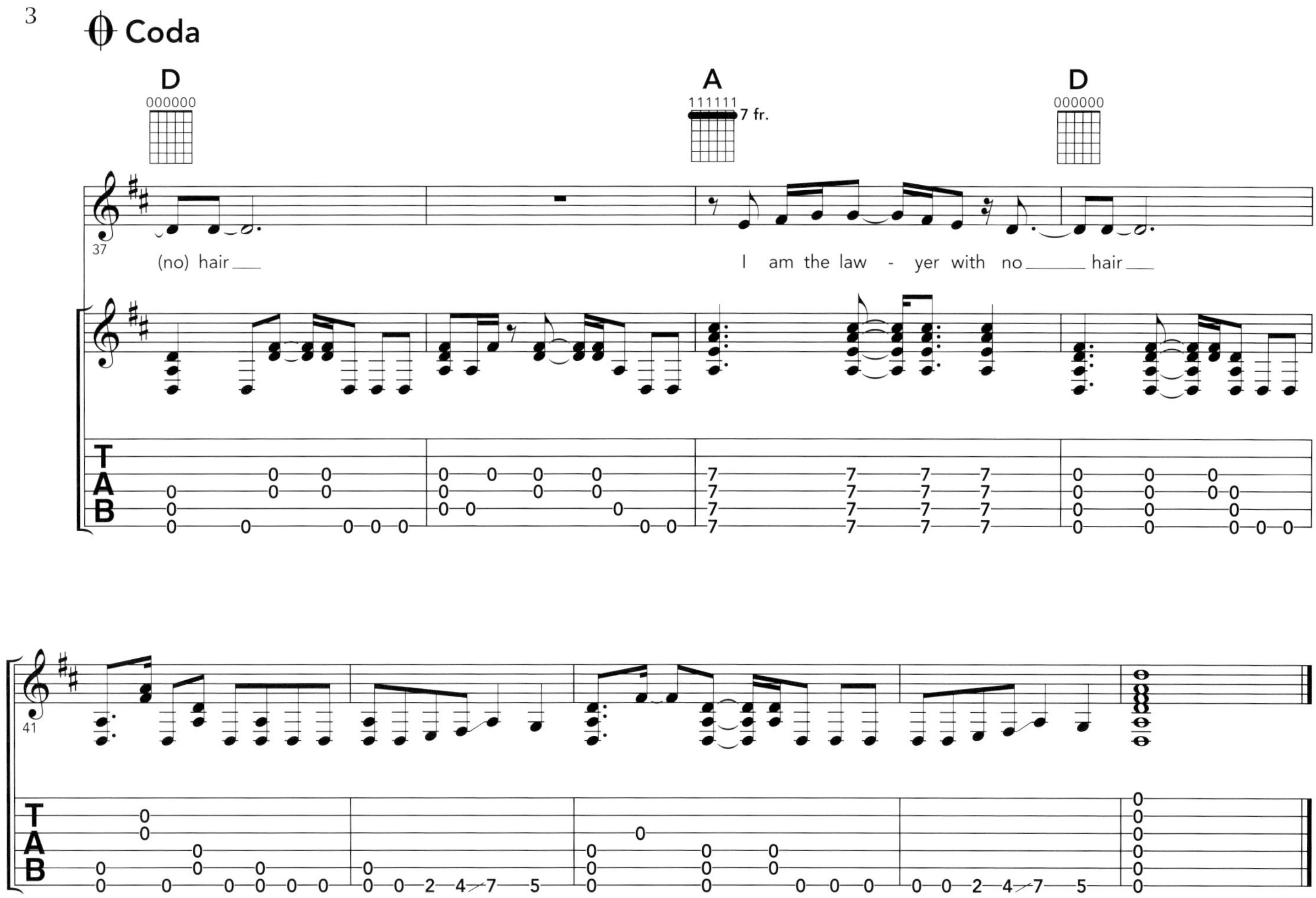

Intro

D

Chorus 1

D
I am your legal guitarist

G A
I'll take you through the legal forest

D
Beware that lawyer over there

G
He's the one who does not care

D
I am the answer to your prayer

A D
I am the lawyer with no hair

D
1. I am not young, I am not old

G
I am a middle creature

A
I can be warm, I can be cold

D
I am a double-feature

D
I was the kid who was so bold

G
To talk back to the teacher

A
And now the law has got my soul

D
And I'm a legal preacher

Pre-Chorus

D A
Hey, say Amen, say Amen

G A
There's no need to run and hide

D G
When a lawyer's on your side

A D
Say Amen, say Amen

Chorus 2

D
I am your legal guitarist

G A
My briefs use up entire forests

D
You see those pine trees over there

G
Pretty soon they'll all be bare

D
This forest doesn't stand a prayer

A D
Against this lawyer with no hair

D
3. I know the law, I know the facts

G
I'm a communicator

A
I'll take you there, I'll bring you back

D
I am a mediator

The hired gun in your gunrack

G
I am a litigator

A
You've just got to catch my act

D
As legal gladiator

Repeat Pre-Chorus

Chorus 3

D
I am your legal guitarist

G A
I'll be the best you'll find by far-est

D G
No summary judgement you need fear

D
As long as I am standing here

I know I am really not that cute

A D
But there's no fact I can't dispute

Repeat Chorus 1

A D
I am the lawyer with no hair

The Love That Lasts

Words and Music by Doc Schneider

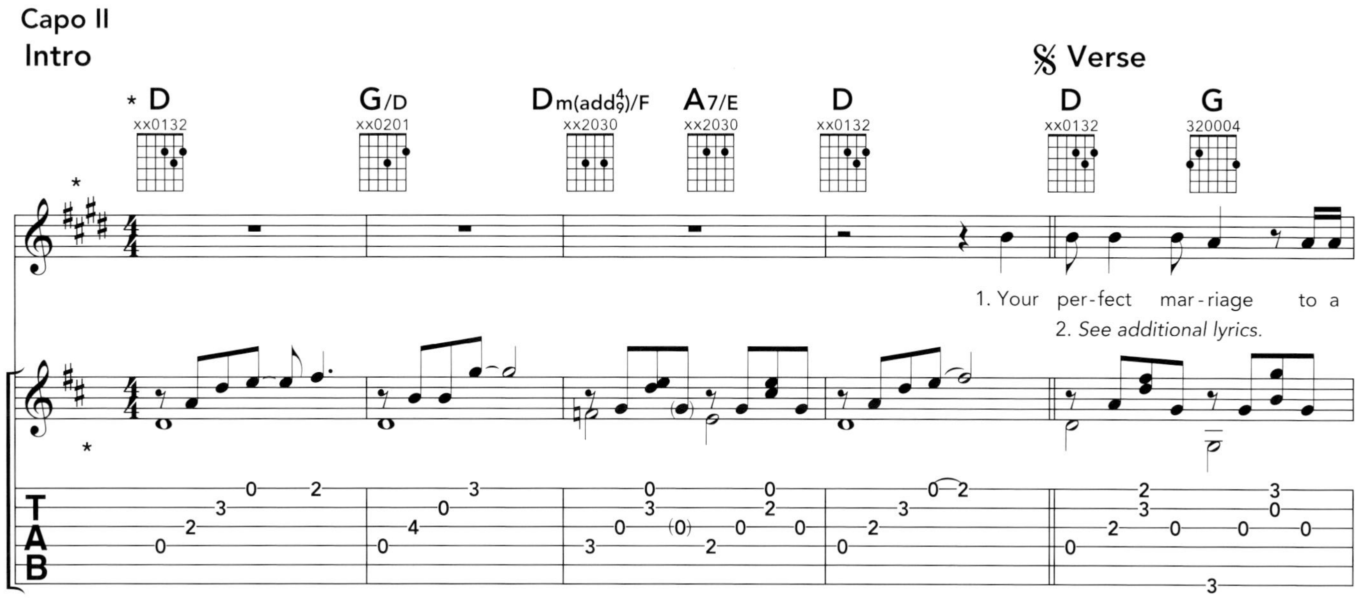

* Vocal written at concert pitch (key of E). Guitar notation, tab, and chords written respective to capoed guitar (key of D).

Chorus
D G A Em Dadd9/F♯ G A
I know I had a late start but I knew I had a good heart
D D/C♯ Dadd9/F♯ G Em Dadd9/F♯ G A
I was wait-ing here on my part in your story-y to be-gin Let all your tears
D G A Em Dadd9/F♯ G A
gone by go fast Let go of your grip on the past
To Coda 2
D D/C♯ D/C Gmaj7/B Em Dadd9/F♯ G A D Dadd9/F♯
I was-n't your first love but I can be the love that lasts Oh dar-ling
D.S. al Coda 1
Em A D G/D A7/E D
let me be the love that lasts

Coda 1
Em A G Dadd9/F♯ G A Em A D
to my arms and it was worth the wait-ing for
And I'm not trying to rush it
Em A Em G Em Bm A
And you want to take it one step at a time
But it's hard for me to slow down my heart
Em Dadd9/F♯ G A
D.S.S. al Coda
For you are my rea - son and you are my rhyme
I know I had
Coda 2
D Dadd9/F♯ Em A D Dadd9/F♯ Em A
Oh yes I can be the love that lasts
Let me try it
let me be the love that lasts
D Dadd9/F♯ Em A D
Now don't de-ny it
let me be the love
that lasts

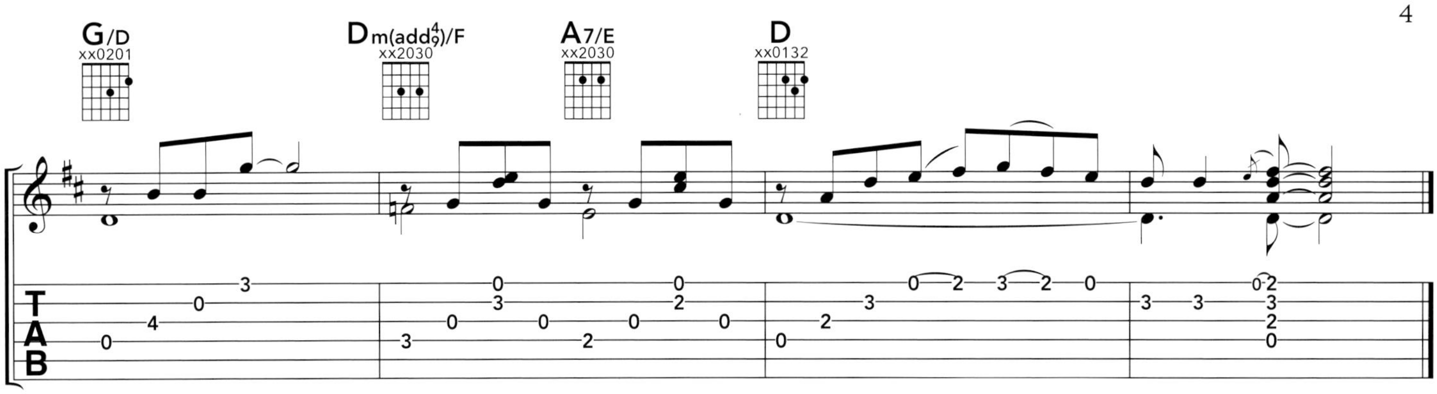

Intro

D G/D Dm(add4[9])/F A7/E D

D G Dadd9/F♯ Em
1. Your perfect marriage to a perfect fool

G D A
Has crumbled in your hands

D G Dadd9/F♯ Em
And you've concluded that love is cruel

G D A
And you frown on our romance

G Dadd9/F♯ Em A
But you are shiny and new to me

D A Em
And it's my turn for the dance

G Dadd9/F♯ Em A
I'm not another in a long line of lovers

G Dadd9/F♯ G A
Please give____ me a chance

Chorus

D G A
I know I had a late start

Em Dadd9/F♯ G A
But I knew I had a good heart

D D/C♯ Dadd9/F♯ G
I was waiting here on my__ part

Em Dadd9/F♯ G
In your story to begin

A D G A
Let all your tears gone by go fast

Em Dadd9/F♯ G A
Let go of your grip on the past

D D/C♯ D/C Gmaj7/B
I wasn't your first love

Em Dadd9/F♯ G A
But I can be the love that lasts

D Dadd9/F♯ Em A D
Oh, darling,____ let me be the love that lasts

D G/D Dm(add4[9])/F A7/E D

D G Dadd9/F♯ Em
2. You've got me singing songs that I

G D A
Have never sung before

D G Dadd9/F♯ Em
And my heart starts sailing and my eyes do shine

G D A
When you walk right through my door

G Dadd9/F♯ Em A
And this sweet feeling has got to be

D A Em
A special love, for sure

G Dadd9/F♯ Em A
The hands of time have brought you to my arms

G Dadd9/F♯ G A
And it was worth the waiting___ for

Bridge

Em A D
And I'm not trying to rush it

Em A Em G
And you want to take it one step at a time

Em Bm A
But it's hard for me to slow down my heart

Em Dadd9/F♯ G A
For you are my reason and you are my rhyme

Repeat Chorus

Em Dadd9/F♯ G A
…But I can be the love that lasts

D Dadd9/F♯ Em A
Oh, yes I can be the love that lasts

D Dadd9/F♯ Em A
Let me try it,____ let me be the love that lasts

D Dadd9/F♯ Em A
Now don't deny it,____ let me be the love that lasts

D G/D Dm(add4[9])/F A7/E D

OLSON
GUITARS
JAMES A. OLSON
JAMES TAYLOR
JAMES TAYLOR SIGNATURE MODEL

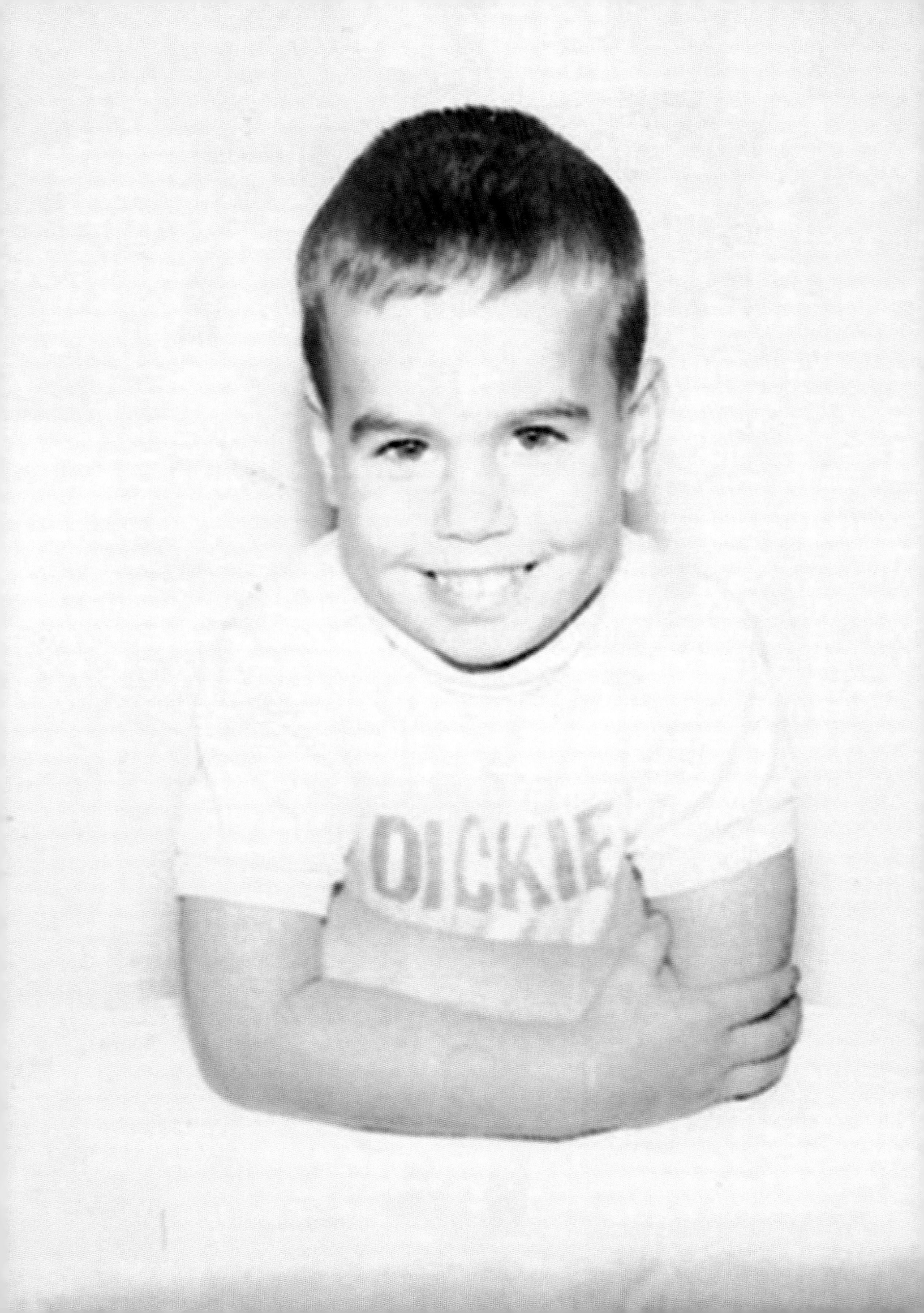
DICKIE

Choices and Chances

Words and Music by Doc Schneider

* Vocal written at concert pitch (key of B). Guitar notation, tab, and chords written respective to capoed guitar (key of G).

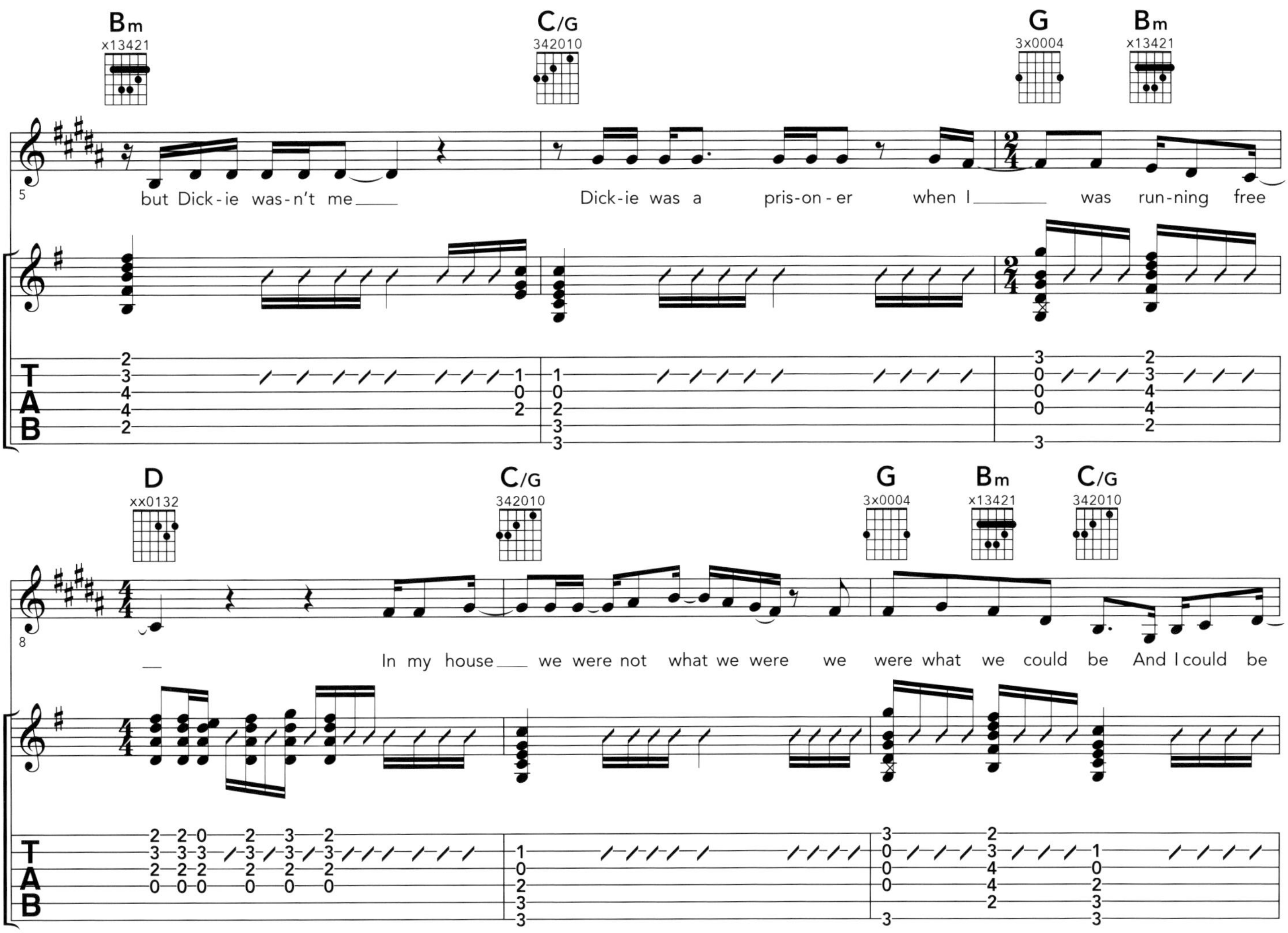

G
Bm
C/G
G
C/G
G
C/G
G
any story I could spin till the truth caught up with me
Chorus
C/G
G
Am
D
Oh the choices that we make mm
Oh the voices that we hear
D.S. (first time, with repeat)
D.S. al Coda (second time, no repeat)
To Coda
C/G
G
C/G
D
G
C/G
G
C/G
G
Sometimes chances slip away
Sometimes choices are not clear
Coda
C/G
D
C/G
Yes all my choices
oh they brought me
G
C/G
G
C/G
G
C/G
G
here

3

Intro

G C/G G C/G G

1. When I was younger I knew Dickie, but Dickie wasn't me
(G, Bm)

Dickie was a prisoner when I was running free
(C/G, G, Bm, D)

In my house we were not what we were, we were what we could be
(C/G, G, Bm, C/G)

And I could be any story I could spin till the truth caught up with me
(G, Bm, C/G)

G C/G G C/G G

2. My father was a diplomat, but a banker by his trade
(G, Bm)

To leave the Foreign Service was the saddest choice he made
(C/G, G, Bm, D)

And he never could forget it, and it haunted him each day
(C/G, G, Bm, C/G)

Till that heart that he inherited so young just took his life away
(G, Bm, C/G, G)

C/G G C/G G

Chorus

Oh, the choices that we make, mm
(C/G, G)

Oh, the voices that we hear
(Am, D)

Sometimes the chances slip away
(C/G, G)

Sometimes choices are not clear
(C/G, D)

G C/G G C/G G

3. I chose to be a lawyer, I'm still a lawyer now
(G, Bm)

Though I know I may not end my days that way somehow
(C/G, G, Bm, D)

Like my Dad before me, I am not what I am
(C/G, G, Bm, C/G)

But I can be any story I can tell, if I can just convince myself
(G, Bm, C/G)

G C/G G C/G G

4. Should have been a poet, I didn't have the faith
(G, Bm)

Could have had a destiny but I never saw the place
(C/G, G, Bm, D)

I worry 'bout my troubles and I waste my time and space
(C/G, G, Bm, C/G)

And when I look into the mirror now I see there are lines upon my face
(G, Bm, C/G, G)

C/G G C/G G

Repeat Chorus

5. But if I had my choices, might have missed my chance
(G, Bm)

The chance that brought my daughters and that gave me my romance
(C/G, G, Bm, D)

The chance that came to save me on a dark Long Island night
(C/G, G, Bm, C/G)

And the chance that brings me here today has singing in the light
(G, Bm, C/G, G)

C/G G C/G G

Chorus

Oh, the choices that we make, mm
(C/G, G)

Oh, the voices that we hear
(Am, D)

Sometimes chances came my way
(C/G, G)

And all my choices brought me here
(C/G, D, G C/G G)

Yes, all my choices, oh, they brought me here
(C/G, D, C/G)

G C/G G C/G G C/G G

In Her Hands

Words and Music by Doc Schneider

To Coda 1
D G/B G Asus4 A D G/B G Asus4 A
All my res-o-lu - tions fall a-part
Bridge 1
Bm D Em D/F♯ G
She does-n't know what I am think-ing At least that's what I'd like to think
Em7 A D Bm Em D/F♯ G6
D.S. al Coda 1
This is a pool of light and dream - ing And I'm just here to take a drink
Coda 1
Bridge 2
Bm E A7sus4
E-very time I come here I swear I won't leave With my head all locked up in some in -
D Bm E
ven - tion of my heart There's no il - lus - ion that my mind won't weave
A7sus4 Dsus2 G A
D.S. al Coda 2
Though I know for cer-tain from the start I'm just a pat-ron of her art

𝄌 Coda 2

Intro

D G/B G Asus4 G
Em D/F♯ G A

D G/B G Asus4
1. She can fix you with her fingers
Em D/F♯ G6
She can soothe you with her hair
D G/B G Asus4
And when she moves and when she lingers
Em D/F♯ G
You can feel her breathing there

Chorus

Bm D/F♯ G
I just came to start my circulation
Em D/F♯ G6
I can't give away my heart
D A Em
I must withstand my inclination
Bm G
To be spellbound by her art
Em DF♯ G6
But in her hands
D G/B G Asus4 A D G/B G Asus4 A
All my_ resolutions fall apart

Bridge 1

Bm D
She doesn't know what I am thinking
Em D/F♯ G
At least that's what I'd like to think
Em7 A D Bm
This is a pool of light and dreaming
Em D/F♯ G6
And I'm just here to take a drink

D G/B G Asus4
2. Your mind wanders as she tells you
Em D/F♯ G6
Some enchantment from her past
D G/B G Asus4
Her hands glide as she unwinds you
Em D/F♯ G
And your tension leaves at last

Repeat Chorus

Bridge 2

Bm   E
Every time I come here I swear I won't leave

A7sus4   D
With my head all locked up in some invention of my heart

Bm   E
There's no illusion that my mind won't weave

A7sus4   Dsus2
Though I know for certain from the start

G   A
I'm just a patron of her art

    D   G/B   G   Asus4
3. She can fix you with her fingers

Em   D/F♯   G6
She can soothe you with her hair

D   G/B   G   A7sus4   D   G/B
And when she moves and when she lingers there

    G   Asus4 A   D
Oh, when she lingers there

G/B   G   Asus4   A   D   G/B
Oh, I hardly can take it when she lingers there

G   Asus4 A D
When she lingers there

Headed Where My Future Meets My Past

Words and Music by Doc Schneider

A Em7 A Em7 A
- way ___ And I'm on my way at last I am head-ed where my ___ fu-ture meets ___ my ___
To Coda 2
Verse
G D Bm G A7sus4 A7 D
___ past to-day ___ 1. Suf-fer-ing in si - lence ___ and in be-tween your lies
2. See additional lyrics.
Em7 A G A Bm G
I could see your as-pi-ra-tions shin-ing in your eyes ___ You were bound to be a writ - er
A7sus4 A7 D C G/B Am G/B
You were bound to be un - done Sit-ting on ___ the shore-line with your hand u-pon the wat -
To Coda 1
Bridge
C G Bm C
er And your hopes out in the sun ___ It was a poem for some-one's ___ daugh-ter ___
Bm A C Bm
It was a chance for some - one's ___ son It was a mo-ment - ar - y tri - umph

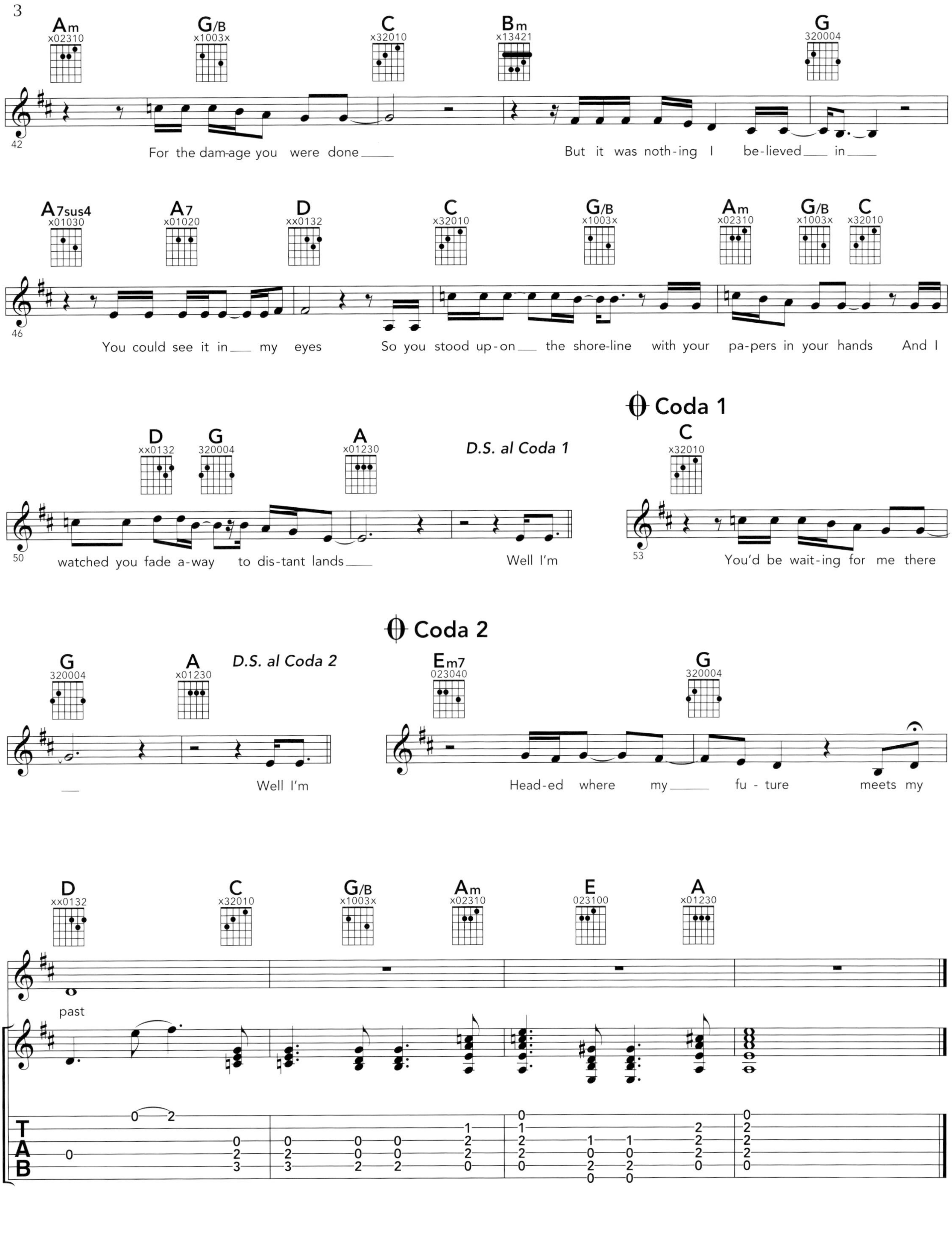
3
Am G/B C Bm G
For the dam-age you were done
But it was noth-ing I be-lieved in
A7sus4 A7 D C G/B Am G/B C
You could see it in my eyes
So you stood up-on the shore-line with your pa-pers in your hands And I
D G A
D.S. al Coda 1
watched you fade a-way to dis-tant lands
Well I'm
Coda 1
C
You'd be wait-ing for me there
G A
D.S. al Coda 2
Well I'm
Coda 2
Em7 G
Head-ed where my fu-ture meets my
D C G/B Am E A
past

Intro

D G/B Em7 Am E A

Chorus

D G D A
Well I'm twenty years behind you and I may be fading fast

Em7 Bm A
All my shackles are behind me

D G
There are bits of broken glass

Em7 A
There are headlights on the highway

Em7 A
And I'm on my way at last

Em7 A G D
I am headed where my future meets my past today

Bm G A7sus4 A7 D
1. Suffering in silence and__ in between your lies

Em7 A G A
I could see your aspirations shining in your eyes

Bm G A7sus4 A7 D
You were bound to be a writer, you were bound to be undone

C G/B Am G/B C
Sitting on the shoreline with your hands upon the water

G
And your hopes out in the sun

Bridge

Bm C
It was a poem for someone's daughter

Bm A
It was a chance for someone's son

C Bm
It was a momentary triumph

Am G/B C
For the damage you were done

Bm G
But it was nothing I believed in

A7sus4 A7 D
You could see it in my eyes

C G/B Am G/B C
So you stood upon the shoreline with your papers in your hands

D G A
And I watched you fade away to distant lands

Repeat Chorus

Bm G A7sus4 A7 D
2. Standing in the darkness, staring at the night

Em7 A G A
I can hear a distant whisper, I can see a distant light

Bm G A7sus4 A7 D
I am racing for the brightness, I can feel it in the air

C G/B Am G/B C
Sitting on the shoreline with your hands upon the water

G
You'll be waiting for me there

G A
You'll be waiting for me there

Repeat Chorus

Em7 G D
Headed where my future meets my past

C G/B Am E A

Nothing Quite Like You

Words and Music by Doc Schneider

Tuning: C G D G B D, Capo I

Intro

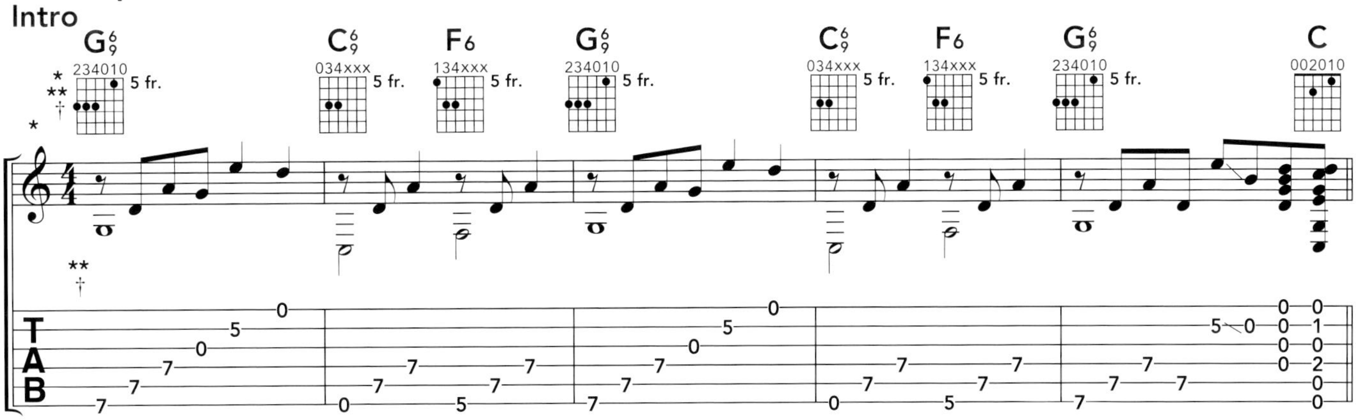

* Vocal written at concert pitch (key of D♭). Guitar notation, tab, and chords written respective to capoed guitar (key of C).

** Fretboards show overall original chords; tab and notation show arrangement of guitar harmony on *Second Chances.*

† Several gtrs. arr. for one.

𝄋 Verse

To Coda 1
Chorus
G
Am9
G
Fadd9
are
I could say the stars are like your eyes paint-ed a-cross
Em
Dm11
G
the sum-mer skies
Those words would nev-er work for me
Am9
G
Fadd9
Em
For if the stars were like your eyes
I would-n't miss you when you're gone
Dm11
G
Fadd9
Am9
I would-n't feel the way I do
There's sim-ply no me-ta-phor
To Coda 2
D.S. al Coda 1
G
Em
Dm11
G
C
G6
to say what I'm search-ing for
Truth is there's noth-ing quite like you
Coda 1
Chorus
Fadd9
Am9
G
Em
There's sim-ply no me-ta-phor
to say what I'm search-ing for

3

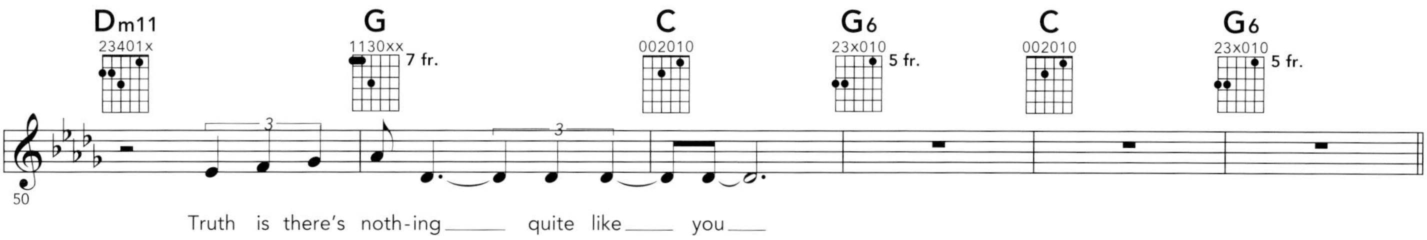

Bridge

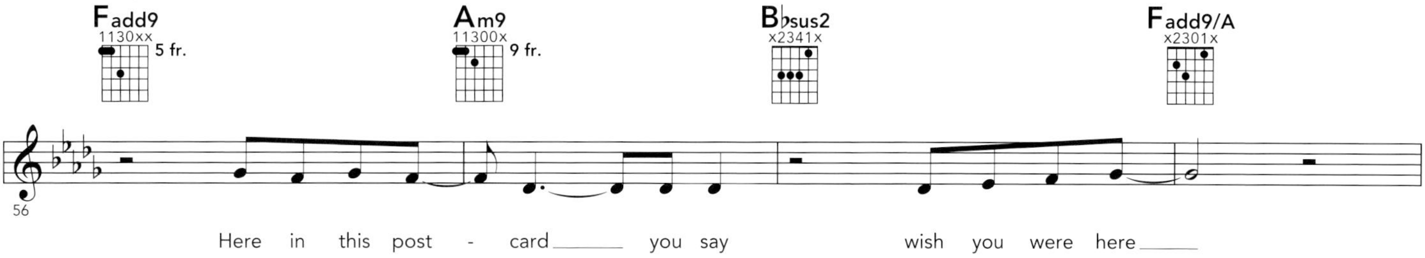

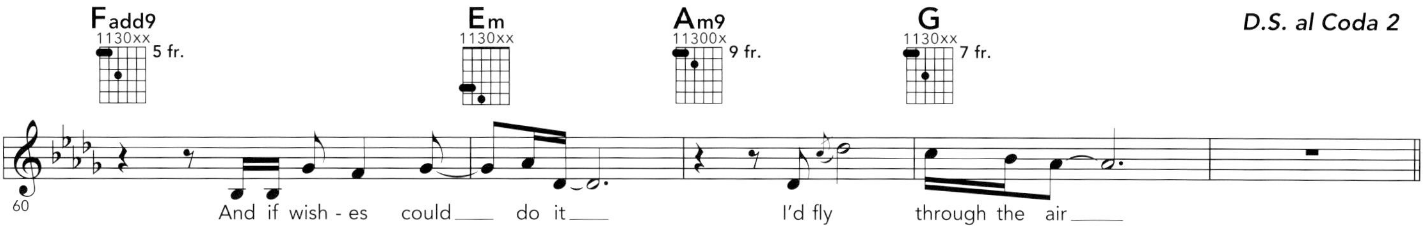

Coda 2

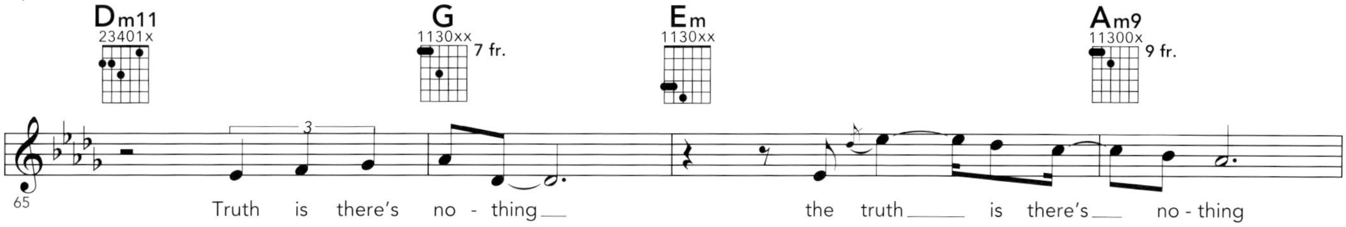

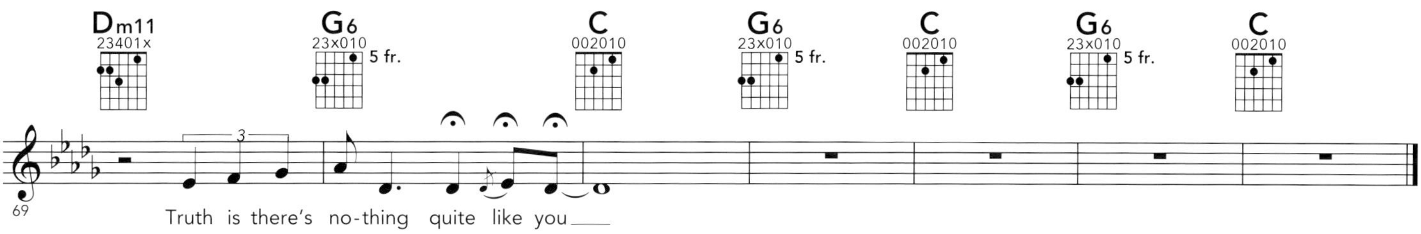

Intro

G6/9 C6/9 F6 G6/9 C6/9 F6 G6/9

C Am9 Fadd9 G
1. The wind in the willows is calling your name

C Am9 Fadd9 G
And the warmth in this meadow is made of your flame

Csus4/B♭ Csus4/A Em9 Fadd9
The sky is a quilted blanket covered in stars

Dm11 G
I wait for the words that will say what you are

Chorus

Am9 G Fadd9 Em Dm11
I could say the stars are like your eyes painted across the summer skies

G
Those words would never work for me

Am9 G Fadd9 Em Dm11
For if the stars were like your eyes, I wouldn't miss you when you're gone

G
I wouldn't feel the way I do

Fadd9 Am9 G Em
There's simply no metaphor to say what I'm searching for

Dm11 G C G6
Truth is there's nothing quite like you

C Am9 Fadd9 G
2. The sense of your leaving empties me out

C Am9 Fadd9 G
The things I'm believing are tempted by doubt

Csus4/B♭ Csus4/A Em9 Fadd9
Here is a magic carpet where we used to fly

Dm11 G
I wait for the stars and the time to go by

Chorus

Fadd9 Am9 G Em
There's simply no metaphor to say what I'm searching for

Dm11 G C G6 C G6
Truth is there's nothing quite like you

Bridge

Fadd9 Am9 B♯sus2 Fadd9/A
Here in this postcard, you say "wish you were here"

Fadd9 Em Am9 G
And if wishes could do it, I'd fly through the air

C Am9 Fadd9 G
3. What summer surrenders, the fall will return

C Am9 Fadd9 G
But it seems like forever for these leaves to turn

Csus4/B♭ Csus4/A Em9 Fadd9
Here is the place I'll take you, after so long

Dm11 G
I'll clear us a space and I'll sing you this song

Chorus

Am9 G Fadd9 Em Dm11
I could say the stars are like your eyes painted across the summer skies

G
Those words would never work for me

Am9 G Fadd9 Em Dm11
For if the stars were like your eyes, I wouldn't miss you when you're gone

G
I wouldn't feel the way I do

Fadd9 Am9 G Em
There's simply no metaphor to say what I'm searching for

Dm11 G Em Am9
Truth is there's nothing, the truth is there's nothing

Dm11 G6 C G6 C G6 C
Truth is there's nothing quite like you

NIMITZ HAL

Coming Home Again

Words and Music by Doc Schneider

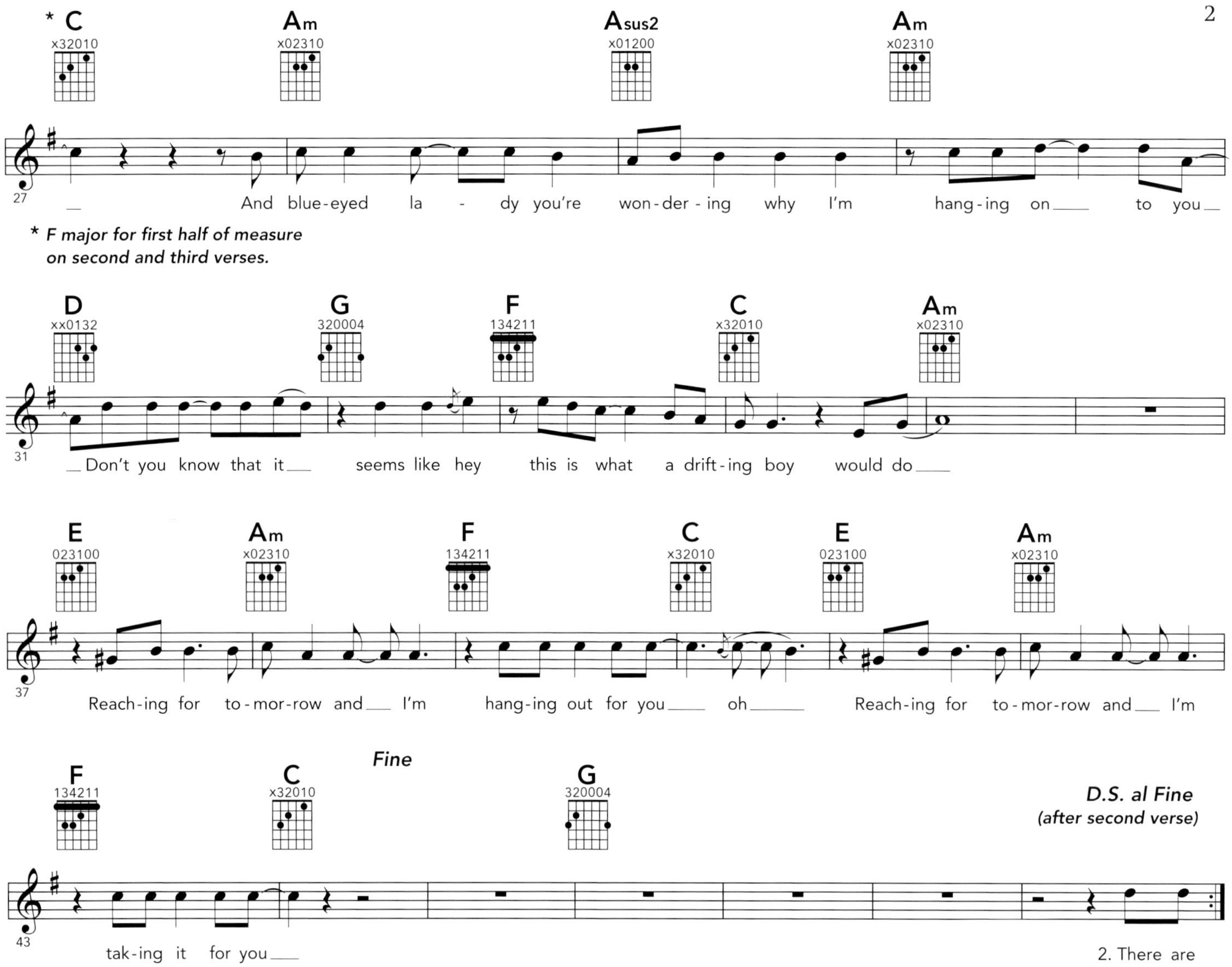

Intro

G

1. **G** Well you're coming home **C** again
Am And you check into the same **D** hotel
G And the maid she knows you **C** well
Am Hell, you've been **D** there before
F And you push through a bruised and **C** battered door
G And you hang up your coat like a **F** mata**C**dor
F And you flick on a **C** neon light
Am But it doesn't cut the **Em** night **E**

Chorus

Am Wondering if I'm really **D** home
G Or if I'm only **C** passing through
Am And blue-eyed lady you're **Asus2** wondering
Am Why I'm hanging on **D** to you
D Don't you know that it **G** seems like
F This is what a **C** drifting boy should **Am** do
E Reaching for **Am** tomorrow
F And I'm hanging out **C** for you, oh
E Reaching for **Am** tomorrow and I'm **F** taking it for **C** you **G**
F And I'm taking **C** it for **G** you

              G   C
2. There are lovers in the hallways

        Am   D
And I hear them whispering

     G   C
I can hear the lovers' songs

             Am   D
That they, oh, so softly sing

     F   C
And all my thoughts come back to me

   G   F   C
I'm here within my memory

     F   C
I can feel you in the room

      Am   E
But it doesn't cut the gloom

Repeat Chorus

           G   C
3. Well, I sang you all my love songs

          Am   D
And I've read you all my poems

          G   C
And I've told you all my stories

        Am   D
Of my sad forsaken home

          F   C
And you heard them like a lover would

          G   F   C
And you did the things that you did so good

    F   C
I can feel you in the room

      Am   E
But it doesn't cut the gloom

Repeat Chorus

If I Can Love Enough

Words and Music by Doc Schneider

Chorus
D Asus4 D Gadd9/B Aadd4/C♯
Some-times there's a shin - y one a dia - mond in the rough
To Coda
G6sus2 Dadd9/F♯ E7sus4 Asus4
Tell me I might reach you there if I can love e - nough If I can love
D Asus4 Gadd9/B
1. Aadd4/C♯ Gadd9/B
e - nough
2. Asus4
Bridge
G6sus2 Asus4 Gadd9/B Aadd4/C♯
And noth - ing lasts for-ev - er You nev - er said it would
D.S. al Coda
G6sus2 Dadd9/F♯ E7sus4 Asus4
But some - times in an old song I still think it should

Intro

D Asus4 Gadd9/B Aadd4/C♯ Gadd9/B

1\. **D** Broken bones **Asus4** beneath my feet **Gadd9/B** are old forgotten **Aadd4/C♯** songs
G6sus2 Words that beat a **Dadd9/F♯** fast **Em11** retreat when no one **Asus4** sang along
D I dig them up like **Asus4** fossil finds **Gadd9/B** and search them for a **Aadd4/C♯** clue
G6sus2 Maybe there's some **Dadd9/F♯** hidden sign that **E7sus4** leads me back to **Asus4** you

Chorus

D Sometimes there's a shiny **Asus4** one, **D** a **Gadd9/B** diamond in the **Aadd4/C♯** rough
G6sus2 Tell me I might **Dadd9/F♯** reach you there if **E7sus4** I can lough **Asus4** enough

If I can love enough

D Asus4 Gadd9/B Aadd4/C♯ Gadd9/B

2\. **D** Like a wound that **Asus4** cut too deep, you **Gadd9/B** wore it on your **Aadd4/C♯** sleeve
G6sus2 A heart I thought I'd **Dadd9/F♯** always keep, I **E7sus4** never heard you **Asus4** leave, no, no
D Make this song my **Asus4** signal flare **Gadd9/B** across the darkening **Aadd4/C♯** sea
G6sus2 Maybe you **Dadd9/F♯** will hear it there **E7sus4** and turn around to **Asus4** me

Chorus

D Sometimes there's a shiny **Asus4** one, **D** a **Gadd9/B** diamond in the **Aadd4/C♯** rough
G6sus2 Tell me I might **Dadd9/F♯** reach you there if **E7sus4** I can lough **Asus4** enough

If I can love enough

D Asus4 Gadd9/B Asus4

Bridge

G6sus2 And nothing lasts **Asus4** forever, **Gadd9/B** you never said it **Aadd4/C♯** would
G6sus2 But sometimes in an **Dadd9/F♯** old song **E7sus4** I still think it **Asus4** should

Chorus

D Sometimes there's a shiny **Asus4** one, **D** a **Gadd9/B** diamond in the **Aadd4/C♯** rough
G6sus2 Tell me I might **Dadd9/F♯** reach you there if **E7sus4** I can lough **Asus4** enough
D Sometimes there's a shiny **Asus4** one, **D** a **Gadd9/B** diamond in the **Aadd4/C♯** rough
G6sus2 Tell me I might **Dadd9/F♯** reach you there if **E7sus4** I can lough **Asus4** enough

Let me love enough

D Asus4 Gadd9/B Aadd4/C♯ Gadd9/B

The Lucky One

Words and Music by Doc Schneider

Open-E Tuning: E B E G♯ B E

Intro

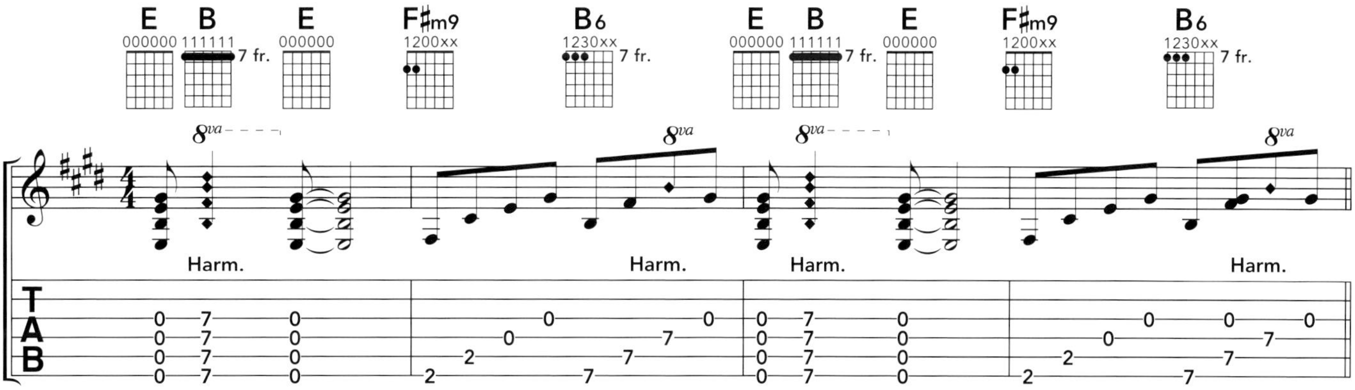

𝄋 Chorus

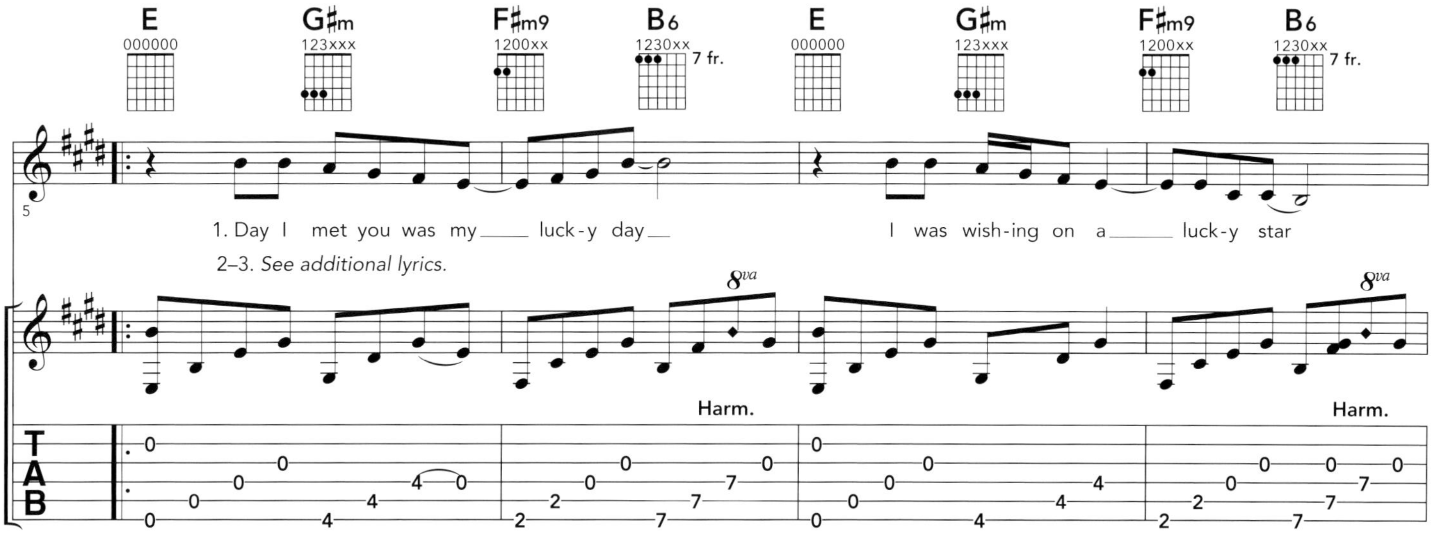

To Coda 𝄌

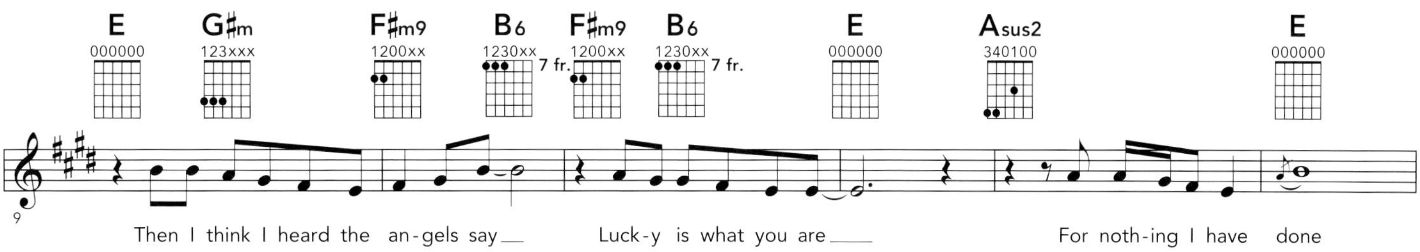

Verse

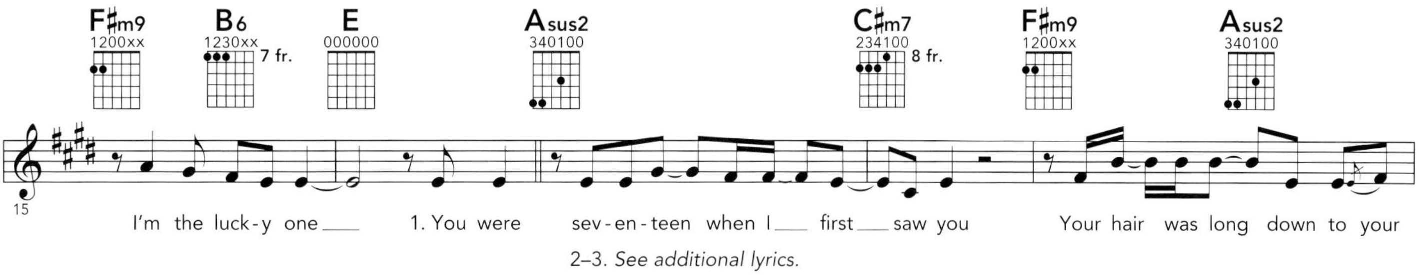

Intro

E B E F♯m9 B6

E B E F♯m9 B6

Chorus

E G♯m F♯m9 B6
Day I met you was my lucky day

E G♯m F♯m9 B6
I was wishing on a lucky star

E G♯m F♯m9 B6
Then I think I heard the angels say

F♯m9 B6 E
"Lucky is what you are"

Asus2 E
For nothing I have done

F♯m9 B6 E
I'm the lucky one

Asus2 C♯m7
1. You were seventeen when I first saw you

F♯m9 Asus2 Badd4
Your hair was long down to your waist

Amaj7 B6 G♯m Asus2
And I looked up from my song and then I saw your smile

F♯m9 Amaj7 Badd4 E
And all that I could think about was how that smile would taste

Asus2 E
And I was basking in the glow of your kindness

F♯m9 Amaj7 Badd4
Hoping you'd be struck by love and all its blindness

Chorus 2

E G♯m F♯m9 B6
My lucky stroke was you were struck that day

E G♯m F♯m9 B6
I never had another lonely day

E G♯m F♯m9 B6
You wore my shirt and took my breath away

F♯m9 B6 E
Each and every day

Asus2 E
For nothing I had done

F♯m9 B6 E
I was the lucky one

Asus2 C♯m7
2. Before you knew it we were married

F♯m9 Asus2 Badd4
And had our babies way too fast

Amaj7 B6 G♯m Asus2
And sometimes I was scared but then I'd you smile

F♯m9 Amaj7 Badd4 E
And all that I was wishing was I hope that this will last

Asus2 E
And I was basking in the glow of your kindness

F♯m9 Amaj7 Badd4
Knowing you'd be struck by love and all its blindness

Chorus 3

E G♯m F♯m9 B6
Inside my heart I keep those summer days

E G♯m F♯m9 B6
To me the picture always looks that way

E G♯m F♯m9 B6
And though the edges may grown worn and gray

F♯m9 B6 E
It's still those summer days

Asus2 E
Still standing in the sun

F♯m9 B6 E
Still the lucky one

Asus2 C♯m7
3. Now sometimes I get lost and you can't find me

F♯m9 Asus2 Badd4
Sometimes I lose those summer days

Amaj7 B6 G♯m Asus2
But I look up from life and see you standing there

F♯m9 Amaj7 Badd4 E
And know that once again my lucky star's been shining clear

Asus2 E
And I'm still basking in the glow of your kindness

F♯m9 Amaj7 Badd4
For your love still brings the warmth and brings the brightness

Bridge

C♯m7 Badd4
Now there are hundreds of hearts that could hold you

A E
There are millions of fish in the sea

G♯m Asus2
There are legions of lovers around you

F♯m9 Amaj7 Badd4
Tell me how does your light fall on me?

Repeat Chorus 1

Rises over You

Words and Music by Doc Schneider

Em Am7 9 fr. Gsus4 F5 5 fr. *Em
nal or a sign to find my way And I'm hop-ing for the night to meet the day
* Am7 on second and third verses.
Chorus
G5 F5 5 fr. E5 G5 7 fr.
And the light that ris-es up is o-ver-due and it
C F5 5 fr. G5 7 fr. C 12 fr.
To Coda
1. G5
ris-es o-ver you
Harm.
C F5 5 fr. G5 7 fr.
2. A bead of gold

2.
F5 G5 G5 C
Bridge
G5 Am7 Em Fadd9 G5 Am7 Fadd9
I know the sun that ris-es Well it just as of-ten falls
But I have seen it shin-ing And I swear I had it all
G5
D.S. al Coda
3. If I could
Coda
F5 G5 G5 C F5 G5
Yes the
F5 E5 G5
light that ris-es up is o-ver-due and it ris-es yes it ris-es o-ver

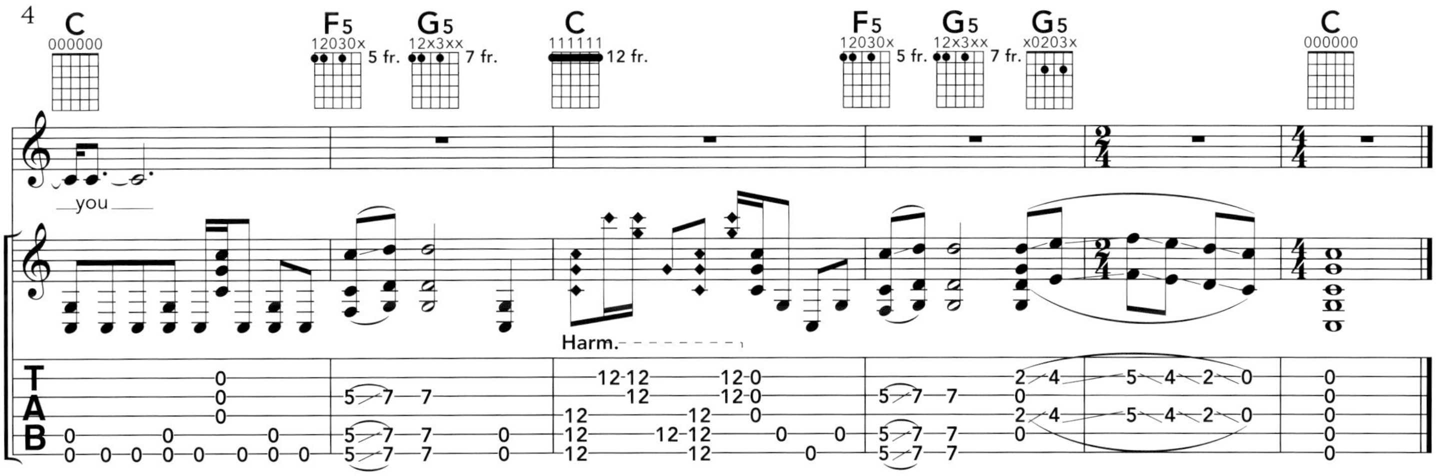

Intro

G5 C F5 G5 C F5 G5
C

1. C Em
In a dream filled with frightened faces
Am7 Gsus4
I feel my eyes fill up with fear
C F5
I lose sight of where I'm going
Am7 Gsus4
And my vision will not clear
F5 Em
So I'm groping for a signal
Am7 Gsus4
Or a sign to find my way
F5 Em G5
And I'm hoping for the night to meet the day

Chorus

F5 Em G5
And the light that rises up is overdue
C F5 G5 C G5
And it rises over you
C F5 G5

2. C Em
A bead of gold slides down your shoulder
Am7 Gsus4
A blade of sunlight paints your hair
C F5
And the sight of your skin glowing
Am7 Gsus4
Well, it's worth the journey there
F5 Em
So I'm reaching for the beauty
Am7 Gsus4
For the beauty is so true
F5 Am7 G5
And I keep it with my memories of you

Chorus

F5 Em G5
And the light that rises up is overdue
C F5 G5 C F5 G5 C
And it rises over you

Bridge

G5 Am7
I know the sun that rises
Em Fadd9
Well, it just as often falls
G5 Am7
But I have seen it shining
Fadd9 G5
And I swear I had it all

3. C Em
If I could see from start to finish
Am7 Gsus4
I might see the master plan
C F5
The little part that's showing
Am7 Gsus4
Is so hard to understand
F5 Em
But the beauty is a beacon
Am7 Gsus4
Like a lighthouse on the land
F5 Am7 G5
And this love is like a power in our hands

Chorus

F5 Em G5
And the light that rises up is overdue
C F5 G5 C F5 G5 C F5 G5
And it rises over you
F5 Em G5
Yes, the light that rises up is overdue
C F5 G5 C F5 G5 C
And it rises, yes it rises over you

Number One Fan

Words and Music by Doc Schneider

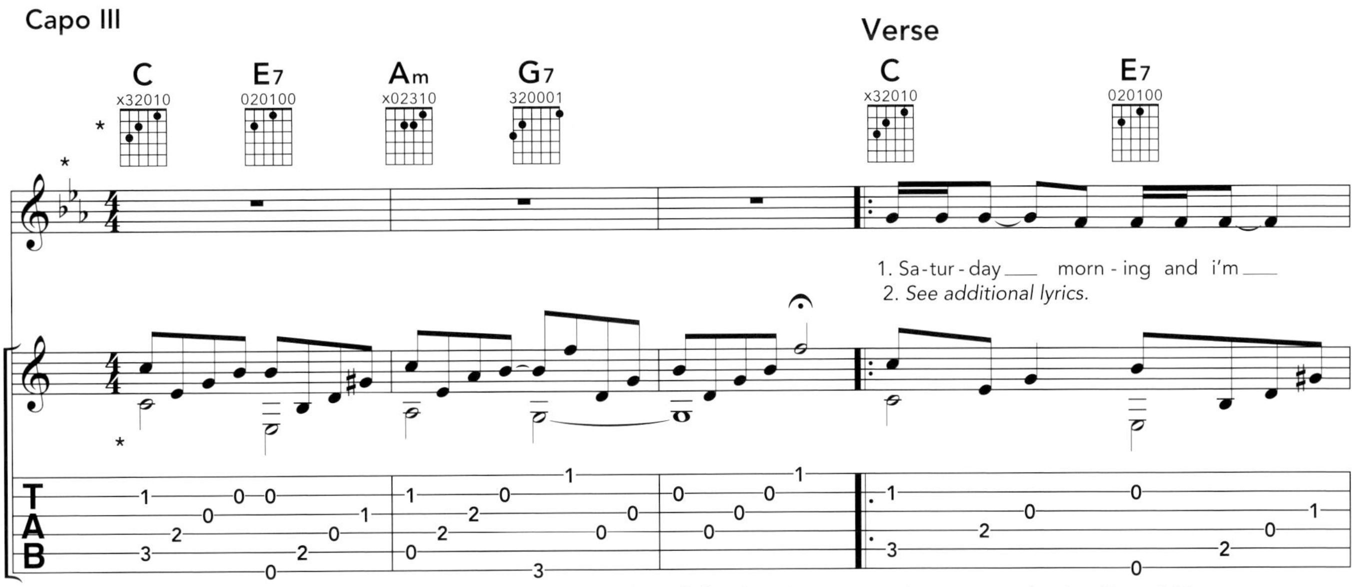

* Vocal written at concert pitch (key of E♭). Guitar notation, tab, and chords written respective to capoed guitar (key of C).

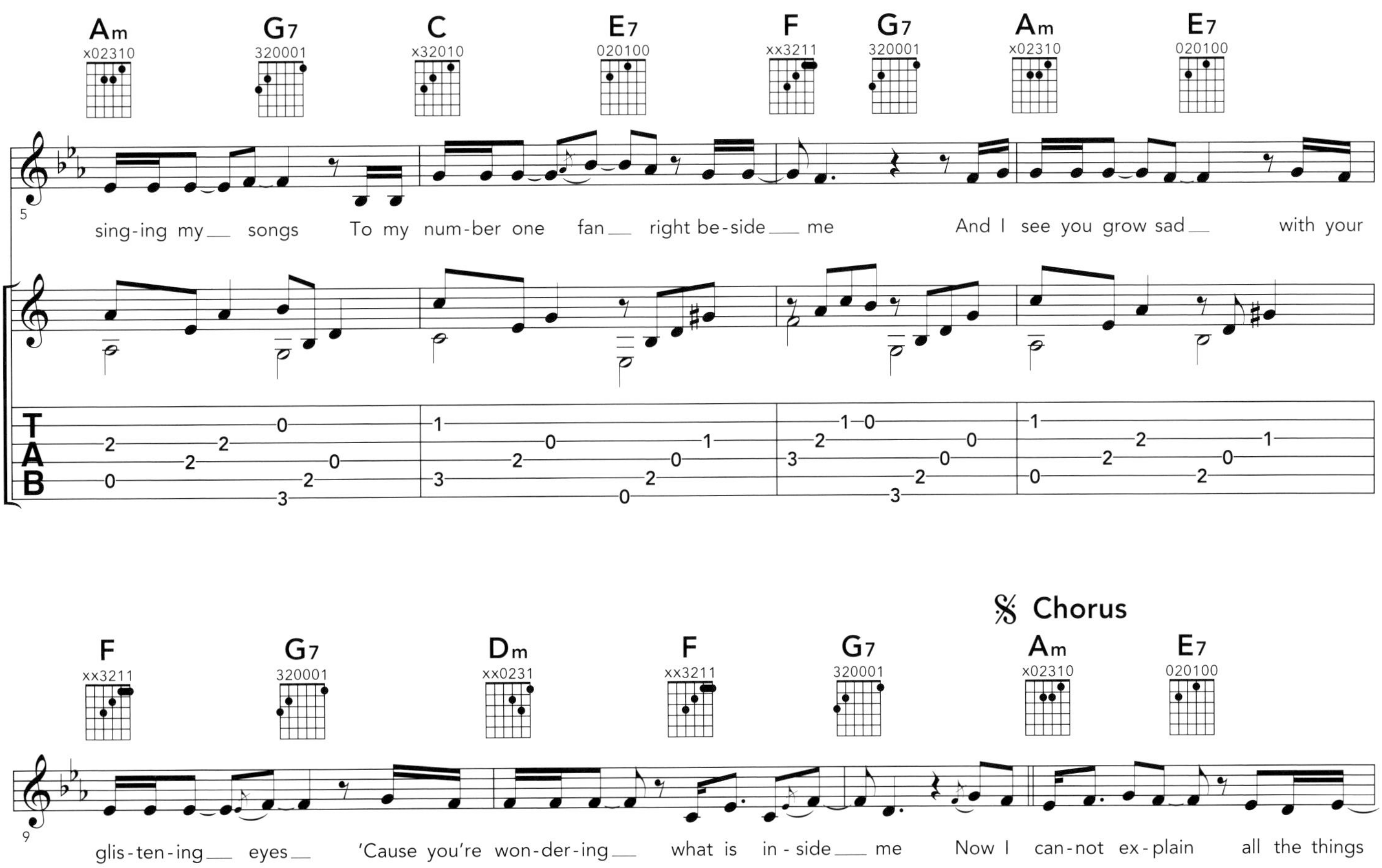

2
F G7 Am E7 F G7 C D7
that I do Or where I am go - ing with mus - sic But let this song wrap my
F G7 To Coda F G7 C
arms a - round you 'Cause there's no way I'm go - ing with-out you 2. I'm
Bridge
Dm G7 E7 Am
Shake off your wor-ries and the doubt - ing you do
Dm G7 E7 Am
Let's see you smile and be-lieve that it's true
F/A G7 D.S. al Coda
There's noth-ing to me with-out you Now I

3

𝄌 Coda

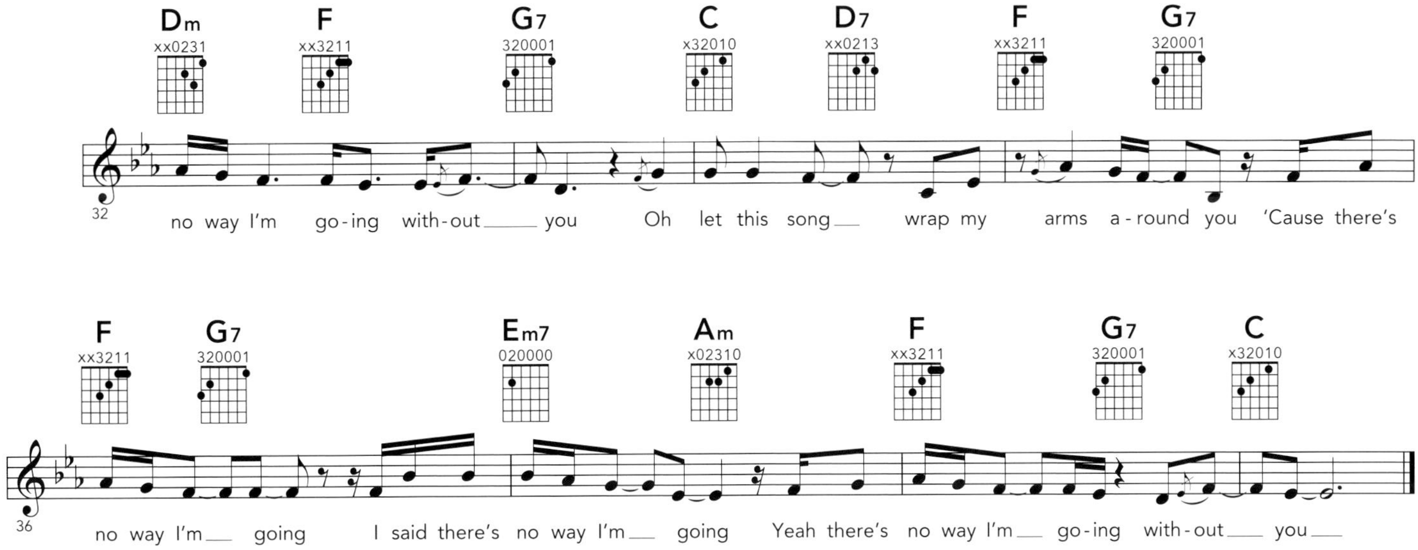

Intro

C E7 Am G7

C E7 Am G
1. Saturday morning and I'm singing my songs
C E7 F G7
To my number one fan right beside me
Am E7 F G7
And I see you grow sad with your glistening eyes
Dm F G7
'Cause you're wondering what is inside me

Chorus

Am E7 F G7
Now I cannot explain all the things that I do
Am E7 F G7
Or where I am going with music
C D7 F G7
But let this song wrap my arms around you
F G7 C
'Cause there's no way I'm going without you

C E7 Am G7
2. I'm here with you now and I'm where I belong
C E7 F G7
I'm your number one fan right beside you
Am E7 F G7
And we'll watch our girls grow glistening eyes
F G7
And go wherever we might decide to

Repeat Chorus

Bridge

Dm G7 E7 Am
Shake off your worries and the doubting you do
Dm G7 E7 Am
Let's see you smile and believe that it's true
F/A G7
There's nothing to me without you

Repeat Chorus

Dm F G7
…'Cause there's no way I'm going without you
C D7 F G7
Oh, let this song wrap my arms around you
F G7 Em7 Am
'Cause there's no way I'm going, I said there's no way I'm going
F G7 C
Yeah, there's no way I'm going without you

Hint of Heaven

Words and Music by Doc Schneider

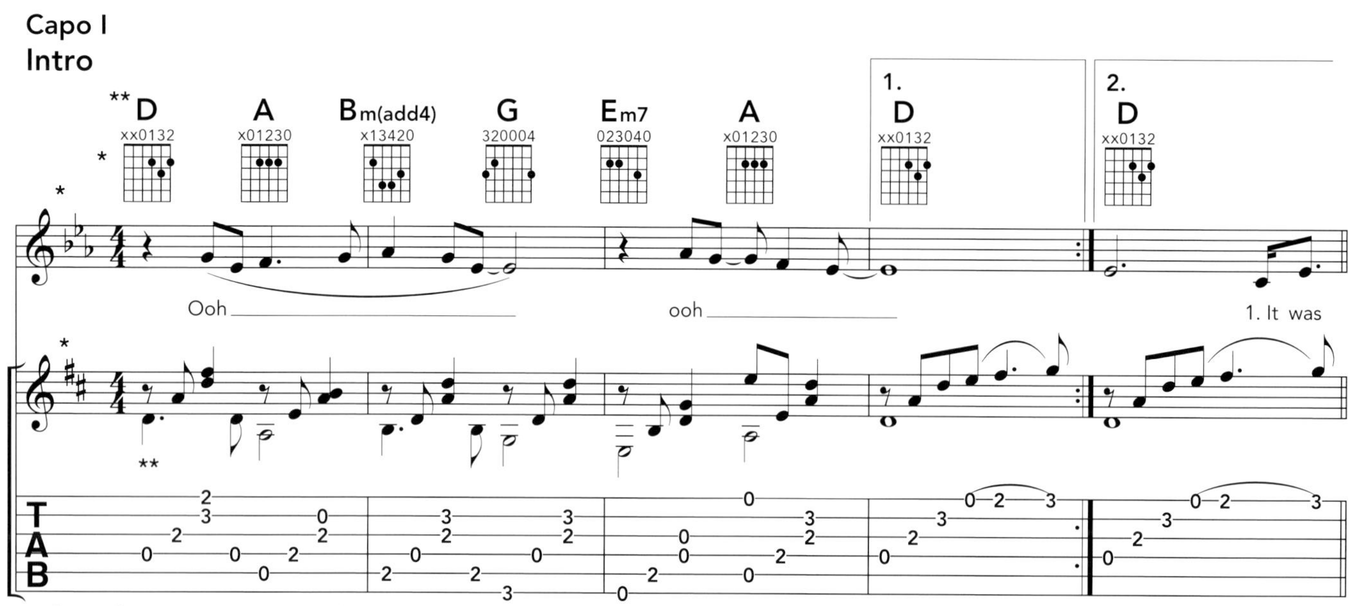

* Vocal written at concert pitch (key of E♭). Guitar notation, tab, and chords written respective to capoed guitar (key of D).

** Fretboards show overall original chords; tab and notation show arrangement of guitar harmony on *Second Chances*.

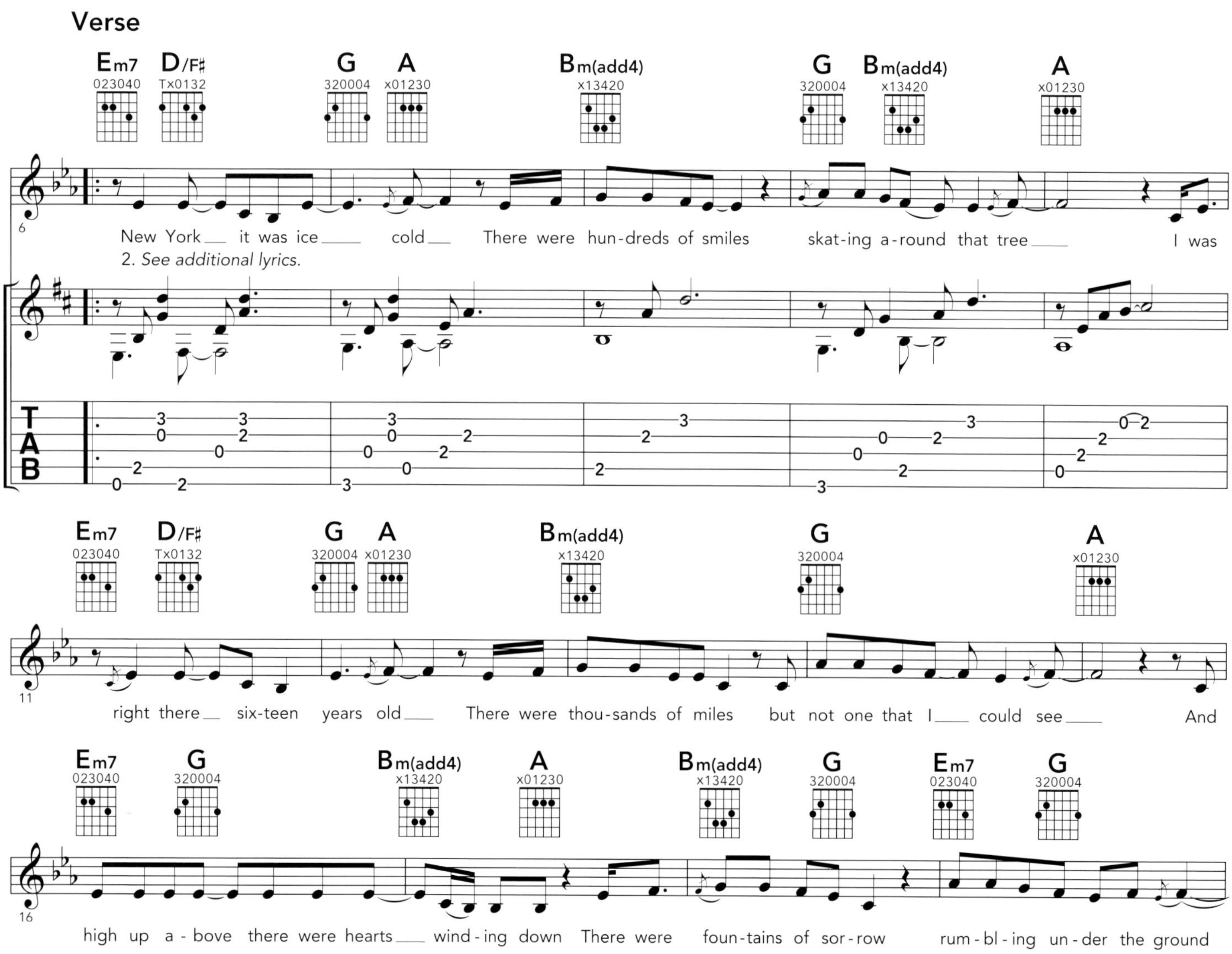

Chorus
G/A Aadd9 D G Em7 A
And you were there to save us Like our catch-er in the rye
Bm(add4) G D G D A
Sing-ing your songs with that hunt-ing had on And the tax-is were fly-ing by I swear I saw a
Bm(add4) G Em7 A
1. D
2. D
hint of heav-en Shin - ing in your eyes 2. Just like There was a song
Bridge
G A Bm(add4) G
for all those peo - ple There was a light in ev - ery eye
D.S. al Coda
Em D/F♯ G G/A Aadd9
Grace e-nough for ev - ery-one E-ven those who won-der why
Coda
D A Bm(add4) G Em7 A D
Oh I swear I saw a hint of heav-en shin - ing in your eyes oh yes I did

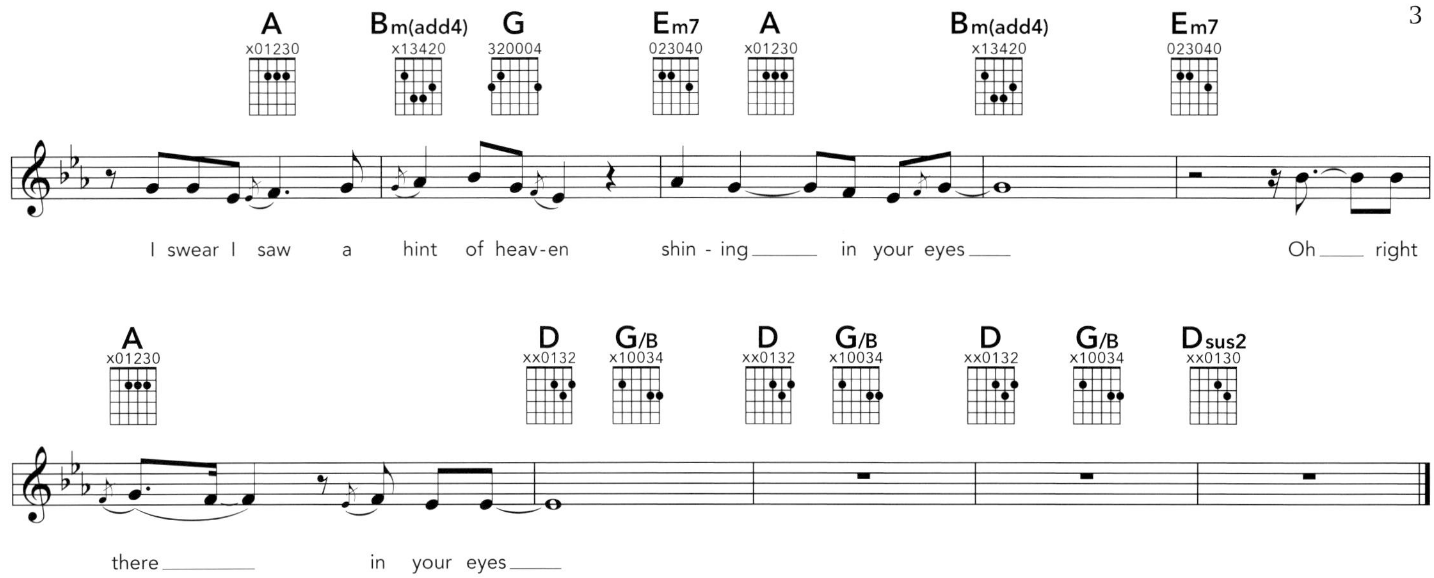

Intro

D A Bm(add4) G Em7 A D
Ooh,_____ ooh___

D A Bm(add4) G Em7 A D
Ooh,_____ ooh___

Em7 D/F♯ G A
1. It was New York, it was ice cold

Bm(add4) G Bm(add4) A
There were hundreds of smiles skating around that tree

Em7 D/F♯ G A
I was right there, sixteen years old

Bm(add4) G A
There were thousands of miles but not one that I could see

Em7 G Bm(add4) A
And high up above there were hearts winding down

Bm(add4) G Em7 G G/A Aadd9
There were fountains of sorrow rumbling under the ground

Chorus

D G
And you were there to save us

Em7 A
Like our catcher in the rye

Bm(add4) G
Singing your songs with that hunting cap on

D G
And the taxis flying by

D A Bm(add4) G
I swear I saw a hint of heaven

Em7 A D
Shining in your eyes

Em7 D/F♯ G A
2. Just like children, round the rosie

Bm(add4) G Bm(add4) A
They were circled around you singing "this is a song for you"

Em7 D/F♯ G A
In that cold air, something told me

Bm(add4) G A
It was more than a moment, down on that avenue

Em7 G Bm(add4) A
And high up above there was grace falling down

Bm(add4) G Em7 G G/A Aadd9
There were anthems of glory lifting us up with their sound

Repeat Chorus

Bridge

G A
There was a song for all the people

Bm(add4) G
There was a light in every eye

Em D/F♯
Grace enough for everyone

G G/A Aadd9
Even those who wonder why

Repeat Chorus

A Bm(add4) G
Oh, I swear I saw a hint of heaven

Em7 A D
Shining in your eyes, oh yes I did

A Bm(add4) G
I swear I saw a hint of heaven

Em7 A Bm(add4)
Shining in your eyes

Em7 A D G/B D G/B D G/B D
Oh, right there in your eyes

Best Year of My Life

Words and Music by Doc Schneider

D G Em7 A
all we could do was laugh Cause there was mu - sic play-ing And there were child - ren sing-ing All the
D G Em7 A
To Coda
trees were sway - ing And the bells were ring - ing And the world was light and bright
1. 2.
Bridge
G A D D F♯7 Bm7
That was the best year of my life life Now the years roll by like a wave of grain
G/B A7 D D/C♯ Bm Em7 A
One by one like an end - less train And I watch each one roll by
Coda
G A D
D.S. al Coda
Roll by the best years of my life
G A G A D
This is the best year This is the best year of my life

Intro
G A7 F♯7 Bm7 G A D

Bm G
1. She was a southern girl
D D/C♯ Bm
Took me in from a different world
Em A
Long out of New York City
D D/C♯ Bm
Never knew a girl who was quite that pretty
Em A
And we were moving way too fast
D G
We were trying to make it last
Em
We were married in September
A
She was pregnant by December
D G
But all we could do was laugh

Chorus
Em7
Cause there was music playing
A
And there were children singing
D
All the trees were swaying
G
And the bells were ringing
Em7 A
And the world was light and bright
G A D
That was the best year of my life

Bm G
2. She was a tiny baby
D D/C♯ Bm
A whole lot of her, and a little me maybe
Em A
Sang her my made up ditty
D D/C♯ Bm
Just another girl who was just that pretty
Em A
And she was growing up so fast
D G
As the time was flying past
Em
She was telling me her letters
A
Did her numbers even better
D G
And all we could do was laugh

Repeat Chorus

Bridge
F♯7 Bm7
Now the years roll by like a wave of grain
G/B A D D/C♯ Bm
One by one like an endless train
Em7 A
And I watch each one roll by
G A D
Roll by the best years of my life

Bm G
3. All of our children grown
D D/C♯ Bm
Off to find what we have known
Em A
Still in this southern city
D D/C♯ Bm
Still here with my girl who is still so pretty
Em A
And the time still going fast
D G
We just grab it going past
Em
We will shower shiny tears
A
On that path of golden years
D G
But all we will do was laugh

Repeat Chorus
G A
…This is the best year of my life
G A D
This is the best year of my life

Just Then

Words and Music by Doc Schneider

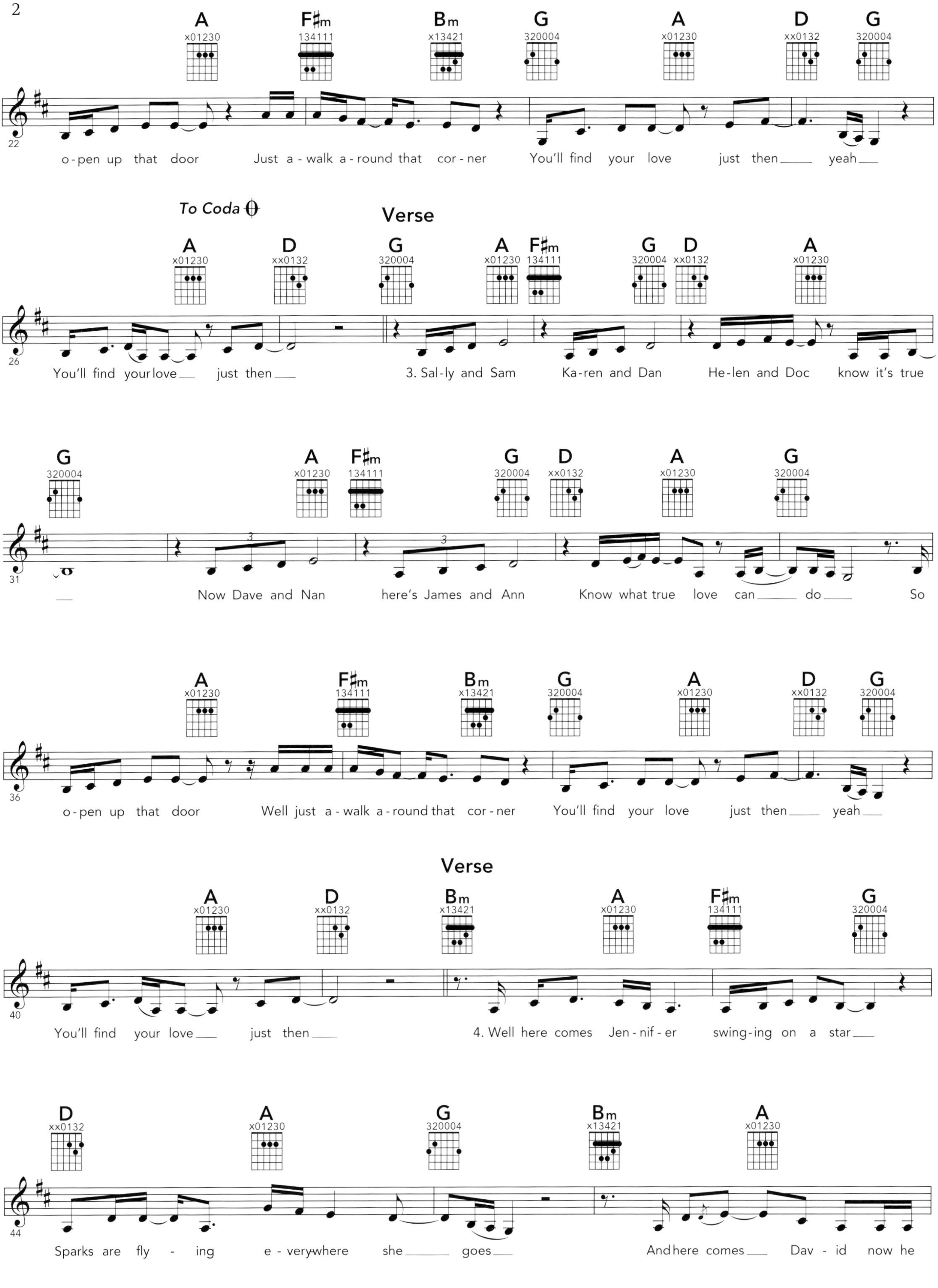
A F♯m Bm G A D G
o-pen up that door Just a-walk a-round that cor-ner You'll find your love just then yeah
To Coda
Verse
A D G A F♯m G D A
You'll find your love just then 3. Sal-ly and Sam Ka-ren and Dan He-len and Doc know it's true
G A F♯m G D A G
Now Dave and Nan here's James and Ann Know what true love can do So
A F♯m Bm G A D G
o-pen up that door Well just a-walk a-round that cor-ner You'll find your love just then yeah
Verse
A D Bm A F♯m G
You'll find your love just then 4. Well here comes Jen-nif-er swing-ing on a star
D A G Bm A
Sparks are fly-ing e-very-where she goes And here comes Dav-id now he

Bm A F♯m G
1. Here comes Jennifer looking so tired
D A F♯m G
A little worn out and a lot uninspired
D Bm
She just needs her heart rewired
G A
To feel that spark again

Bm A F♯m G
2. There goes David dragging his lonely
D A F♯m G
He never has met his one and his only
D Bm
He hopes he hasn't missed his moment
G A
But he feels that way again

Pre-Chorus

D
Unbeknownst to them, right around the corner
G D A
There's a path that leads them each to each
G D/F♯ A F♯m Bm
And right before their eyes the come upon each other
G A
And see that there's a love that they can reach

Chorus

G Bm G
Cause love always knows it will find every heart to fill
D A G
Though nobody knows quite when
A F♯m Bm
So open up that door, just walk around that corner
G A D G
You'll find your love just then, yeah
A D
You'll find your love just then

G A F♯m G
2. Sally and Sam, Karen and Dan
D A G
Helen and Doc know it's true
A F♯m G
Now Dave and Nan, here's James and Ann
D A G
Know what true love can do
A F♯m Bm
So open up that door, well, just walk around that corner
G A D G
You'll find your love just then, yeah
A D
You'll find your love just then

```
    Bm                A       F♯m            G
4.  Well, here comes Jennifer swinging on a star

    D            A                   G
    Sparks are flying everywhere she goes

    Bm             A             F♯m                G
    And here comes David now he won't know who you are

                         D    A      G    A
    Cause Jennifer's the only one he knows
```

Repeat Chorus

```
   G              A         F♯m              Bm
So open up that door, just walk around that corner

G               A        D      G
You'll find your love just then, yeah

                A       D
You'll find your love just then
```

If You Must Leave Me Now

Words and Music by Doc Schneider

G A D D/C♯ Bm G A
stars in-side your shoes Take a-way the whole damn world And just leave me with my blues
Em7 A D Em7 A
If you must leave me If you must leave me now
D To Coda Em7 A D 1.
Why must you leave me now
2. Bridge
Dsus4 G A Bm G
And I know I must hard - en my heart So I can

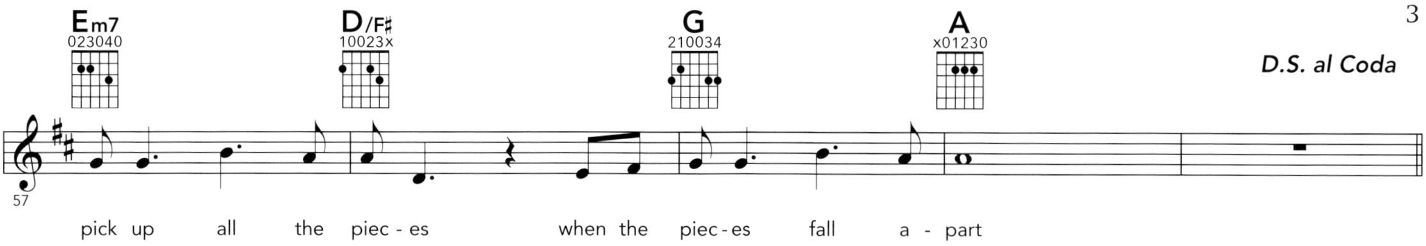

𝄌 Coda

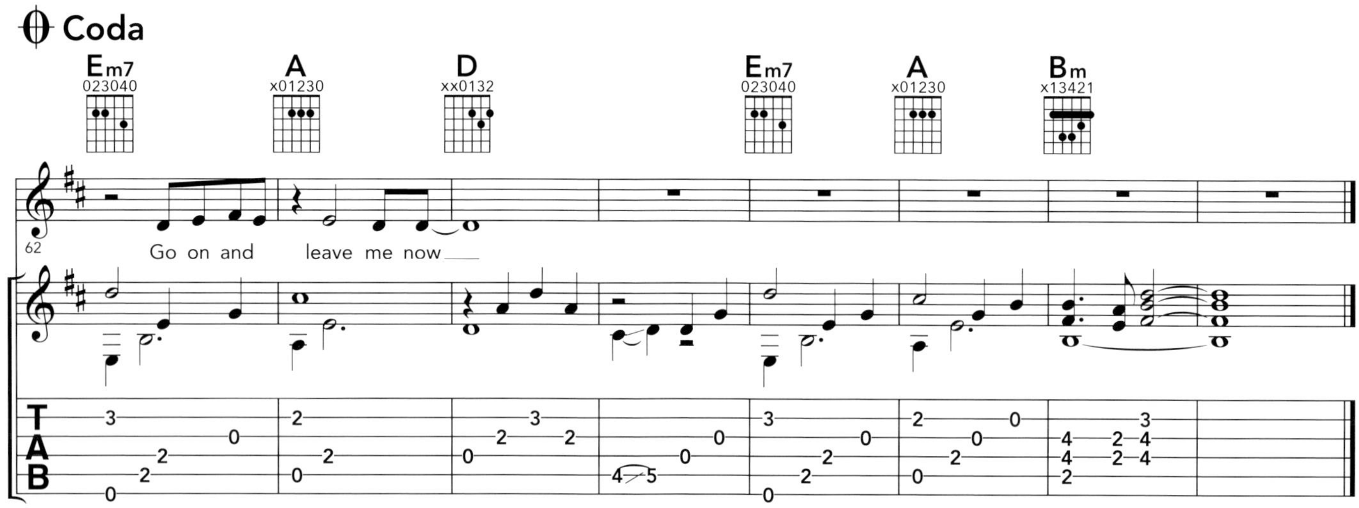

Intro

Em7 A7 Bm
Em7 A7 Bm

```
   Em7            A7  Bm
1. Watching your eyes, you're watching the door
   Em7        A7  Bm
   Telling me why it's not there anymore
   G                   D            A                 Bm
   And you say you're leaving, I don't want to hear those words
   G          D           A               Bm
   Try to believe in it was something else I heard
                       Em7        A
   There is no reason to leave me this way
```

Chorus

```
Em7             A          D
But if you must leave me now
           D/C♯              Bm
Pack the moon inside your suitcase
          G            A
Stick the stars inside your shoes
D    D/C♯        Bm
Take away the whole damn world
           G               A
And just leave me with my blues
Em7       A       D
If you must leave me
Em7       A        D
If you must leave me now
Em7          A         D
Why must you leave me now?
```

```
   Em7                   A7  Bm
2. Remember that day, declaring our love
   Em7                          A7  Bm
   When words wouldn't say what we tried to speak of
   G                 D                 A                Bm
   Now every new sweet love surely some day will be gone
   G                D                   A                  Bm
   But there is a true love left for those who will hold on
                         Em7          A
   There is no reason to give up this way
```

Chorus

```
Em7             A          D
But if you must leave me now
           D/C♯         Bm
Can you take me to that moment
        G               A
When I gave away my heart
D        D/C♯     Bm
Can you take this love away
        G              A
And don't ever let it start?
Em7        A       D
If you must leave me
Em7        A        D
If you must leave me now
Em7           A         D   Dsus4
Why must you leave me now?
```

Bridge

G A Bm G
And I know I must harden my heart

Em7 D/F♯ G A
So I can pick up all the pieces when the pieces fall apart

Em7 A7 Bm
3. Turn out the light, turn on the dark

Em7 A7 Bm
Letting in the night steal your last spark

G D A Bm
The sight of you leaving slowly cuts me like a knife

G D A Bm
And every good feeling is now bleeding from my life

Em7 A
Tell me the reason it hurts me this way

Chorus

Em7 A D
And if you must leave me now

D/C♯ Bm
Pack the moon inside your suitcase

G A
Stick the stars inside your shoes

D D/C♯ Bm
Take away the whole damn world

G A
And just leave me with my blues

Em7 A D
If you must leave me

Em7 A D
If you must leave me now

Em7 A D
Go on and leave me now

Em7 A Bm

Bitter Brew

Words and Music by Doc Schneider

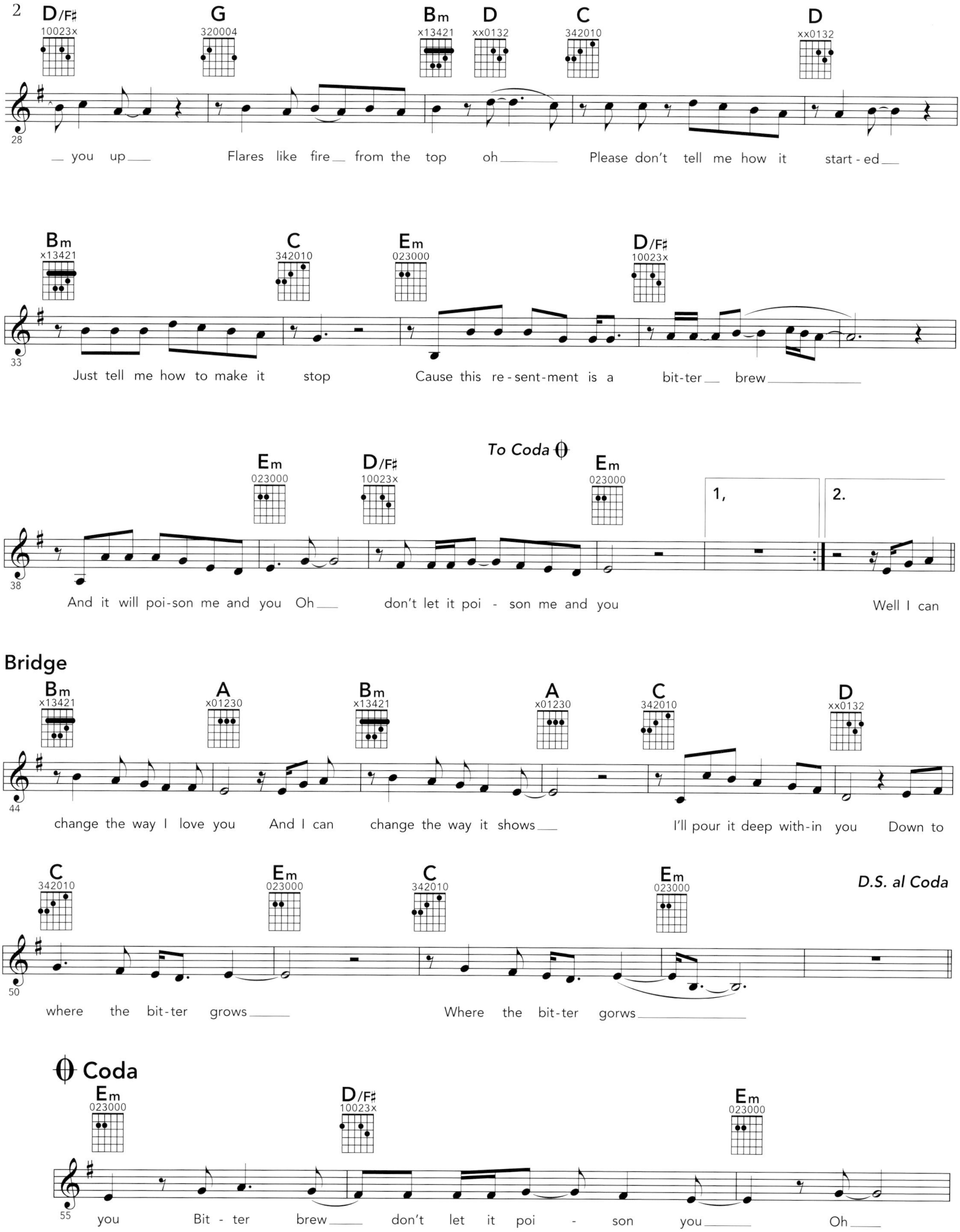
2
D/F♯ G Bm D C D
you up Flares like fire from the top oh Please don't tell me how it start-ed
Bm C Em D/F♯
Just tell me how to make it stop Cause this re-sent-ment is a bit-ter brew
To Coda
Em D/F♯ Em
1, 2.
And it will poi-son me and you Oh don't let it poi - son me and you Well I can
Bridge
Bm A Bm A C D
change the way I love you And I can change the way it shows I'll pour it deep with-in you Down to
C Em C Em
D.S. al Coda
where the bit-ter grows Where the bit-ter gorws
Coda
Em D/F♯ Em
you Bit - ter brew don't let it poi - son you Oh

Intro

C♯m Em C♯m Em
C♯m Em C♯m

C♯m A
1. You feel my eyes ignore you, you grow dissatisfied

C♯m A
You mark it on your ledger and you never let it rise

Bm G C D
While I wallow in my ego where I cower and I hide

C G Em Bm
Your anger won't let me go and it tears you up inside

Chorus

C D
This resentment is a bitter brew

Bm C
You fill the bottle drop by drop

Em D/F♯
And pretty soon it fills you up

G Bm D
Flares like fire from the top, oh

C D
Please don't tell me how it started

Bm C
Just tell me how to make it stop

Em D/F♯
Cause this resentment is a bitter brew

Em
And it will poison me and you

D/F♯ Em
Oh, don't let it poison me and you

C♯m A
2. Now sometimes you confront me and you tally up my faults

C♯m A
And I become the wounded one and your words rub in like salt

Bm G C D
I do nothing to dissuade you, I just hope it goes away

C G Em Bm
But it never quite blows over, it just smolders on that way

Repeat Chorus

Bridge

Bm A
Well I can change the way I love you

Bm A
And I can change the way it shows

C D
I'll pour it deep within you

C Em
Down to where the bitter grows

C Em
Where the bitter grows

C♯m A
3. The truth is I'm to blame here but that's a truth that I don't say

C♯m A
My self-indictment is my secret, I keep it weak that way

Bm G C D
So I wrap myself in silence and I flee the light of day

C G Em Bm
Your heart is left in darkness and the love just bleeds away

Repeat Chorus

D/F♯ Em
Bitter brew, don't let it poison me and you

D/F♯ Em
Oh, don't let it poison me and you

We're Still Standing Here

Words and Music by Doc Schneider

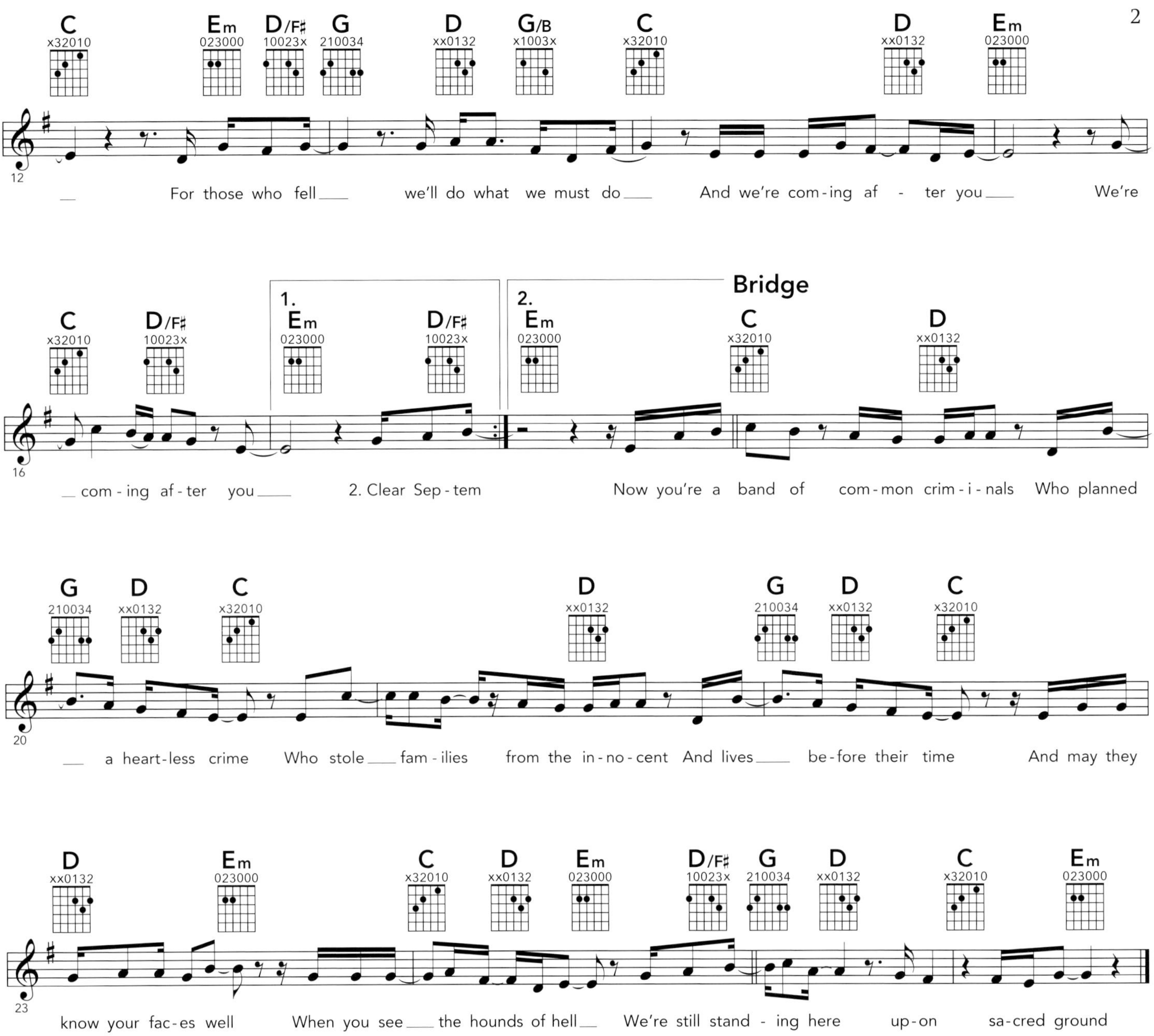

Em7 D/F♯ G D C Em
1. We're still standing here upon sacred ground

D C D/F♯ G
Well, did you really think you'd knock us down?

G/B D/F♯ D Em
When those buildings fell to zero ground

D C Em D/F♯ G
Well, every heart stood up in every town

Chorus

D/F♯ Em C D
And every town is coming after you

G D/F♯ Em D C
For every cop and firefighter, too

Em D/F♯ G D G/B C
For those who fell, we'll do what we must do

D Em
And we're coming after you

C D/F♯ Em
We're coming after you

Em D/F♯ G D C Em
2. Clear September sky and those morning planes

D C D/F♯ G
And all the heroes die, but not in vain

G/B D/F♯ D Em
And on the cell phone lines, the brave goodbye

D C Em D/F♯ G
And the tears that fall from every eye

Chorus

D/F♯ Em C D
And eye for eye, we're coming after you

G D/F♯ Em D C
For every cop and firefighter, too

Em D/F♯ G D G/B C
For those who fell, we'll do what we must do

D Em
And we're coming after you

C D/F♯ Em
We're coming after you

Bridge

C D
Now you're a band of common criminals

G D C
Who planned a heartless crime

D
Who stole families from the innocent

G D C
And lives before their time

D Em
And may they know your faces well

C D Em
When you see the hounds of hell

Em D/F♯ G D C Em
We're still standing here upon sacred ground

choices & chances

The Liner Notes

This CD was a long time coming. This collection of songs was written over the period from 1974 to 2002. The songs cover a whole range of subjects from the power of first love, to the exuberant joy of marriage and family, to my philosophy on love and life to the mixture of sadness, anger and pride that I think we all felt and still feel about September 11, 2001. I have included one song that is nearly 30 years old—Coming Home Again, which is the first song I ever wrote at age 19 (I did not consider myself a songwriter back then, and this song just fell out of my guitar and my heart accidentally). I thank my Naval Academy Prep School classmates, the Urrutia family and Helen (then Schroll and forever Schneider) for seeming to like my early songs, and planting the seed that gave rise to other songs in the years ahead. All of the other songs date from 1992 forward, when I started writing songs again in earnest, with much more care and attention to the effort required.

These songs do not compare to those of my heroes—James Taylor, David Wilcox, Don McLean, Paul Simon, Carole King, Pierce Pettis, Dar Williams and so many others—but they are inspired by them. And there is a song or two in this collection that tips my hat to them. Hint of Heaven, for example, is my portrait of James Taylor performing on a very cold day in New York City outside on the Good Morning America Show in 2000, with a furry hat pulled down over his ears, straps dangling, and a heavy coat—singing soft songs into the cold air surrounded by a holy host of others—grace personified.

I am thankful to so many people who supported my effort to put together this collection. First and foremost, I thank Helen who has always tolerated my endless gazing at the green light, and encouraged my songwriting—and has been at the center of many of my songs, just as she is at

the center of my life. I thank my daughters, Heather and Kristin, who would always listen to the recordings of my latest songs in their cars and in their rooms, even when I was not there—which convinced me that they really did enjoy them. I thank my little grandchildren to date—McKenzie, Madison, Zoe, and Zachary—for continuing the circle of life, and giving me a whole new universe to search for songs. (I am sure that I have just killed runaway sales by admitting that this collection is being released by a grandfather—albeit a very, very young grandfather!) I thank David Romine and Songbird Studios in Atlanta for being my friend and supporter for all these years. There are few souls as warm and talented and generous as David Romine, and I thank him and Onnie for their helping hands. Some of the songs in this collection reflect David's painstaking orchestrations (like Just Then, for example), and they add variety to what otherwise is me pulling up to a mic at Songbird, guitar on my knee and giving it all I have. I thank the Schroll family for listening to my songs over the years and letting me do beach concerts year after year—and even having favorites (like Shea's affection for Choices and Chances)—that meant the world to me. And last but not least, I thank my niece Jenny Garland (nee Schroll), who was the talented project manager and creative graphic designer for this project, and who designed the look and feel of this album, produced a wonderful lyric book and a great overall concept for this collection of songs, and then did all the legwork to reproduce 1000 copies to insure that we would not sell out the first day or ever. I often dreamt of what a well-produced CD with my music might look like, and then Jenny exceeded my dreams. Thank you.

And to all who listen to this CD, I will tell you this. I wrote these songs for me, but in truth, I wrote them for you too. I hope you enjoy them.

Doc

SECO
C
Intro & Riff
o the wheel is turni
rns this world
l the stars
nce fell

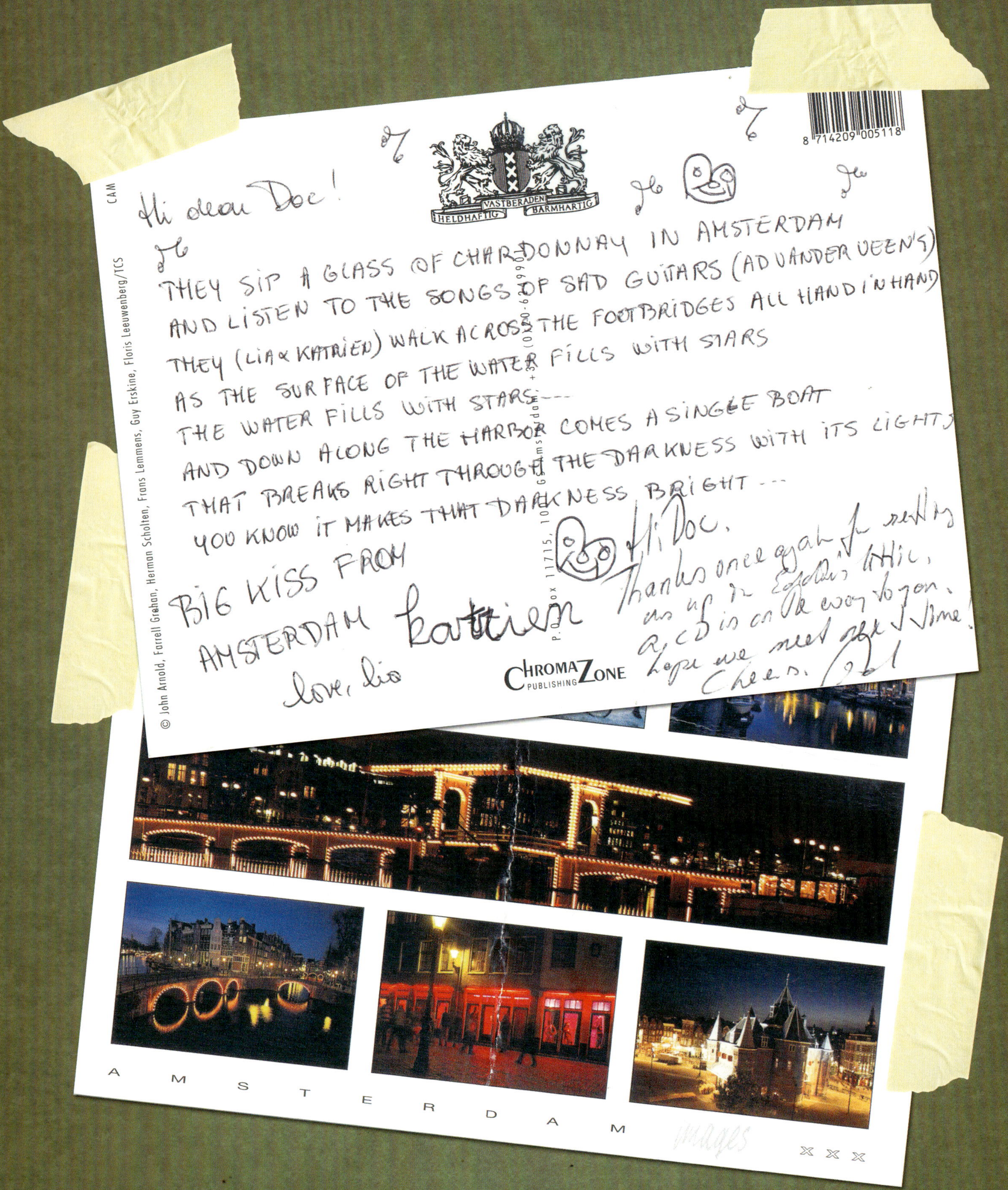
Hi dear Doc!
THEY SIP A GLASS OF CHARDONNAY IN AMSTERDAM
AND LISTEN TO THE SONGS OF SAD GUITARS (AD VANDER VEEN'S)
THEY (LIA & KATRIEN) WALK ACROSS THE FOOTBRIDGES ALL HAND IN HAND
AS THE SURFACE OF THE WATER FILLS WITH STARS
THE WATER FILLS WITH STARS---
AND DOWN ALONG THE HARBOR COMES A SINGLE BOAT
THAT BREAKS RIGHT THROUGH THE DARKNESS WITH ITS LIGHTS
YOU KNOW IT MAKES THAT DARKNESS BRIGHT ---
BIG KISS FROM
AMSTERDAM
Katrien
love, lia
Hi Doc,
Thanks once again for setting us up in Eglise Lille,
a CD is on the way to you.
Hope we meet again some time!
Cheers,
CHROMA ZONE
PUBLISHING
VASTBERADEN
HELDHAFTIG
BARMHARTIG
8 714209 005118
CAM
© John Arnold, Farrell Grehan, Herman Scholten, Frans Lemmens, Guy Erskine, Floris Leeuwenberg/TCS
A M S T E R D A M
images
x x x

A Second Chance

Words and Music by Doc Schneider

Chorus
2
Cadd9 D Em7 Cadd9 G D/F♯ Em(add9) Cadd9 Dsus4
Give them a se-cond chance be-neath the paint-ed sky For if they had
To Coda
1.
D.S.
Cadd9 Em7 Cadd9 D Em D/F♯ Gadd9
a se-cond chance may-be this time they would fly 3. They
2.
Bridge
Cadd9 D G D/F♯ Em7 D/F♯ G Cadd9
may-be this time they would fly So brave the way the heart fights back
Em7 D/F♯ Gsus2 D/F♯ Em7 D/F♯ G Cadd9 G D/F♯
For e-very-thing it knows Shines on bright a-gainst the black The fire and the rose
Guitar Solo (nylon-string)
Em(add9) Fadd9 Gadd9 D/F♯ Em7 C
the fire and the rose
Gsus2 D/F♯ Em7 C Gsus2
D.S. al Coda
5. There's a

3 **Coda**

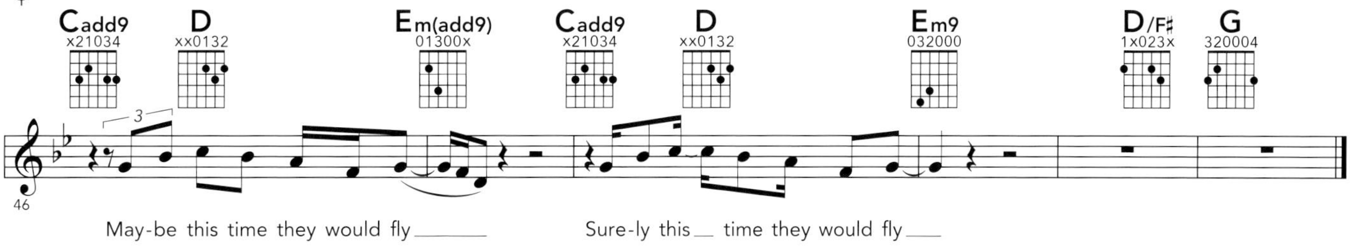

Intro

Gsus2 C6(9) Gsus2 C6(9)

Gsus2 D/F♯
1. There's a young man holding tightly to a ray of hope
Em A13sus4 Csus2
Writing novels that are woven with his past
Gadd9 D/F♯
Lost his father way too early, found him way too late
Em A13sus4 Csus2
Sometimes the losing is the only thing that lasts
Gsus2
The only thing that lasts

Gsus2 D/F♯
2. He asks the pretty mochachino if she likes to dance
Em A13sus4 Csus2
Tries to touch her perfect fingers with the change
Gadd9 D/F♯
And he says he'd like to take her to the coast of France
Em A13sus4 Csus2
But she just thinks the novelist is strange
G
The novelist is strange

Chorus

Cadd9 D Em7 Cadd9
Give them a second chance
G D/F♯ Em(add9)
Beneath the painted sky
Cadd9 D Cadd9 Em7
For if they had a second chance
Cadd9 D Em D/F♯ Gadd9
Maybe this time they would fly

G D/F♯
3. They sip a glass of chardonnay in Amsterdam
Em A13sus4 Csus2
And listen to the songs of sad guitars
Gadd9 D/F♯
They walk across the footbridges all hand in hand
Em A13sus4 Csus2
As the surface of the water fills with stars
Gsus2
The water fills with stars

Gsus2 D/F♯
4. And soon she reads his novel on the coast of France
Em A13sus4 Csus2
And lets a silver tear begin to fall
Gadd9 D/F♯
And every time she thinks about their Starbuck's dance
Em A13sus4 Csus2
She knows that love was waiting after all
Gadd9
Love was waiting after all

Repeat Chorus

Cadd9 D G
…Maybe this time they would fly

Bridge

D/F♯ Em7 D/F♯ G Cadd9
So brave the way the heart fights back
Em7 D/F♯ Gsus2
For everything it knows
D/F♯ Em7 D/F♯ G Cadd9
Shines on, bright against the black
G D/F♯ Em(add9) F
The fire and the rose, the fire and the rose

Nylon-String Guitar Solo

Gadd9 D/F♯ Em7 C
Gsus2 D/F♯ Em7 C Gsus2

Gadd9 D/F♯
5. There's a young man holding tightly to his ray of hope
Em Dadd4 Csus2
She brushes back her hair and says goodnight
G D/F♯
And down along the harbor comes a single boat
Em Dadd4 Csus2
That breaks right through the darkness with its light
Gadd9
You know it makes that darkness bright

Repeat Chorus

Cadd9 D Em(add9)
…Maybe this time they would fly
Cadd9 D Em9 D/F♯ G
Surely this time they would fly

Homemade Song

Words and Music by Doc Schneider

Intro

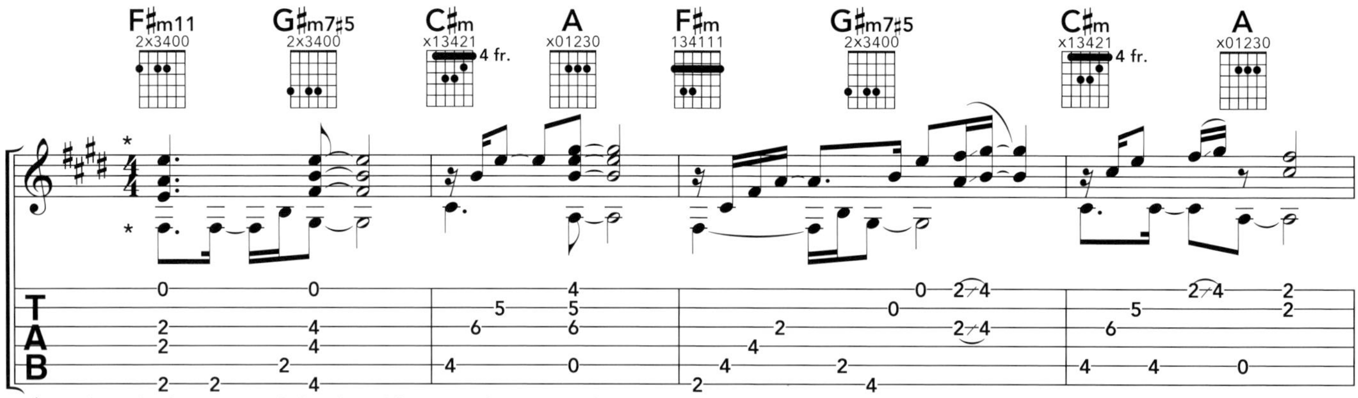

* Fretboards show original chords; tablature and notation show version from *Second Chances* arranged for guitar in standard tuning without capo.

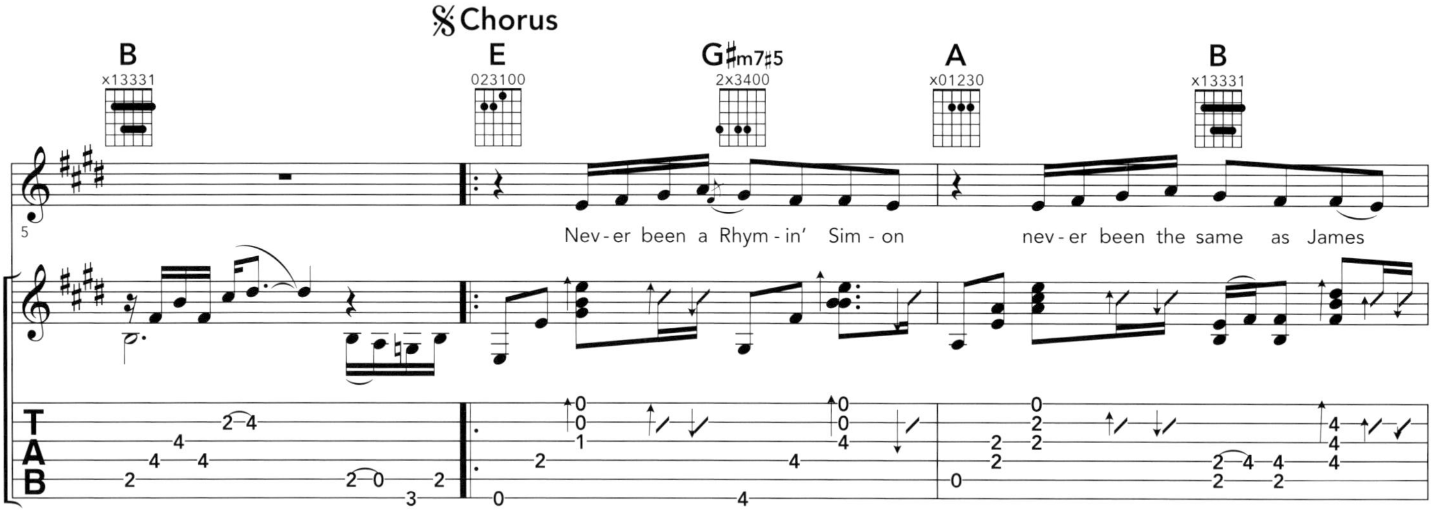

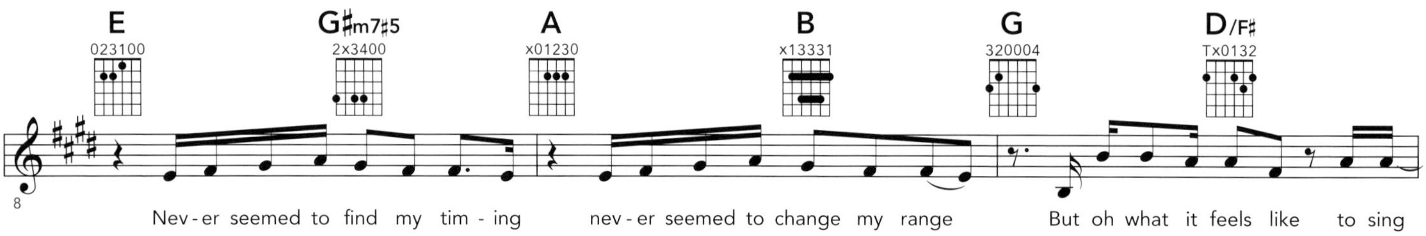

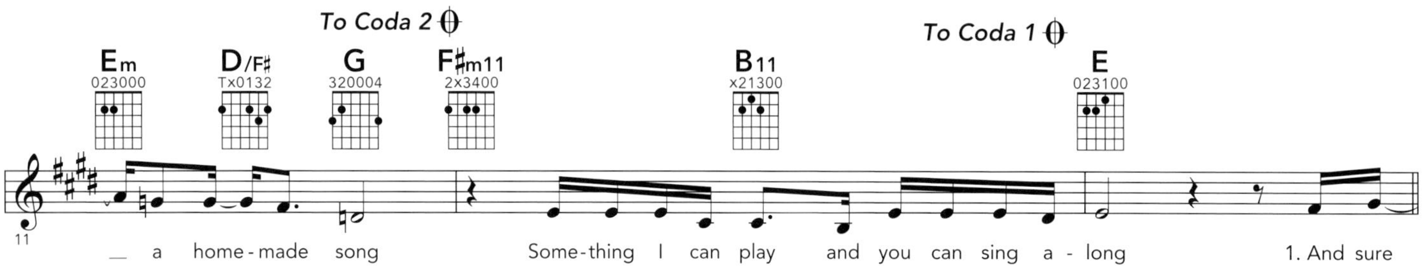

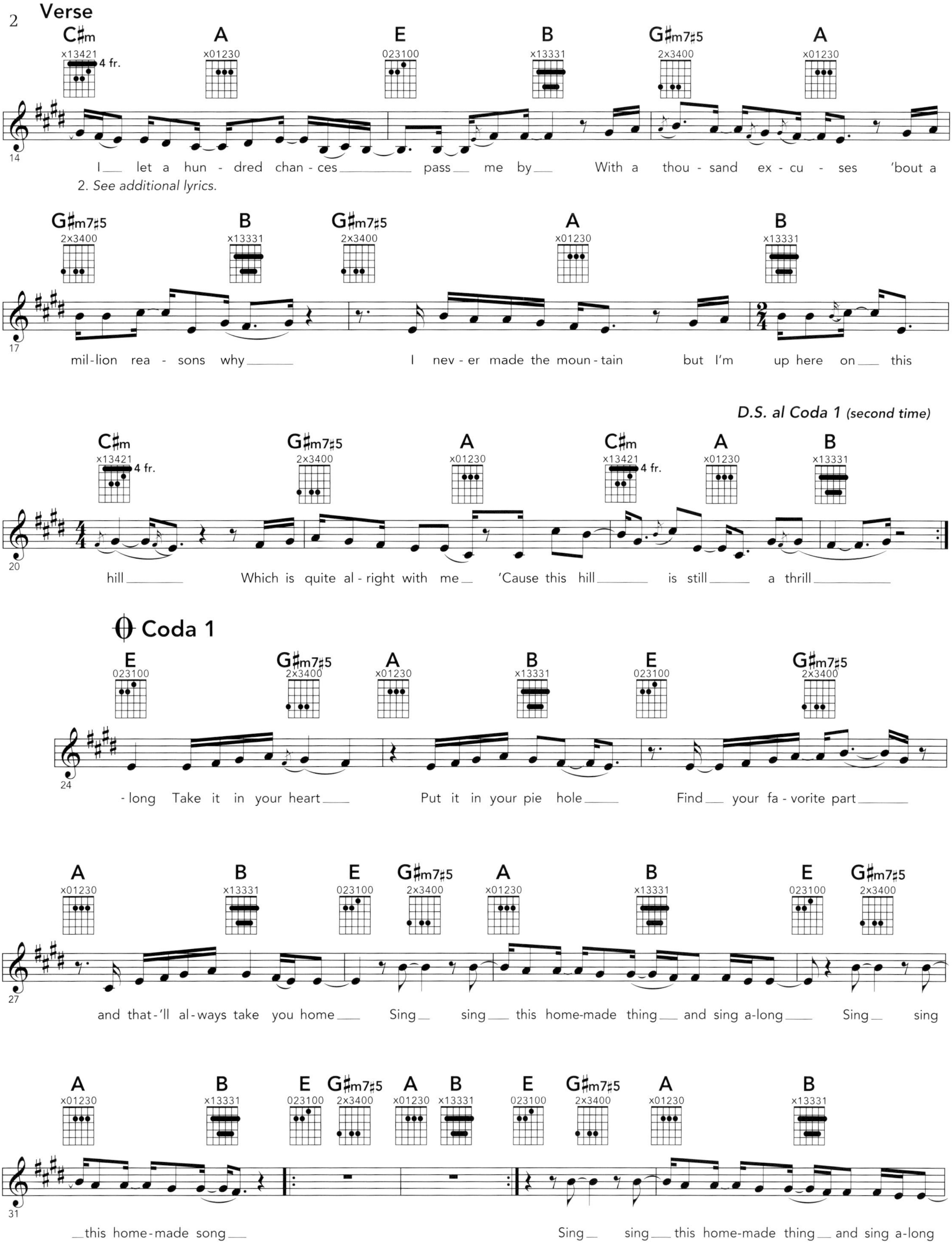
2 Verse
C♯m A E B G♯m7♯5 A
I let a hun - dred chan - ces pass me by With a thou - sand ex - cu - ses 'bout a
2. See additional lyrics.
G♯m7♯5 B G♯m7♯5 A B
mil - lion rea - sons why I nev - er made the moun - tain but I'm up here on this
D.S. al Coda 1 (second time)
C♯m G♯m7♯5 A C♯m A B
hill Which is quite al - right with me 'Cause this hill is still a thrill
Coda 1
E G♯m7♯5 A B E G♯m7♯5
- long Take it in your heart Put it in your pie hole Find your fa - vorite part
A B E G♯m7♯5 A B E G♯m7♯5
and that-'ll al - ways take you home Sing sing this home-made thing and sing a-long Sing sing
A B E G♯m7♯5 A B E G♯m7♯5 A B
this home-made song Sing sing this home-made thing and sing a-long

Intro

F♯m11 G♯m7♯5 C♯m A
F♯m11 G♯m7♯5 C♯m A B

Chorus

```
E                G♯m7♯5
Never been a Rhymin' Simon
A           B
Never been the same as James
E                 G♯m7♯5
Never seemed to find my timing
A                 B
Never seemed to change my range
G              D/F♯         Em    D/F♯       G
But, oh, what it feels like to sing a homemade song
F♯m11          B11                  E
Something I can play, and you can sing along
```

```
         C♯m         A          E          B
1.  And sure I let a hundred chances pass me by
        G♯m7♯5        A          G♯m7♯5            B
    With a thousand excuses 'bout a million reasons why
    G♯m7♯5            A                B              C♯m
    I never made the mountain, but I'm up here on this hill
               G♯m7♯5         A
    Which is quite alright with me
              C♯m   A     B
    Cause this hill is still a thrill
```

Chorus

```
E                G♯m7♯5
Never been a Rhymin' Simon
A           B
Never been the same as James
E                    G♯m7♯5
The trouble's always been my timing
A                 B
I never heard the next chord change
G              D/F♯         Em    D/F♯       G
But, oh, what it feels like to sing a homemade song
F♯m11          B11                  E
Something I can sing, and you can sing along
```

    C♯m   A   E   B
2. And sure I've passed my time and prime for writing songs

      G♯m7♯5   A   G♯m7♯5   B
But then something still moves me and floats my soul along

G♯m7♯5   A   B   C♯m
And suddenly I'm singing, and back up on this hill

    G♯m7♯5   A
And once more, like before

  C♯m   A   B
This hill is still a thrill

Repeat First Chorus

              G♯m7♯5 A   B
Take it in your heart, put it in your pie hole

E   G♯m7♯5 A   B   E
Find your favorite part and that'll always take you home

 G♯m7♯5 A   B   E
Sing, sing this homemade thing and sing along

 G♯m7♯5 A   B
Sing, sing, this homemade song

E   G♯m7♯5   A   B   E   G♯m7♯5   A   B   E

 G♯m7♯5 A   B   E
Sing, sing this homemade thing and sing along

 G♯m7♯5 A   B
Sing, sing, this homemade song

      A   G♯m7♯5
And if it's only me and you and we're up here on this hill

   C♯m   B
Will I sing the song for two? You know I will

Repeat First Chorus

Marie

Words and Music by Doc Schneider

2
Csus2 D5 Csus2 G D5 G Em7 Csus2
on-ly for one night Oh but I did not be-lieve that dream I nev-er thought I'd e-ver find my way
D5 Em7 Csus2 G D5 Csus2
And when it seemed too late you o-pened up the gate and set me free I
Chorus
Am7 Em7 F6/9 G Em7
can't be-lieve that you came back for me Ma-rie I have loved you for-ev-er Ma-
To Coda
1.
Csus2 G D/F♯ Am11 Em7 F6/9 G
rie we can walk out to-geth-er Ma-rie I can't be-lieve that you came back for me
2.
Bridge
G Em Am(add4) C D5
for me I've got a pock-et full of songs that I can sing you I
G Em7 D5 Em7 C
have this heart that I nev-er gave a-way I have a head full of dreams that I can

Em7 D5 Em7 Cadd9 G D5
D.S. al Coda
bring you And now these words I fi - nally get to say Ma
Coda
G Em7 Csus2
Ma-rie I have loved you for - ev - er Ma - rie we can
G D/F♯ Am11 Em7 F6/9
walk out to - geth - er Ma - rie I can't be - lieve that you came back
Em(add9) C(♯4) Gmaj7 D5 Em(add9) C(♯4)
for me you came back for me
Gmaj7 D5 Em(add9) C(♯4) Gmaj7 D5 Cadd9 D
you came back for me

4

Intro

Em(add9) C(♯4) Gmaj7 D/F♯
Em(add9) C(♯4) Gmaj7 D/F♯

Em(add9) Csus2
1. Your voice was like a river

G D5 Csus2
Rolling out across the land

Am7 Em(add9)
Sometimes I could hear you

Csus2 D/F♯
Calling for my hand, calling for my hand

G Em7
Just to take me past the bars and walls

Csus2 D5
That locked me up inside

G Em7
And then at last I'd see it all

Csus2 D5
If only for one night

Csus2 G D5 G
Oh, but I did not believe that dream

Em7 Csus2 D5
I never thought I'd ever find my way

Em7 Csus2
And when it seemed too late

G D5 Csus2
You opened up the gate and set me free

Am7 Em7 F6(9)
I can't believe that you came back for me

Chorus

G Em7
Marie, I have loved you forever

Csus2 G D/F♯
Marie, we can walk out together

Am11 Em7 F6(9) G
Marie, I can't believe that you came back for me

Em(add9) C(♯4) Gmaj7 D5
Em(add9) C(♯4) Gmaj7 D5

Em(add9) Csus2
2. And so the wheel is turning

G D5 Csus2
That turns this world around

Am7 Em(add9)
And all the stars are burning

Csus2 D/F♯
That once fell to the ground, that once fell to the ground

G Em7
Here beneath the sky you begin to dance

Csus2 D5
Where I'd dreamed you'd danced before

G Em7
Only you and I in an old romance

Csus2 D5
What else are chances for?

Csus2 G D5 G
Oh, and I, I do believe that dream

Em7 Csus2 D5
I never thought I'd find my way

Em7 Csus2
And when it seemed too late

G D5 Csus2
You opened up the gate and set me free

Am7 Em7 F6(9)
I can't believe that you came back for me

Repeat Chorus

Bridge

Em(add9) Am(add4) G D5
I've got a pocket full of songs that I can sing you

G Em7 D5
I have this heart that I never gave away

Em7 C Em7 D5
I have a head full of dreams that I can bring you

Em7 Cadd9 G D5
And now these words I finally get to say

Repeat Chorus (two times)

F6(9) Em(add9) C(♯4) Gmaj7
…that you came back for me

D5 Em(add9) C(♯4) Gmaj7
You came back for me

D5 Em(add9) C(♯4) Gmaj7 D5 Cadd9 D
You came back for me

Turn the World Around

Words and Music by Doc Schneider

Drop-D Tuning: D A D G B E, Capo II

Intro

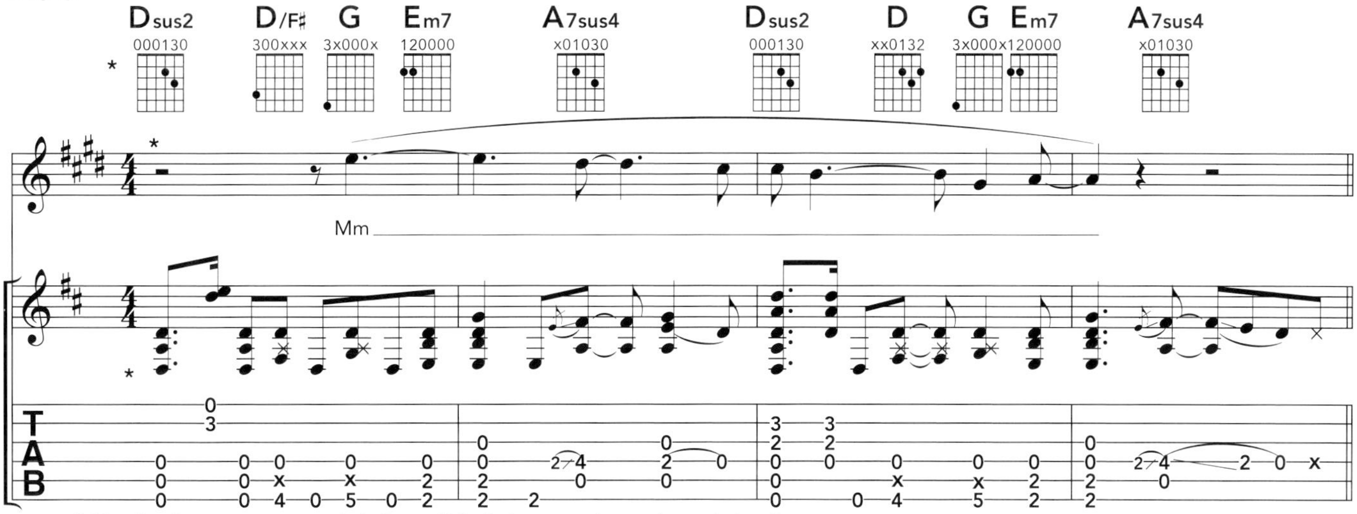

* Vocal written at concert pitch (key of E). Guitar notation, tab, and chords written respective to capoed guitar (key of D).

Verse

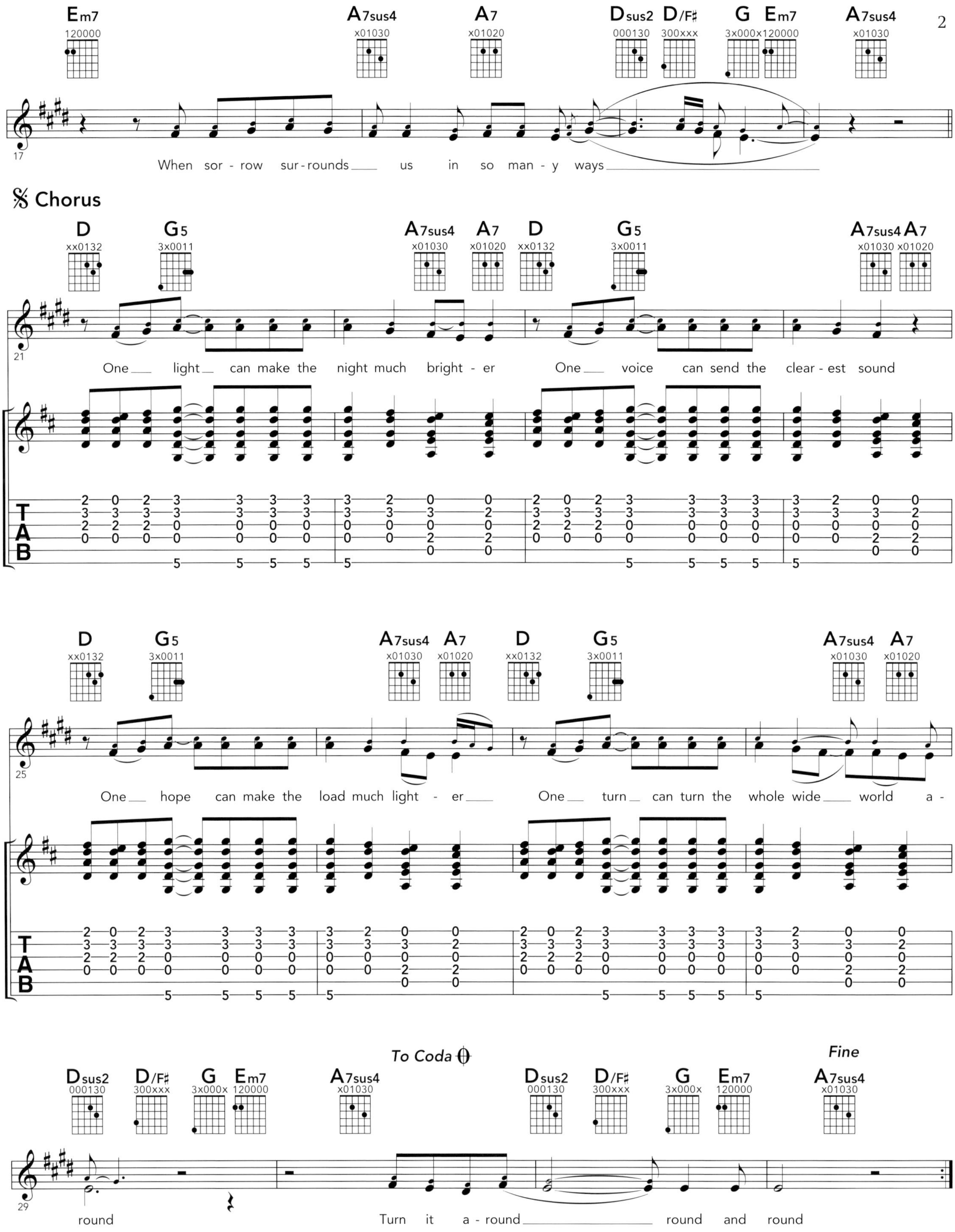
Em7 A7sus4 A7 Dsus2 D/F♯ G Em7 A7sus4
When sor - row sur - rounds us in so man - y ways
Chorus
D G5 A7sus4 A7 D G5 A7sus4 A7
One light can make the night much bright - er One voice can send the clear - est sound
D G5 A7sus4 A7 D G5 A7sus4 A7
One hope can make the load much light - er One turn can turn the whole wide world a -
To Coda
Fine
Dsus2 D/F♯ G Em7 A7sus4 Dsus2 D/F♯ G Em7 A7sus4
round Turn it a - round round and round

Bridge
3
Bm11 D/G D/F♯ Asus4 Bm11
In thou - sands of ti - ny hands the cray - ons are cry - ing And each of them
D/G D/F♯ Asus4 Em7 G
un - der - stands their fa - milies are dy - ing Some - one needs to stop this
Dsus2 D/F♯ G Em7 G Em7 A7
Some - one needs to stop this now Do you think that you're some - one who could turn it all a -
D.S. al Coda
Dsus2 D/F♯ G Em A7sus4 Dsus2 D/F♯ G Em7 A7sus4
- round turn it a - round
Coda
D G5 A7sus4 A7 D G5 A7sus4 A7
One voice can send the clear - est sound One hope can set the load much light - er

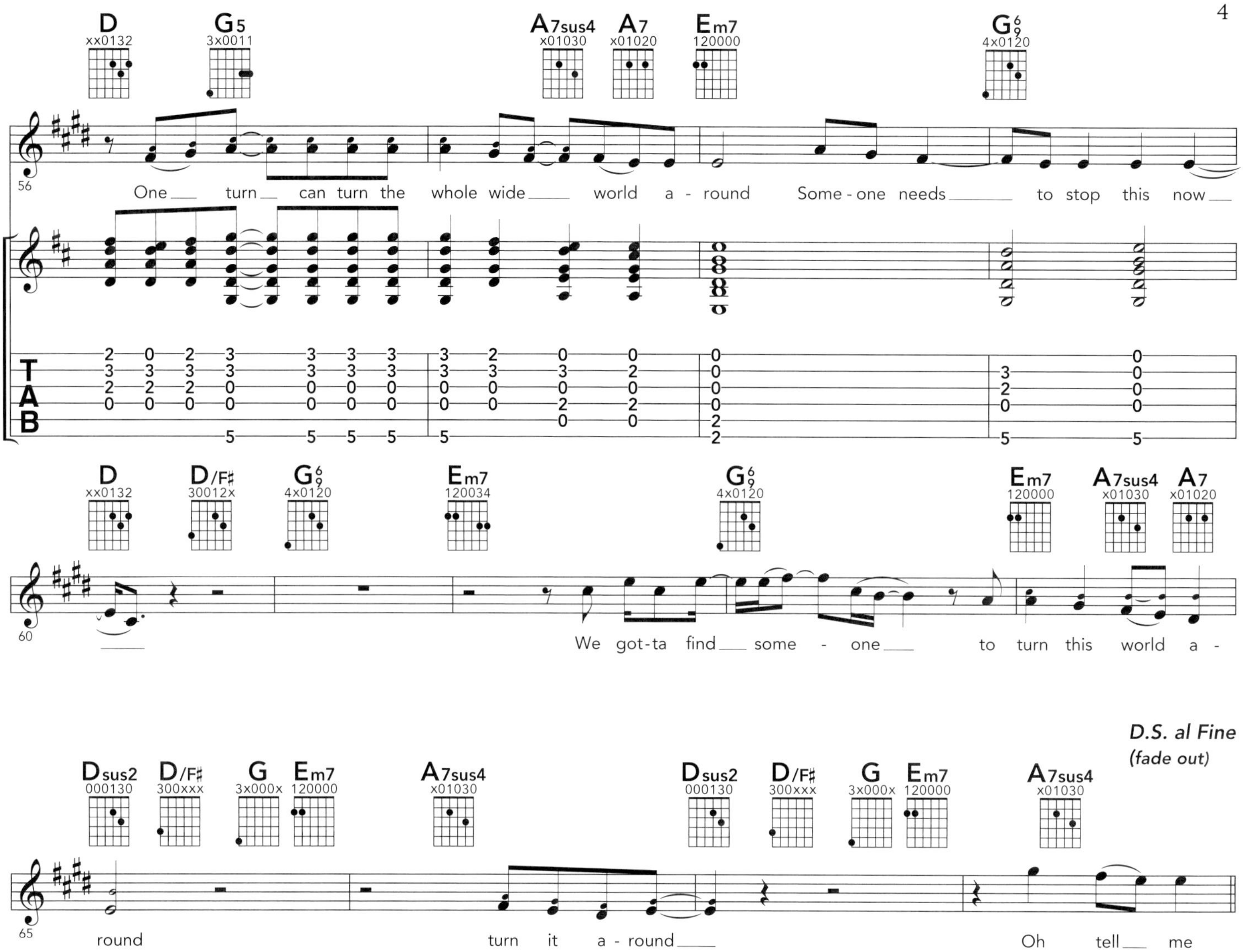

Intro

Dsus2 D/F♯ G Em7 A7sus4
Mm
Dsus2 D/F♯ G Em7 A7sus4

Dsus2 D/F♯ G A7sus4
1. In the heart of a war torn nation

Dsus2 D/F♯ G A7sus4
In the faces worn by pain

Em7 A7sus4 A7 Dsus2
Where it takes so much strength to face it again,

D/F♯ G Em7 A7sus4
mm

Dsus2 D/F♯ G A7sus4
In the eyes of the desperate children

Dsus2 D/F♯ G A7sus4
In the thick of these troubled days

Em7 A7sus4 A7 Dsus2
When sorrow surrounds us in so many ways

D/F♯ G Em7 A7sus4

Chorus

D G5 A7sus4 A7
One light can make the night much brighter

D G5 A7sus4 A7
One voice can send the clearest sound

D G5 A7sus4 A7
One hope can make the load much lighter

D G5 A7sus4 A7 Dsus2 D/F♯ G Em7
One turn can turn the whole wide world around

A7sus4 Dsus2 D/F♯ G Em7 A7sus4
Turn it around, round and round

5

Dsus2 D/F♯ G A7sus4
2. In the tears shed by shattered mothers

Dsus2 D/F♯ G A7sus4
From the many and the few

Em7 A7sus4 A7 Dsus2
When the eyes of the wounded are looking at you,

D/F♯ G Em7 A7sus4
oh

Dsus2 D/F♯ G A7sus4
In the dream of the frightened child

Dsus2 D/F♯ G A7sus4
In the back of her broken heart

Em7 A7sus4 A7 Dsus2
There is a hope with which you can start,

D/F♯ G Em7 A7sus4
yeah

Bridge

Bm11 D/G D/F♯ Asus4
In thousands of tiny hands, the crayons are crying

Bm11 D/G D/F♯ Asus4
And each of them understands their families are dying

Em7 G
Someone needs to stop this

Dsus2 D/F♯ G
Someone needs to stop this now

Em7 G Em7 A7 Dsus2
Do you think that you're someone who could turn it all around?

D/F♯ G Em A7sus4 Dsus2 D/F♯ G Em7 A7sus4
Turn it around

Repeat Chorus

A7sus4
…Turn it around,

D G5 A7sus4 A7
One voice can send the clearest sound

D G5 A7sus4 A7
One hope can make the load much lighter

D G5 A7sus4 A7 Em7
One turn can turn the whole wide world around

G6(9) D D/F♯ G6(9)
Someone needs to stop this now

G6(9) Em7 A7sus4 A7 Dsus2
We gotta find someone to turn this world around

D/F♯ G Em7 A7sus4 Dsus2 D/F♯ G Em7
Turn it around

A7sus4
Oh tell me

Repeat Chorus (and fade out)

I Wanted Everything

Words and Music by Doc Schneider

Tune down one half step: E♭ A♭ D♭ G♭ B♭ E♭

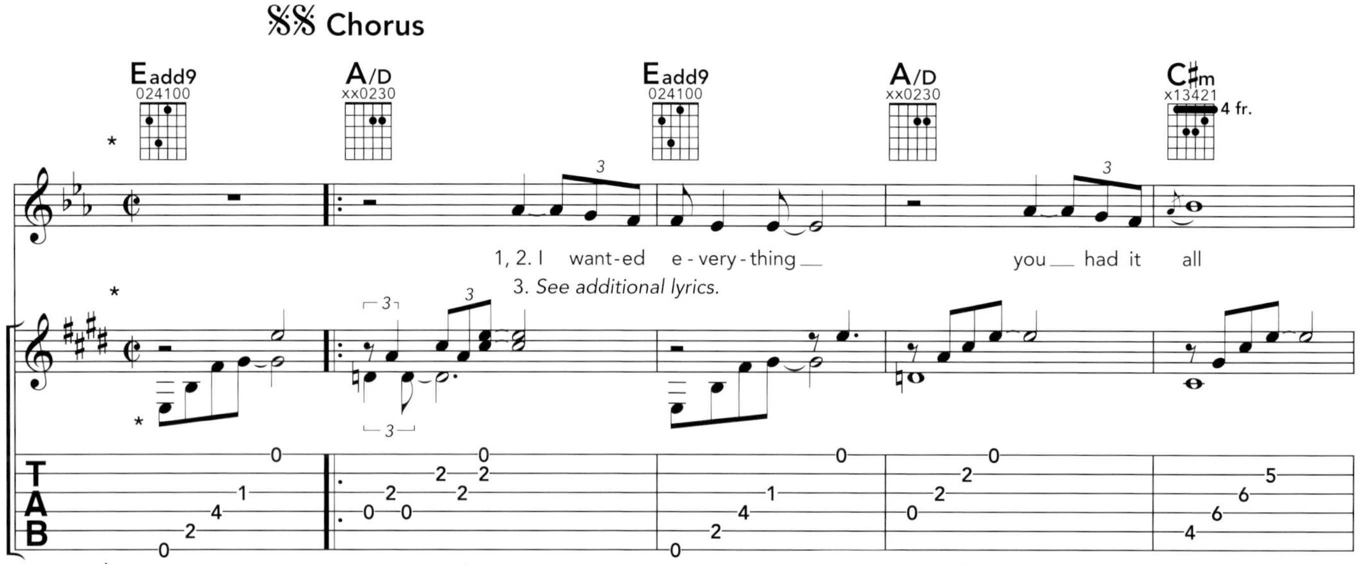

* Vocal written at concert pitch (key of E♭). Guitar notation, tab, and chords written respective to de-tuned guitar (key of E).

** Several gtrs. arr. for one.

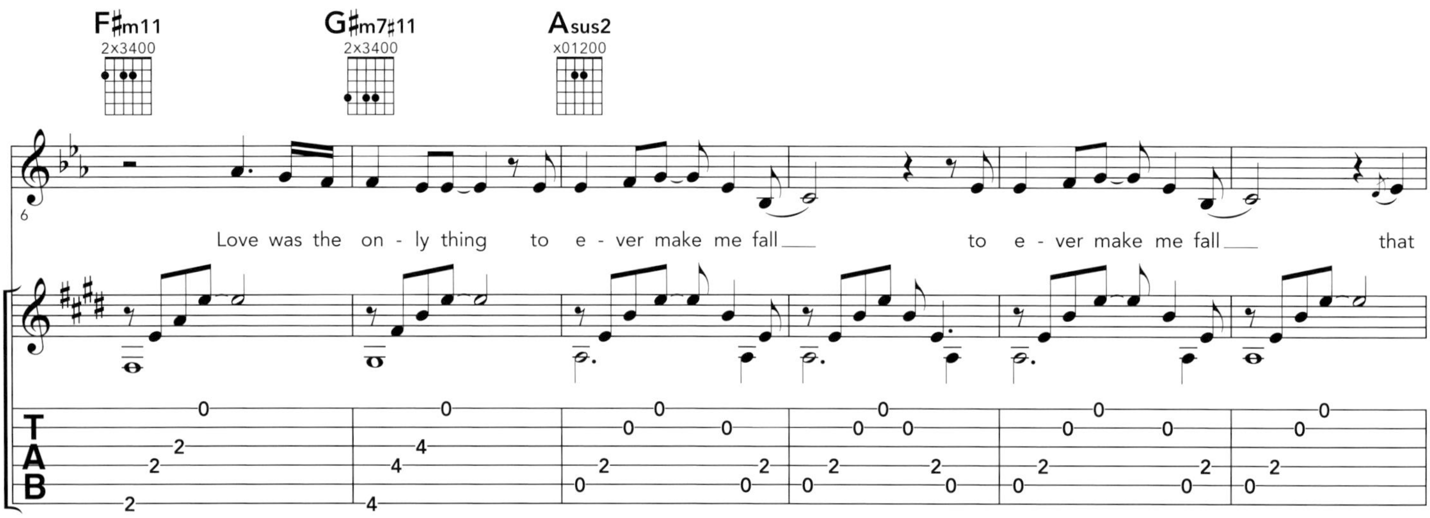

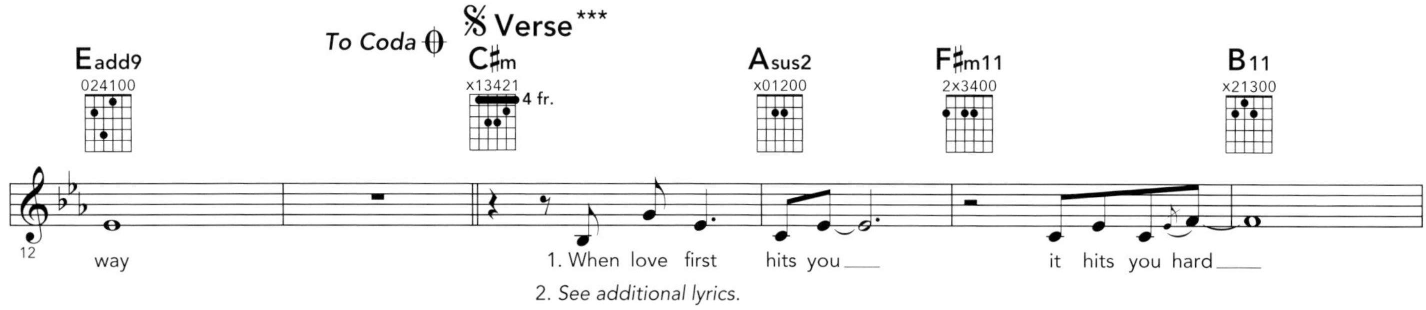

*** Instrumental, second time.

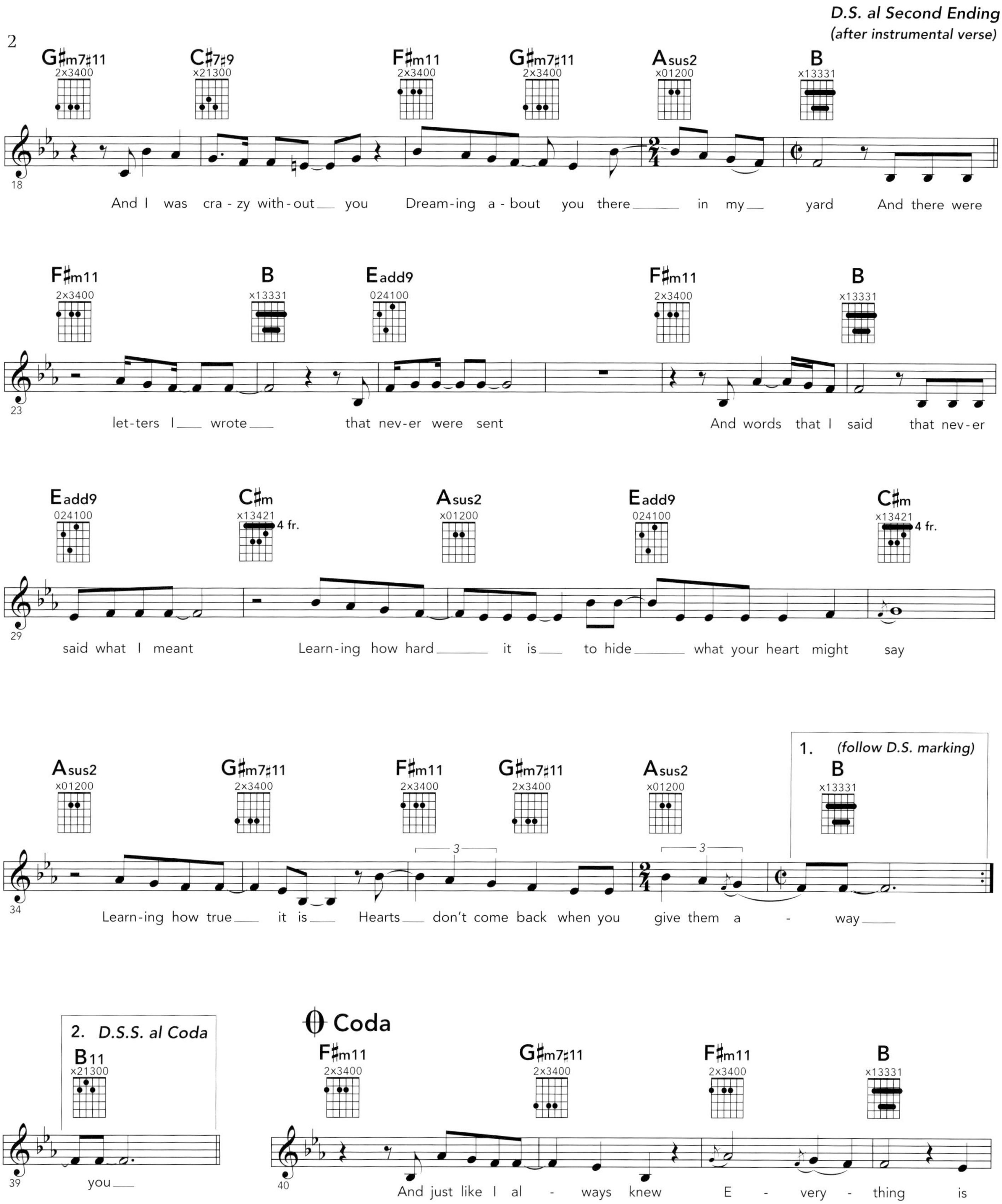
D.S. al Second Ending
(after instrumental verse)
2
G♯m7♯11 C♯7♯9 F♯m11 G♯m7♯11 Asus2 B
And I was cra - zy with - out you Dream - ing a - bout you there in my yard And there were
F♯m11 B Eadd9 F♯m11 B
let - ters I wrote that nev - er were sent And words that I said that nev - er
Eadd9 C♯m Asus2 Eadd9 C♯m
said what I meant Learn - ing how hard it is to hide what your heart might say
Asus2 G♯m7♯11 F♯m11 G♯m7♯11 Asus2
1. (follow D.S. marking) B
Learn - ing how true it is Hearts don't come back when you give them a - way
2. D.S.S. al Coda
B11
you
Coda
F♯m11 G♯m7♯11 F♯m11 B
And just like I al - ways knew E - very - thing is

Eadd9

Chorus

A/D Eadd9 A/D C♯m
I wanted everything, you had it all

F♯m11 G♯m7♯11 Asus2
Love was the only thing to ever make me fall

Eadd9
To ever make me fall that way

C♯m Asus2 F♯m11 B11
1. When love first hits you, it hits you hard

G♯m7♯11 C♯7♯9
And I was crazy without you

F♯m11 G♯m7♯11 Asus2 B
Dreaming about you there in my yard

F♯m11 B Eadd9
And there were letters I wrote that never were sent

F♯m11 B Eadd9
And words that I said that never said what I meant

C♯m Asus2 Eadd9 C♯m
Learning how hard it is to hide what your heart might say

Asus2 G♯m7♯11
Learning how true it is

F♯m11 G♯m7♯11 Asus2 B
Hearts don't come back when you give them away

Repeat Chorus

Instrumental (over first nine bars of verse)

C♯m Asus2 F♯m11 B11
2. Before we knew it, time slipped away

G♯m7♯11 C♯7♯9
And I was destined to lose you

F♯m11 G♯m7♯11 Asus2 B
Watching them choose you and get in my way

F♯m11 B Eadd9
And there were years that went by before that letter you sent

F♯m11 B Eadd9
Telling me tales of all the places you went

C♯m Asus2 Eadd9 C♯m
There on your final page you ask if my dreams came true

Asus2 G♯m7♯11
Finally you hear me say

F♯m11 G♯m7♯11 Asus2 B
All of my life my dream has been you

Chorus

A/D Eadd9 A/D C♯m
Suddenly everything comes into view

F♯m11 G♯m7♯11 Asus2
Such an amazing thing to watch the change in you

Eadd9
And see my dreams come true with you

F♯m11 G♯m7♯11
And just like I always knew

F♯m11 B Eadd9
Everything is you

Everything Gold

Words and Music by Doc Schneider

G Bm7 A G Bm7 A
talk to me by___ the moon___ You're just like a moon - light la - dy You
2–3. See additional lyrics.
* Two gtrs. arr. for one.
Dsus4 D Dsus4 D G Em7 Asus4 A
take me back you take me back And some-how we stayed___ in___ tune___ With
D A Bm7 To Coda Dsus4 D A Bm7
dreams made be-neath___ that___ moon___ in the long a-go___ and far a - way Where
G Asus4 A 1. D 2. D
e - very-thing gold must stay 2. We stay
Bridge
Em Bm7 Cadd9 D
Oh___ time still holds us___ in that mo - ment long a-go___ I___
Em7 Bm7 Cadd9 Asus4
___ feel it shin - ing like the moon - light___ on___ that snow___

Intro

D A Bm7 Em7 Bm7 A
F♯m7 G Em7 A Em7 D

1.
G Bm7 A
You talk to me by the moon
G Bm7 A
You're just like a moonlight lady
Dsus4 D Dsus4 D
You take me back, you take me back
G Em7 Asus4 A
And somehow we stayed in tune
D A Bm7
With dreams made beneath that moon
Dsus4 D A Bm7
In the long ago and far away
G Asus4 A D
Where everything gold___ must stay

2.
G Bm7 A
We lived us a life between
G Bm7 A
And picures on separate pages
Dsus4 D Dsus4 D
There's you, there's me, there's you, there's me
G Em7 Asus4 A
And somehow we stayed in tune
D A Bm7
With dreams made beneath that moon
Dsus4 D A Bm7
In the long ago and far away
G Asus4 A D
Where everything gold___ must stay

4

Bridge

Em7 Bm7 Cadd9 D
Oh, time still holds us in that moment long ago

Em7 Bm7 Cadd9 Asus4 A
I feel it shining like the moonlight on that snow

Repeat Intro

G Bm7 A
3. We walk on this middle ground

G Bm7 A
It's something just like forever

Dsus4 D Dsus4 D
It's gold again, it's gold again

G Em7 Asus4 A
And somehow we stay in tune

D A Bm7
With dreams made beneath that moon

Dsus4 D A Bm7
In the long ago and far away

Dsus4 D A Bm7
It was long ago and far away

G D A Bm7
It was long ago and far away

G A Bm7 G D A
Where everything gold must stay,__ yeah, yeah

Bm7 G D A
Let it stay,__ yeah *(repeat and fade w/ ad-lib vocals)*

Original Chords (Capo II)

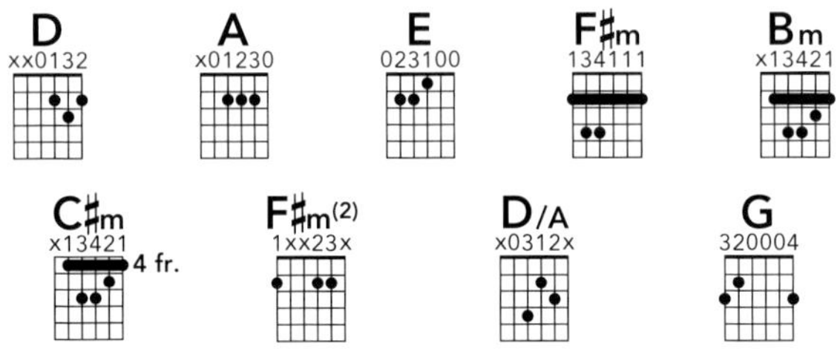

Intro and Verse Pattern (first two measures)

Intro

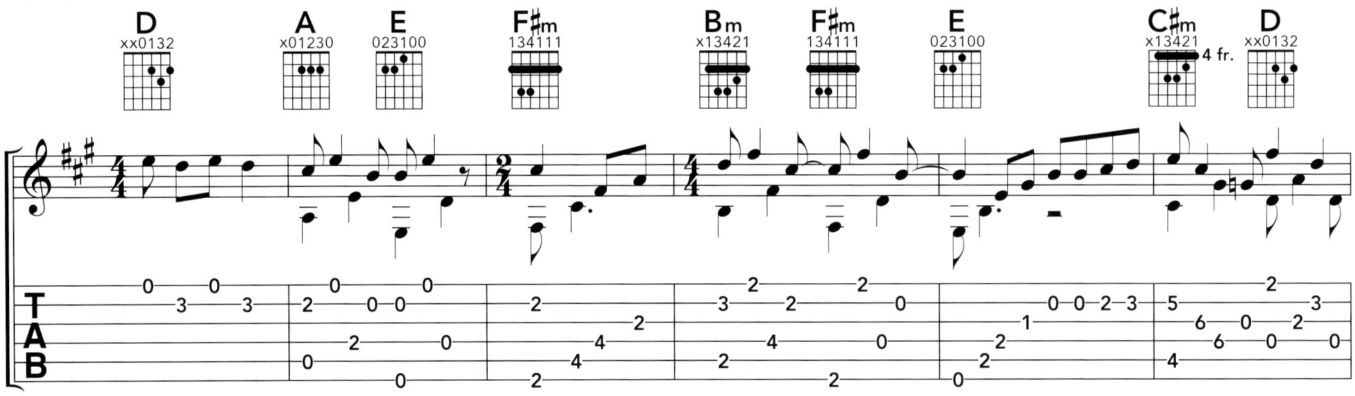

Verse

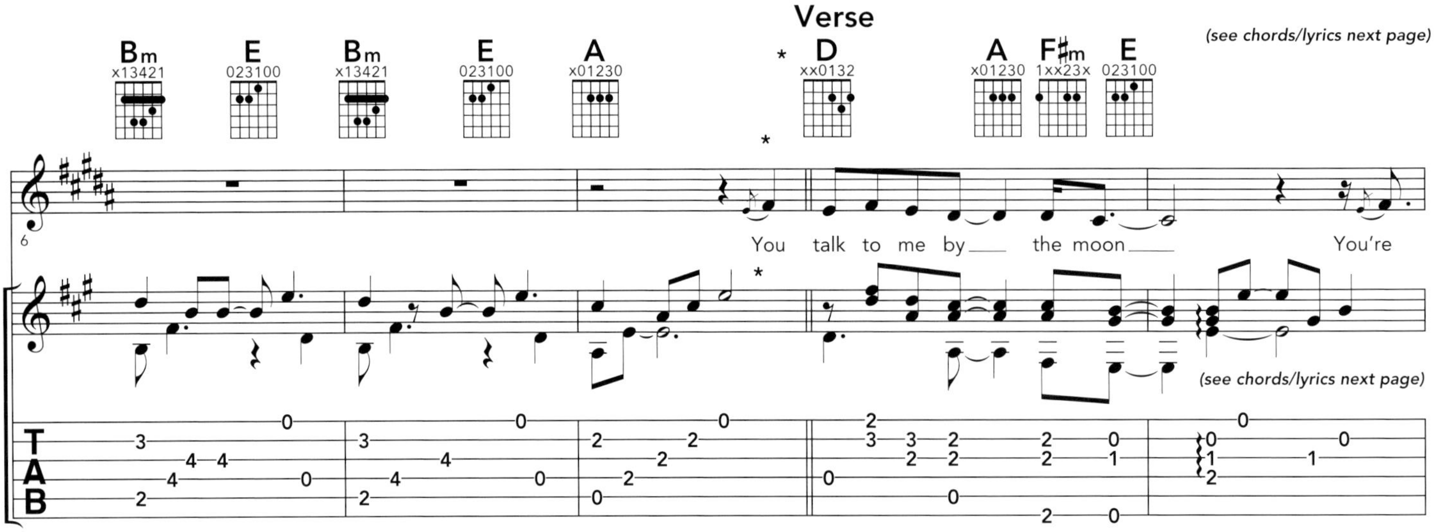

* Vocal written at concert pitch (key of B). Guitar notation, tab, and chords written respective to capoed guitar (key of A).

5 *Intro*

D A E F♯m Bm F♯m E
C♯m D Bm E Bm E A

D A F♯m(2) E
1. You talk to me by the moon

D A F♯m(2) E
You're just like the moonlight lady

D/A A D/A A
You take me back, you take me back

D Bm E
And somehow we stayed in tune

A E F♯m
With dreams made beneath that moon

D A E F♯m
In the long ago and far away

D E A
Where everything gold must stay

D A F♯m(2) E
2. We lived us a life between

D A F♯m(2) E
In pictures on separate pages

D/A A D/A A
There's you, there's me, there's you, there's me

D F♯m E
But somehow we stayed in tune

A E F♯m
With dreams made beneath that moon

D A E F♯m
In the long ago and far away

D E A
Where everything gold must stay

Bridge

Bm F♯m G A
Oh, time still holds us in that moment long ago

Bm F♯m G E
I feel it shining like the moonlight on that snow

Repeat Intro

D A *F♯m(2) E
3. We walk on this middle ground

D A *F♯m(2) E
It's something just like forever

D/A A D/A A
It's gold again, it's gold again

D Bm E
And somehow we stay in tune

A E F♯m
With dreams made beneath that moon

D A E F♯m
In the long ago and far away

D A E F♯m
It was long ago and far away

D A E F♯m
It was long ago and far away

D E F♯m D A E
Where everything gold must stay,__ yeah, yeah

F♯m D A E F♯m D A E
Let it stay,__ yeah, let it stay,__ yeah, yeah

D E A D E A
Where everything gold must stay

*** Play bass note only.**

Massapequa

Words and Music by Doc Schneider

Chorus
2
Fadd9 T0301x
Gadd9 3x020x
Em(add9) 0140xx
Fadd9 T0301x
Gadd9 3x020x
22
wait - ed long e - nough to tell you Mas - sa - pe - qua Mas - sa - pe - qua
G/B x2000x Csus2 x3001x G/B x2000x D/F♯ Tx013x
G 32004x Csus2 x3001x G/B x2000x D/F♯ Tx013x
1.
2.
3
27
Oh mm hm Oh 2. Mas - sa Great
Bridge
Em(add9) 0140xx
Bm7 x1023x
Dadd4/A x0201x
Em(add9) 0140xx
Bm7 x1023x
32
wa - ter land they called you in their na - tive tongue But they left their land be - hind
Em(add9) 0140xx
Am7 x02010
Am7/G 3x201x
D/F♯ Tx013x
D.S. al Coda
37
them Just like me when they were young 3. Mas - sa
Coda
G/B x2000x Csus2 x3001x G/B x2000x D/F♯ Tx013x
G 32004x Csus2 x3001x G/B x2000x D/F♯ Tx013x
41
Oh mm hm Oh I've wait - ed long e - nough
G/B x2000x Csus2 x3001x G/B x2000x D/F♯ Tx013x
G 32004x Csus2 x3001x G/B x2000x D/F♯ Tx013x
play three times
46
Oh I've wait - ed long e - nough Oh I've wait - ed long e - nough

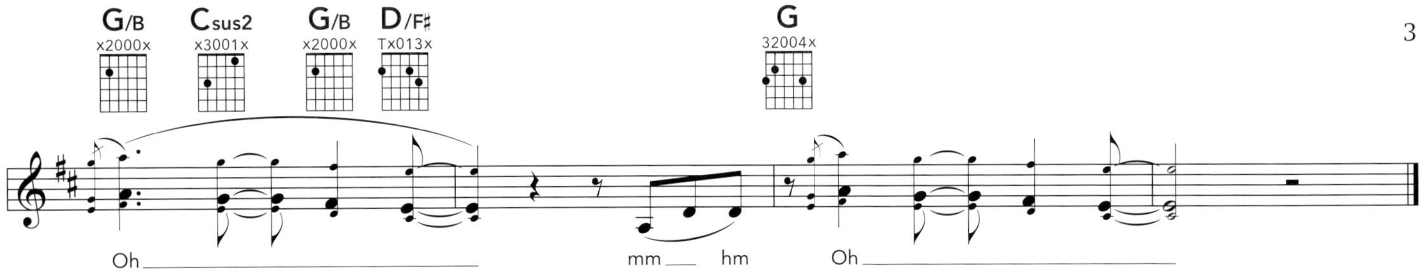

Intro
G Bm7 E7sus4 Am7 Am7/G D/F♯

1.
Gadd9 Bm7
Massapequa, you're my home

Am7 Am7/G D/F♯
But you're not home to me

Gadd9 Bm7
I can walk down your tree-lined streets

Am7 Am7/G D/F♯
But sad is all I see

Em(add9) Fadd9 Gadd9
And I know it's not your fault

Bm7 Csus2 Cmaj7sus2
But I blame you just the same

Am7 Am7/G D/F♯
Which is why my heart still breaks

Am7 D/F♯ Gadd9
Every time I say your name

Chorus

Fadd9 Gadd9
And I've waited long enough to tell you

Em(add9) Fadd9 Gadd9
Massapequa, Massapequa

G/B Csus2 G/B D/F♯
Oh,__________ mm hm

G Csus2 G/B D/F♯
Oh,__________

2.
Gadd9 Bm7
Massapequa, please forgive me

Am7 Am7/G D/F♯
If I don't forgive myself

Gadd9 Bm7
For leaving on my own

Am7 Am7/G D/F♯
And saving no one else

Em(add9) Fadd9 Gadd9
And there are days I don't remember

Bm7 Csus2 Cmaj7sus2
In every picture frame

Am7 Am7/G D/F♯
Which is why my heart still breaks

Am7 D/F♯ Gadd9
Every time I say your name

Repeat Chorus

Bridge

Em(add9) Bm7
"Great water land," they called you

Dadd4/A Em(add9)
In their native tongue

Bm7 Em(add9)
But they left the land behind them

Am7 Am7/G D/F♯
Just like me, when they were young

3.
Gadd9 Bm7
Massapequa, one dark night

Am7 Am7/G D/F♯
You gave a chance to me

Gadd9 Bm7
I stood upon the shoreline

Am7 Am7/G D/F♯
And I headed out to sea

Em(add9) Fadd9 Gadd9
And those days I don't remember

Bm7 Csus2 Cmaj7sus2
They flicker a flame

Am7 Am7/G D/F♯
Which is why my heart still breaks

Am7 D/F♯ Gadd9
Every time I say your name

Repeat Chorus

G/B Csus2 G/B D/F♯
Oh,__________ mm hm

G Csus2 G/B D/F♯
Oh,__________ I've waited long enough

Repeat last two lines three more times (w/ ad-lib vocals)

G/B Csus2 G/B D/F♯
Oh,__________ mm hm

G
Oh,__________

HOTEL D'AUBUSSON

THE INCREDIBLES

COLTS

One Heckuva Little Girl

Words and Music by Doc Schneider

* Vocal written at concert pitch (key of E). Guitar notation, tab, and chords written respective to capoed guitar (key of D).
** Fretboards show overall original chords; tab and notation show arrangement of guitar harmony on *Second Chances.*
† Several gtrs. arr. for one.

Em7 A7sus4 A7 D D/C♯ Bm Am7 D
she has me sing-ing And just when I knew I was o-ver and through She takes me back
G D/F♯ Em7 A7sus4 A7 D
Bridge
E C♯m F♯m
yes she does All the way to the be-gin-ning And who knew one lit-tle girl
Bm E7sus4 E7 A7sus4 A7 F♯m E C♯m D
Could come and rock my world And I'm here to say right here to-day She's one
Em7 A7sus4 A7 Bm E7 Em7 A7sus4 A7
To Coda
1. D
heck-uv-a lit-tle girl yes she is now now She's one heck-uv-a lit-tle girl 2. When it
2. D D/C♯ Bm Am7 D G D/F♯ Em7 A7sus4 A7
La la la la la la la la la la la la la la La la la oh la la la la la la La la
D.S. al Coda
D D/C♯ Bm Am7 D G D/F♯ Em7 A7sus4 A7
la la la la la la la la la la la la la la la la La la la oh

Coda

1. Em7 A Asus2 A
She was not what I was planning on
Bm A Asus2 A
In this world that I was standing on
D D/C Bm
When the pathway took a turn into the woods
Em A7sus4
And the forest and the trees
A7 Bm G
Man, they look all the same to me
Em7 A7sus4 A7 Bm
I never knew that this could be something so good

Chorus

A D D/C♯ Bm Am7
And just when I thought I was out of songs
D G
She comes along, here she is
D/F♯ Em7 A7sus4 A7
Oh, and now she has me singing
D D/C♯ Bm Am7
And just when I knew I was over and through
D G
She takes me back, yes she does
D/F♯ Em7 A7sus4 A7
All the way to the beginning

Bridge

D E C♯m F♯m
And who knew one little girl
Bm E7sus4 E7 A7sus4 A7
Could come and rock my world
F♯m E C♯m D
And I'm here to say, right here, today
Em7 A7sus4 A7 Bm E7
She's one heckuva____ little girl, yes she is now, now
Em7 A7sus4 A7 D
She's one heckuva____ little girl

2. Em7 A Asus2 A
When it seemed like we were lost at sea
Bm A Asus2 A
And nothing was as it should be
D D/C Bm7
It seemed like we might never find our way
Em7 A7sus4
Well, then, suddenly the light
A7 Bm G
It chased away the scary night
Em7 A7sus4 A7 Bm
And has me singing here inside the light of day

Repeat Chorus

Repeat Bridge

D/C♯ B♯m Am7 D G
La la la, la la la la la la la la la la la

D/F♯ Em7 A7sus4 A7
La la la la, oh, la la la la_____ la

D D/C♯ B♯m Am7 D G
La la la la, la la la la__ la la la la la la la la la la

D/F♯ Em7 A7sus4 A7
La la la, oh

Repeat Bridge

Bm E7
Yes she is, now, now

Em7 A7sus4 A7
So take your diamonds and your rubies

Bm E7
And all the money in the world

Em7 A7sus4 A7 D
She's one heckuva_____ little girl

D/C♯ B♯m Am7 D G
La la la, la la la la la la la la la la la

D/F♯ Em7 A7sus4 A7 D
Oh

I'll Take You Back

Words and Music by Doc Schneider

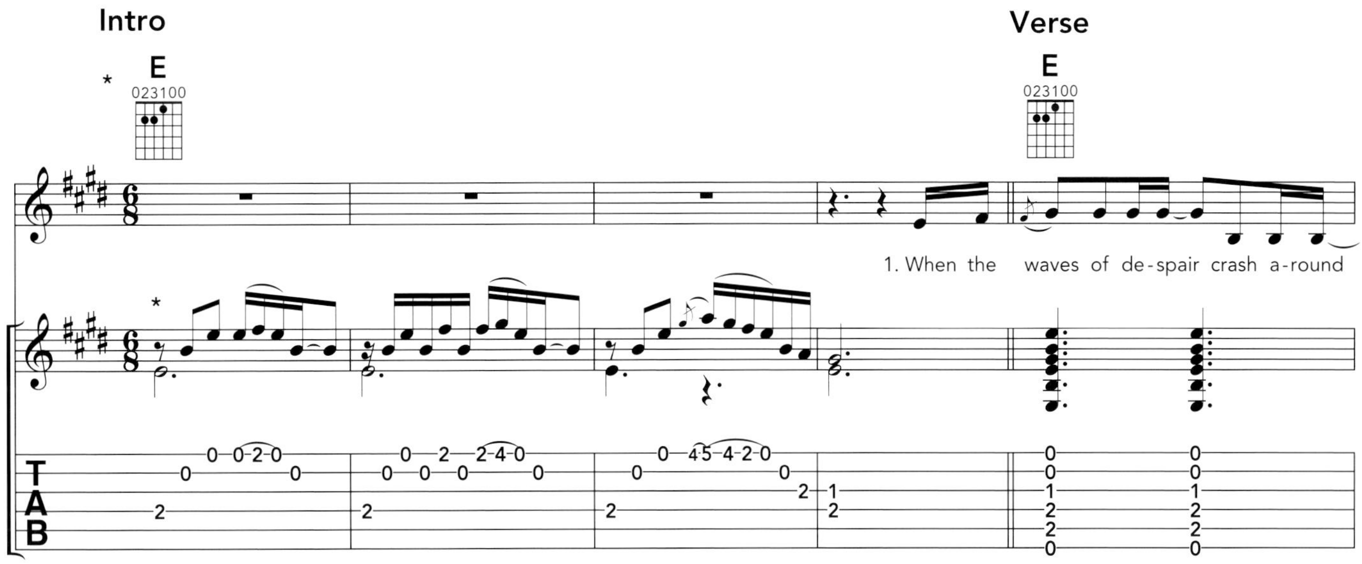

* Fretboards show overall original chords; tab and notation show piano intro on *Second Chances* arranged for guitar.

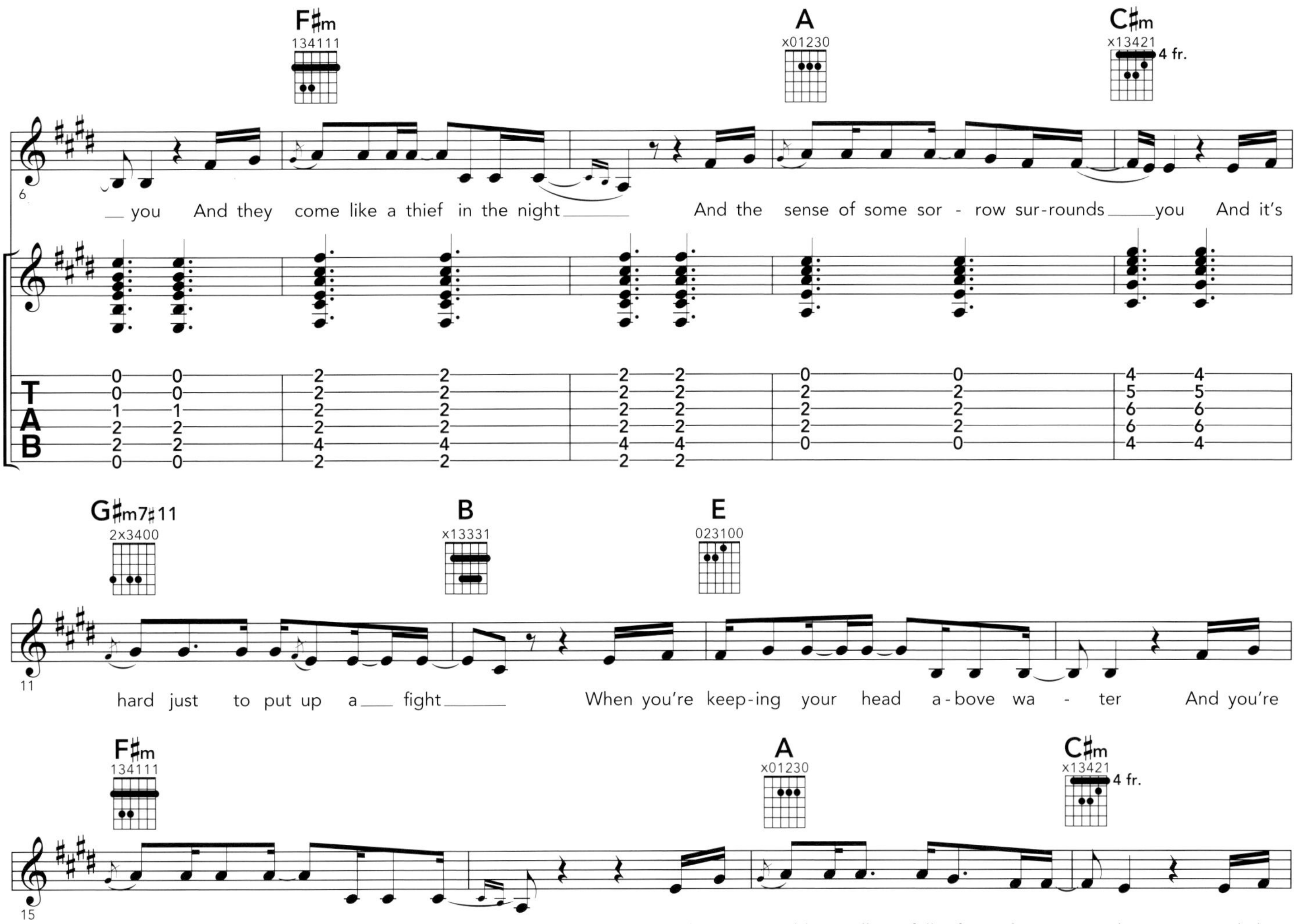

G♯m7♯11 B
Chorus
E
life that you knew seems all gone___ I'll take___ you back just like it was___
C♯m Asus2 C♯m B E C♯m
___ Just like a boat___ that___ can car - ry two I'll take you back keep you a - float I'll lead you
To Coda 2
Asus2 C♯m B Asus2 B F♯m11
through I've been there too you know___ and There is a shin - ing shore___ you've seen it in___ your dreams that
B7add4 Asus2 C♯m Asus2 C♯m Asus2 C♯m Asus2
___ And you'll make it there___ once more___ once more___ As hard to be - lieve as that
To Coda 1
F♯m11 B7add4 E
Verse
E
___ now seems___ 2. Now the strength of your soul___ will sur - prise you And the
F♯m A C♯m G♯m7♯11
hope that you hold deep in-side___ There in the dis - tance a-ris - ing is the glow of a beck-on-ing light

Intro
E

```
       E
1. When the waves of despair crash around you
       F♯m
   And they come like a thief in the night
        A                  C♯m
   And the sense of some sorrow surrounds you
          G♯m7♯11          B
   And it's hard just to put up a fight

       E
   When you're keeping your head above water
          F♯
   And you're finding it hard to hold on
          A                 C♯m
   And your world is all full of disorder
              G♯m7♯11                 B
   And the life that you knew seems all gone
```

Chorus

E C♯m
I'll take you back just like it was

Asus2 C♯m B
Just like a boat that can carry two

E C♯m
I'll take you back, keep you afloat

Asus2 C♯m B
I'll lead you through, I've been there too, you know

Asus2 B F♯m11 B7add4
And there is a shining shore, you've seen it in your dreams

Asus2 C♯m Asus2 C♯m Asus2
And you'll make it there once more, once more

C♯m Asus2 F♯m11 B7add4 Eadd9
As hard to believe as that__ now seems

E
2. Now the strength of your soul will surprise you

F♯m11
And the hope that you hold deep inside

A C♯m
There in the distance, arising

G♯m7♯11 B
Is the glow of a beckoning light

E
Now your faith is a way of believing

F♯m11
That you have an unbreakable soul

A C♯m
And this life is a blanket you're weaving

G♯m7♯11 B
Grows strong when you sew up the holes

Repeat Chorus

Bridge

F♯m11
So hold on my golden girl

Asus2 E
We're gonna sail past that darker world

C♯m Asus2
And here's what your father's for

A G♯m7♯11 C♯m B
To hold up the light on that shining shore

Final Chorus

E C♯m
I'll take you back just like it was

Asus2 C♯m B
Just like a boat that can carry two

E C♯m
I'll take you back, keep you afloat

Asus2 C♯m B
I'll lead you through, I've been there too, you know

E
I'll take you back

Deeper

Words by John Mayer
Music by Doc Schneider

Capo V
Intro
Half Time Feel

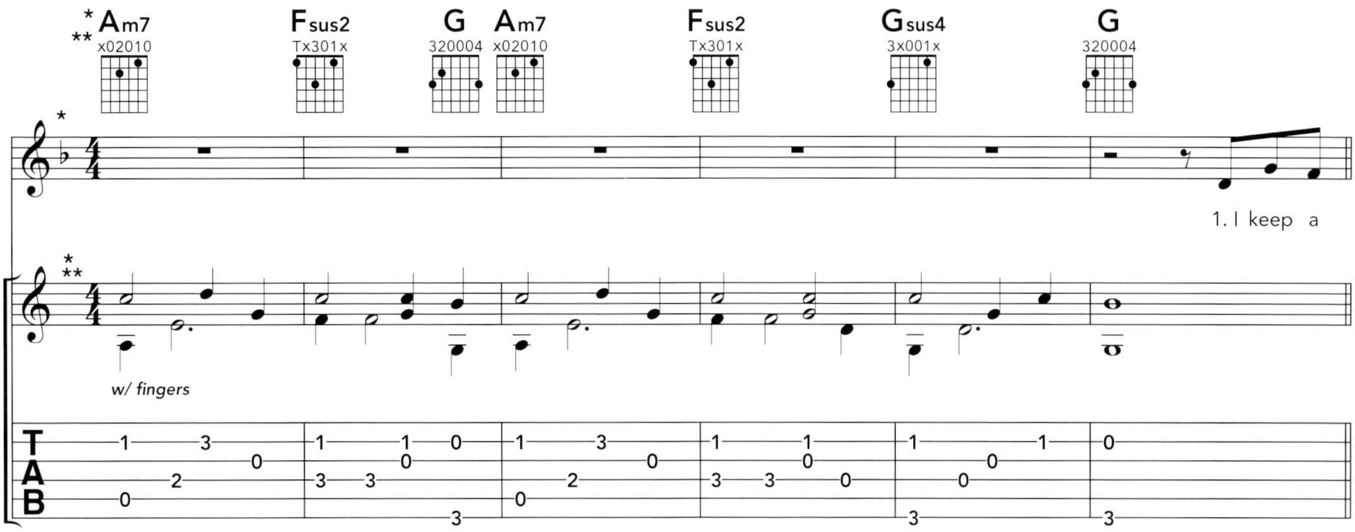

* Vocal written at concert pitch (key of Dm). Guitar notation, tab, and chords written respective to capoed guitar (key of Am).
** Arrangement from *Second Chances* shown here; fretboards for overall original chords shown on fourth page of transcsription.

𝄋 Verse

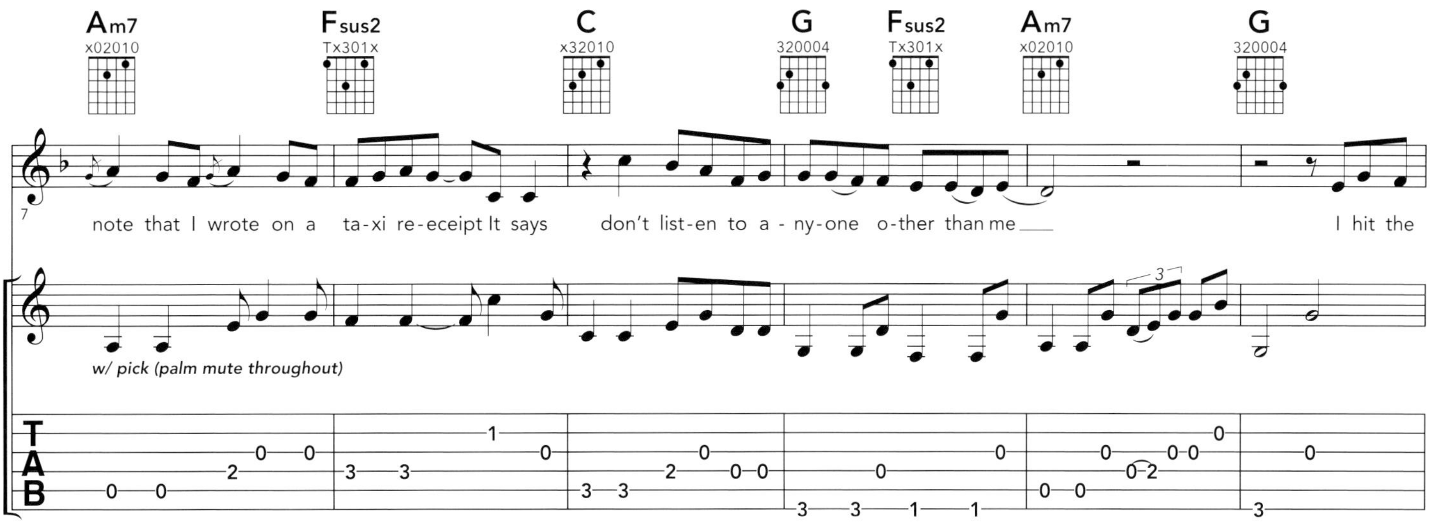

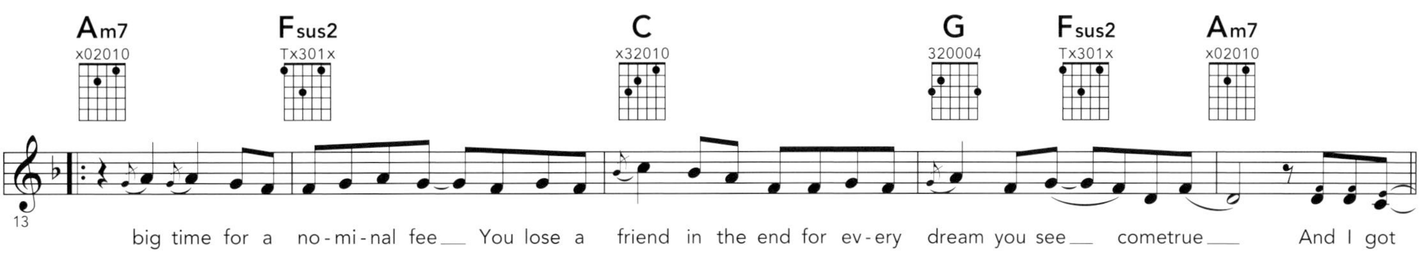

2. *See additional lyrics.*

Chorus
G C Am7 G C G
scars up-on scrapes And I got bruis-es on breaks
Dm E7 Am7 Am7/G Fsus2 Dm E7
Ma-so-chi-sti-cally com-mit-ted to see how much of this I'll take Three years un-der wa-
Am7 C G Am7 E7 Fsus2 G
ter And I ain't ev-en got the shakes I'm go-ing deep-er deep-er and deep-
Am7
er
1.
Fsus2 G Am7 Fsus2 G
2. I got some
2, 3.
Am7/G Fsus2
I'm go-ing deep-er
Bridge
G Am7 Fsus2 C G Am7
deep-er and deep-er Down down down down down down
Fsus2 C G Am7 Fsus2 C
Down down down down down down Down down down down

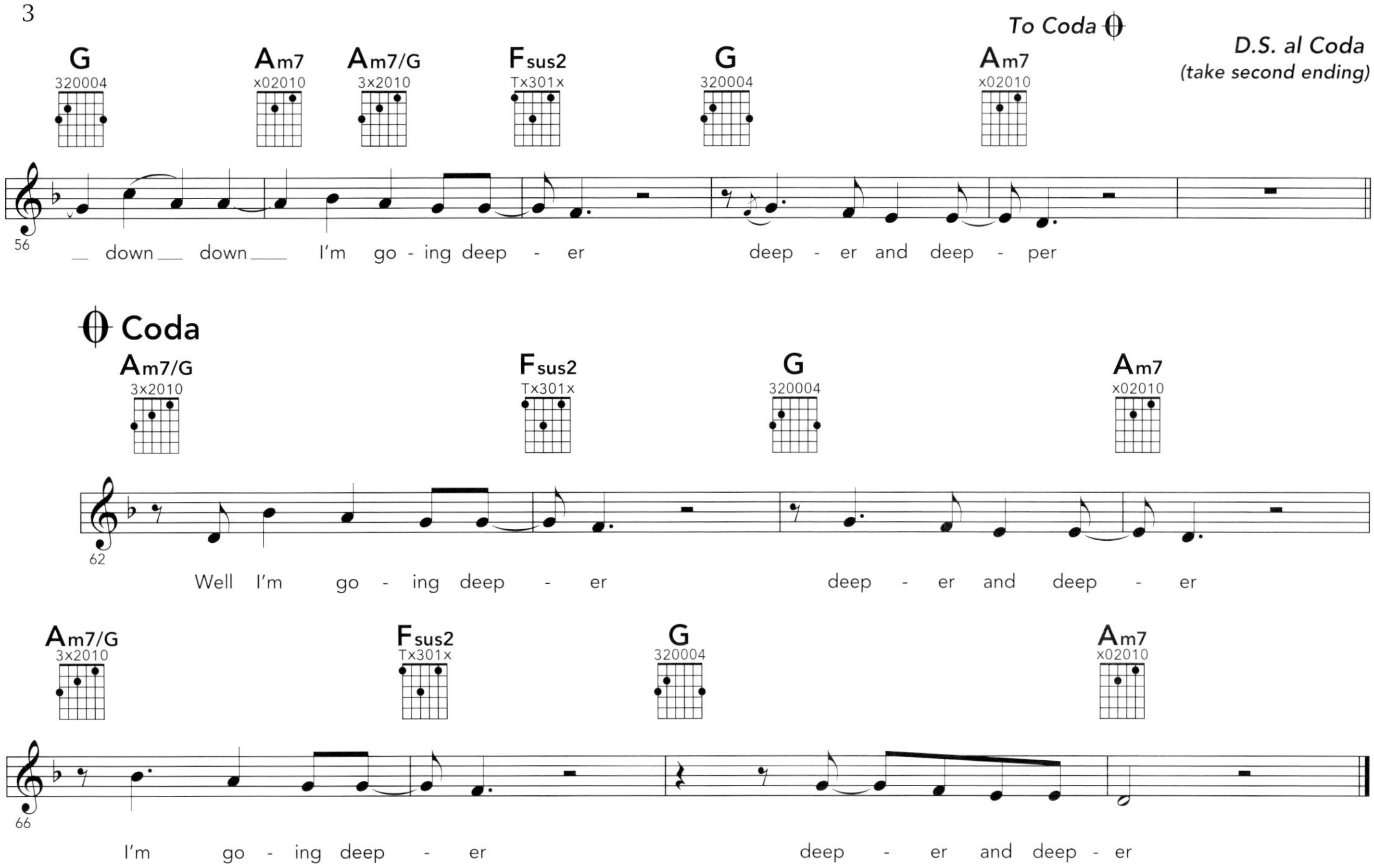

Intro

Am7 Fsus2 G Am7 Fsus2 Gsus4 G

1. Am7 Fsus2
I keep a note that I wrote on a taxi receipt
C G Fsus2 Am7 G
It says "don't listen to anyone other than me"
Am7 Fsus2
I hit the big time for a nominal fee
C G Fsus2 Am7
You lose a friend in the end for every dream you see come true

Chorus

G C Am7
And I got scars upon scrapes
G C G Dm
And I got bruises on breaks
E7 Am7/G Am7 Fsus2
Masochistically committed to see how much of this I'll take
Dm E7 Am7
Three years under water
C G Am7
And I ain't even got the shakes
E7 Fsus2 G Am7
I'm going deeper, deeper and deeper

Fsus2 G Am7 Fsus2

2. Am7 Fsus2
I got some dreams to remember, got some days to forget
C G Fsus2 Am7
I got some phone calls to God but he ain't called me back just yet

Repeat Chorus

Am7/G Fsus2 G Am7
I'm going deeper, deeper and deeper

Bridge

Fsus2 C G Am7
Down, down, down, down, down, down
Fsus2 C G Am7
Down, down, down, down, down, down
Am7/G Fsus2 G Am7
I'm going deeper, deeper and deeper

Instrumental (over Verse progression)

Repeat Chorus

Repeat Bridge

Am7/G Fsus2 G Am7
Well, I'm going deeper, deeper and deeper
Am7/G Fsus2 G Am7
I'm going deeper, deeper and deeper

4

Original Chords (no capo)

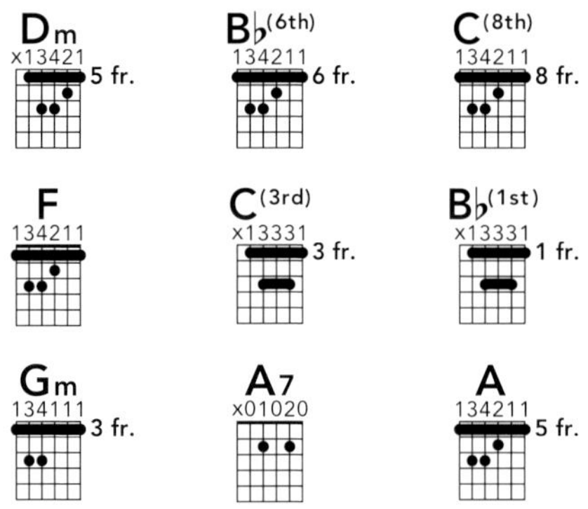

Intro

Dm B♭(6th) C(8th) Dm B♭(6th) C(8th)

Dm B♭(6th)
1. I keep a note that I wrote on a taxi receipt

F C(8th) B♭(6th) Dm B♭(6th) C(8th)
It says "don't listen to anyone other than me"

Dm B♭(6th)
I hit the big time for a nominal fee

F C(8th) B♭(6th) Dm
You lose a friend in the end for every dream you see come true

Chorus

C(3rd) B♭(1st) Dm
And I got scars upon scrapes

C(3rd) F C(3rd) Gm
And I got bruises on breaks

A7 Dm C(3rd) B♭(1st)
Masochistically committed to see how much of this I'll take

Gm A7 Dm
Three years under water

F C(8th) Dm B♭(6th)
And I ain't even got the shakes

A B♭(6th) C(8th) Dm
I'm going deeper, deeper and deeper

B♭(6th) C(8th) Dm B♭(6th)

Dm B♭(6th)
2. I got some dreams to remember, got some days to forget

F C(8th) B♭(6th) Dm
I got some phone calls to God but he ain't called me back just yet

Repeat Chorus

B♭(6th) A B♭(6th) C(8th) Dm
I'm going deeper, deeper and deeper

Bridge

B♭(1st) F C(8th) Dm
Down, down, down, down, down, down

B♭(1st) F C(8th) Dm
Down, down, down, down, down, down

C(8th) B♭(6th) C(8th) Dm
I'm going deeper, deeper and deeper

Instrumental (over Verse progression)

Repeat Chorus

Repeat Bridge

C(8th) B♭(6th) C(8th) Dm
Well, I'm going deeper, deeper and deeper

C(8th) B♭(6th) C(8th) Dm
I'm going deeper, deeper and deeper

Song for the Morning

Words and Music by Doc Schneider

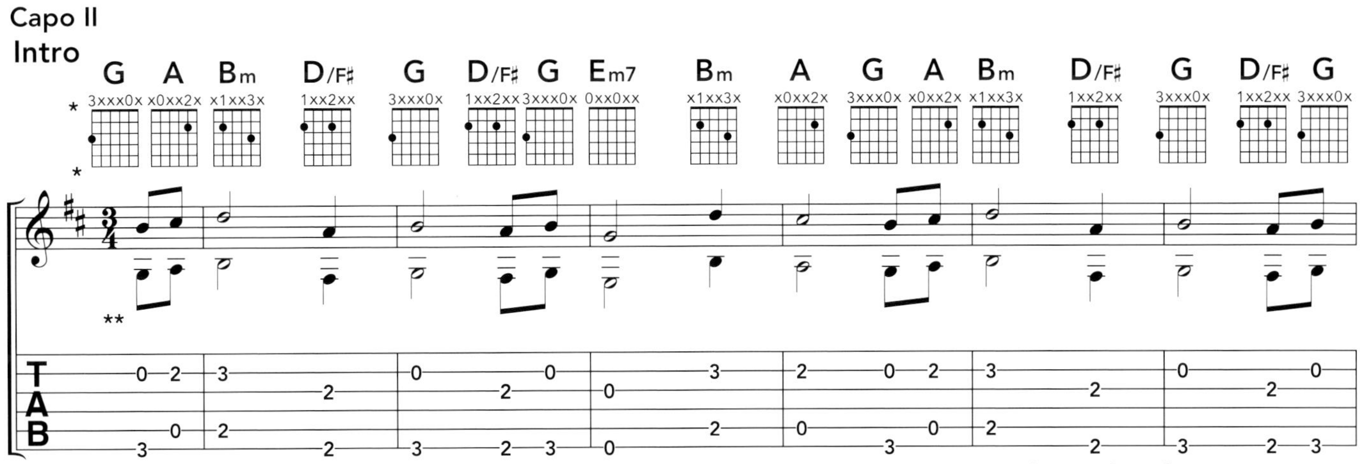

* Vocal written at concert pitch (key of E). Guitar notation, tab, and chords written respective to capoed guitar (key of D).

** Several guitars arranged for one.

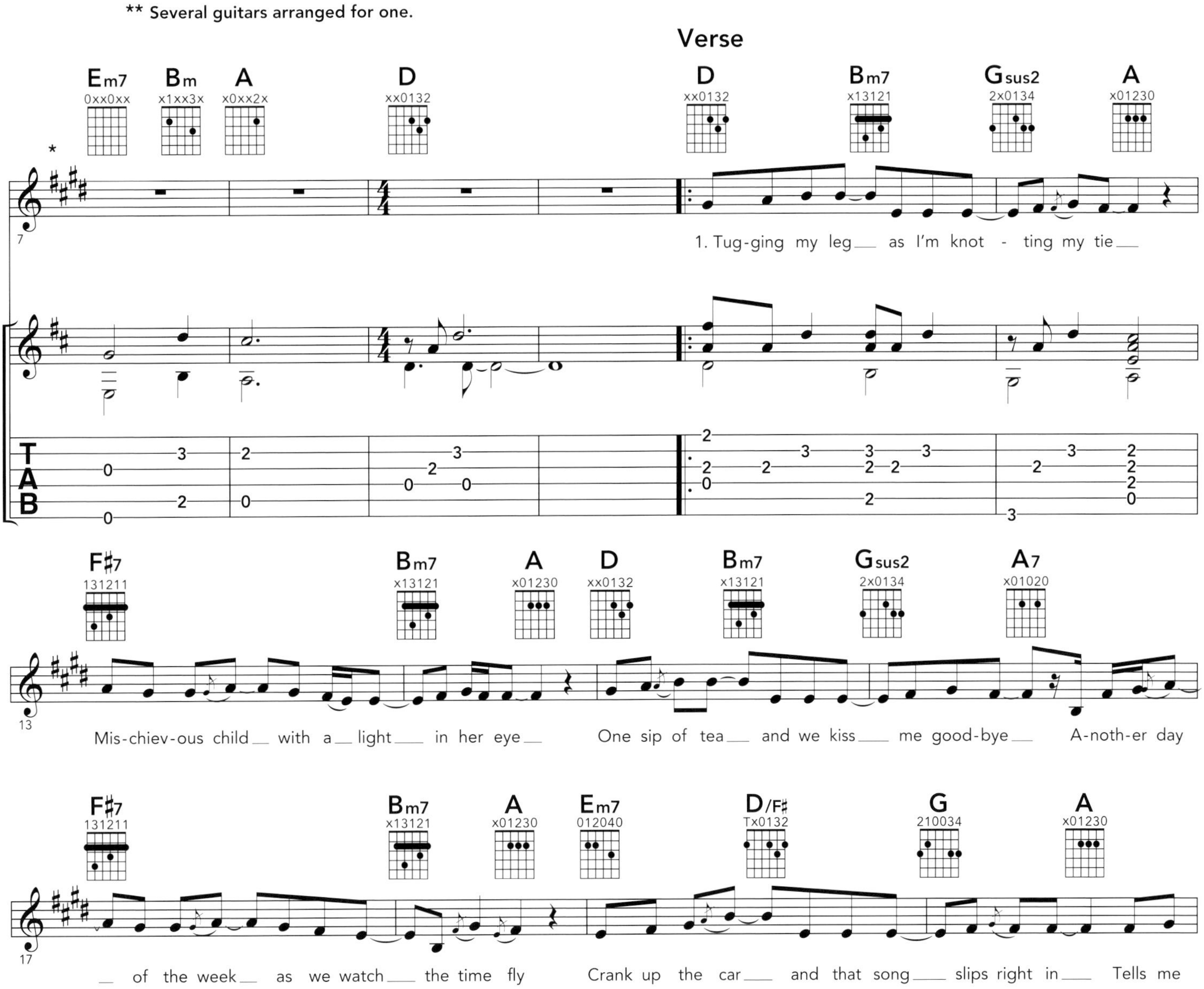

Chorus
Em7 D/F♯ G A D D/C♯ Bm7 Gsus2 A
21
stop where you are this is where I be-gin This is a song for the morn-ing And
Em7 D/F♯ G A7sus4 A7 D D/C♯ Bm7 Gsus2 A
26
this is a song for the day Kis - ses you warm with-out warn - ing
Em7 A7sus4 A7 A7sus2 A7 G A
30
And sud-den-ly takes you a - way This song is like a life - line It's a
To Coda
Em7 D/F♯ G A7 G A7
34
sound you can't mis - take Ech-oes of my life - time make the mu - sic that I make
Bridge
D Bm7 G A7 1. 2. Bm7 D/G Em7
39
Now some songs take so long to get here And
D/F♯ A7sus4 A7 D Bm7 G Asus4 A Em7 D/F♯
45
I nev-er know where they roam I'm al-ways rea-dy to wel - come them in Like fa-mily and friends com-

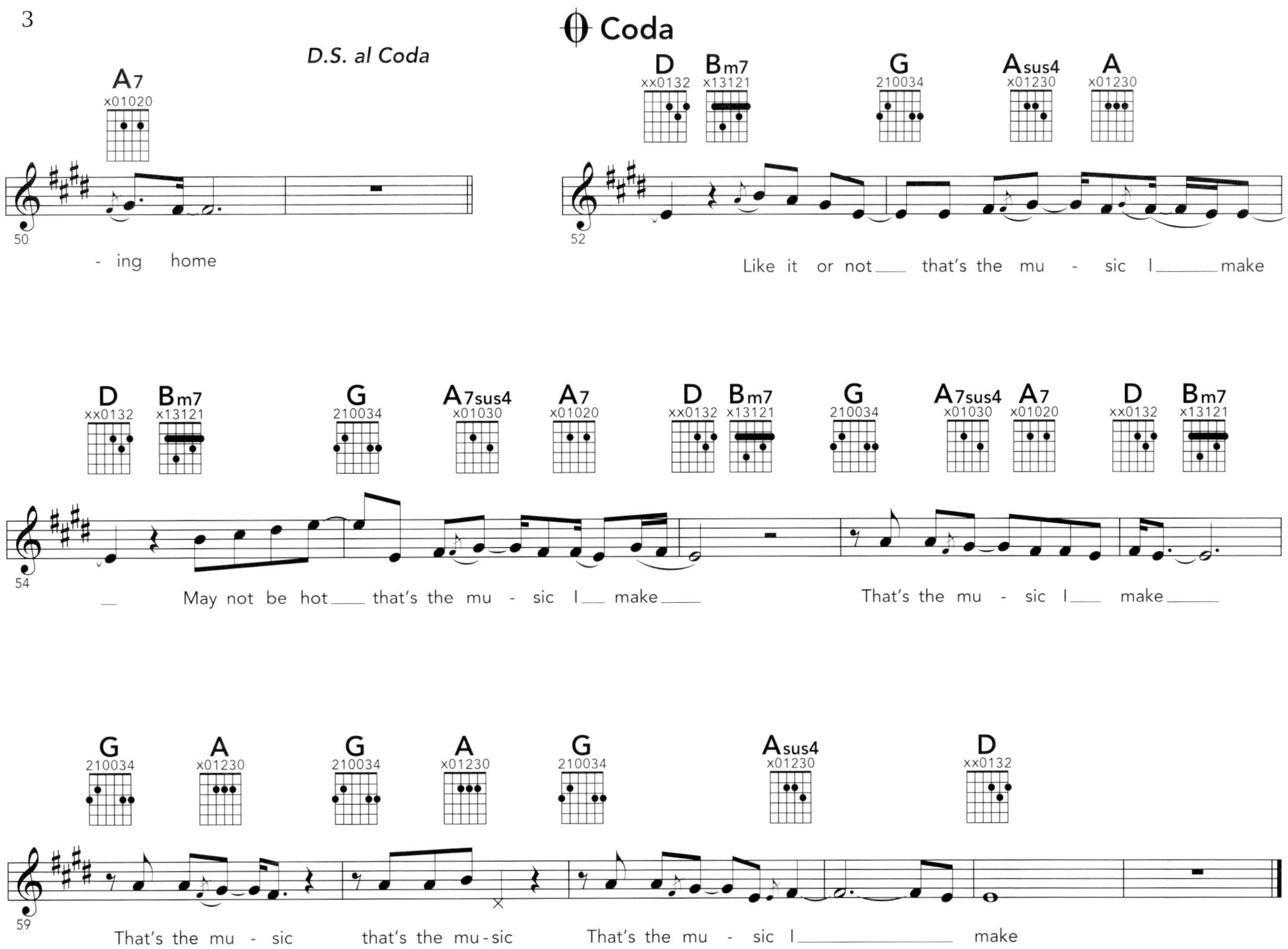

Intro

G A Bm D/F♯ G D/F♯ G Em7 Bm A
G A Bm D/F♯ G D/F♯ G Em7 Bm A D

D Bm7 Gsus2 A
1. Tugging my leg as I'm knotting my tie

F♯7 Bm7 A
Mischievous child with a light in her eye

D Bm7 Gsus2 A7
One sip of tea and we kiss me goodbye

F♯7 Bm7 A
Another day of the week as we watch the time fly

Em7 D/F♯ G A
Crank up the car and that song slips right in

Em7 D/F♯ G A
Tells me stop where you are, this is where I begin

Chorus

D D/C♯ Bm7 Gsus2 A
This is a song for the morning

Em7 D/F♯ G A7sus4 A7
And this is a song for the day

D D/C♯ Bm7 Gsus2 A
Kisses you warm without warning

Em7 A7sus4 A7 Asus2 A7
And suddenly takes you away

G A Em7 D/F♯ G
This song is like a lifeline, it's a sound you can't mistake

A7 G A7
Echoes of my lifetime make the music that I make

D Bm7 G A7

```
    D             Bm7            Gsus2       A
2.  Tied to my desk with my ear on the phone

    F♯7                        Bm7        A
    Mischievous child never leaves me alone

    D              Bm7      Gsus2       A7
    I shake my head and I tell myself no

          F♯7                      Bm7          A
    Then I flip on the mute and I hum soft and low

              Em7           D/F♯           G              A
    And then I kick the door closed and that song slips right in

         Em7          D/F♯          G         A
    Says I know how it goes and I'm back here again
```

Repeat Chorus

Bridge

```
         Bm7                          D/G
    Now some songs take so long to get here

    Em7        D/F♯        A7sus4   A7
    And I never know where they roam

    D           Bm7       G           Asus4  A
    I'm always ready to welcome them in

        Em7          D/F♯      A7
    Like family and friends coming home
```

Repeat Chorus

```
    Bm7       G           Asus4 A      D
    Like it or not, that's the music I make

    Bm7        G           Asus4 A      D    Bm7
    May not be hot, that's the music I make

    G        Asus4 A      D  Bm7
    That's the music I make

    G        A      G        A
    That's the music, that's the music

    G         Asus4   D
    That's the music I make
```

Who Took Our Eyes Away

Words and Music by Doc Schneider

F G C F G C G/B
What made the muse wan - der on
Why can't I say what I used to
Am F G A
To Coda
1, 3.
say
Where has my in - no - cence gone
Bridge
2.
D F♯m Bm Em F
But I tremble at the sight of beeu-ty
I'm af - flic - ted with an old at - trac - tion
I'd give it all
C F G Bm
for a slight dis - trac - tion
But I know it all just blows a - way
God I know it all just blows a - way
C G A D G Bm
Beau - ty is the on - ly truth I know
But it flick - ers when it calms your soul

3

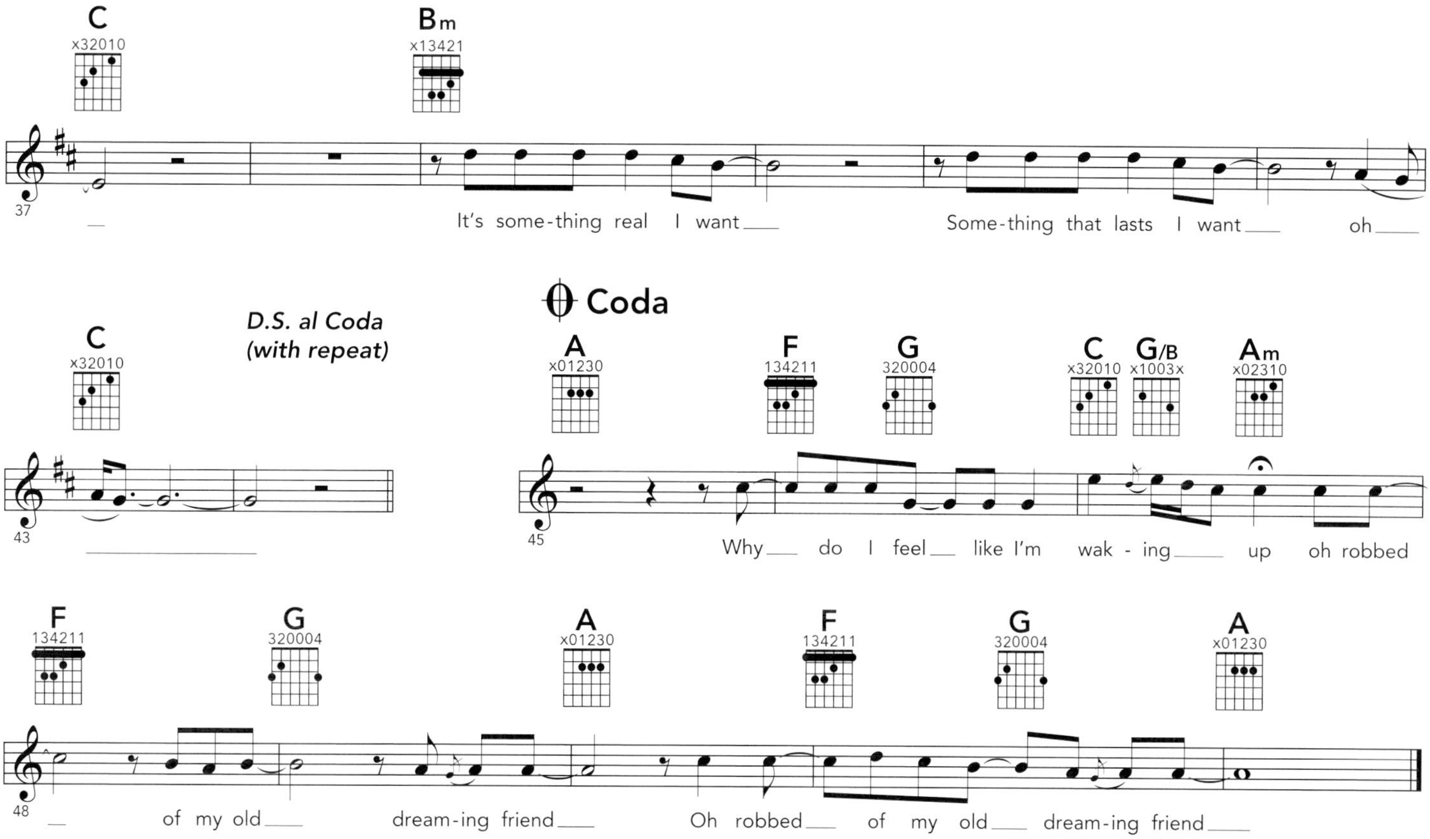

Intro

C

C

1. What ever happened to J. Alfred Prufrock

A D

And all of the dreams on the green?

F G C G/B F

And what ever happened to me and to you?

Chorus

C G/B Am

Who took our eyes away?

F G C

What made the muse wander on?

F G C G/B Am

Why can't I say what I used to say?

F G A

Where has my innocence gone?

C

2. And what ever happened to Eleanor Rigby

A D

And the black and white shades of my youth?

F G C G/B F

And what ever happened to saving the world?

Chorus

C G/B Am

Who took our eyes away?

F G C

What made the dream fade from sight?

F G C G/B Am

Why do I feel like a wounded child

F G A

Suddenly left in the night?

Bridge

D F♯m Bm

But I tremble at the sight of beauty

Em F

I'm afflicted with an old attraction

C F G

I'd give it all for a slight distraction

Bm

But I know it all just blows away

C

God, I know it all just blows away

G A D

Beauty is the only truth I know

G Bm C

But it flickers when it calms your soul

Bm

It's something real I want

C

Something that lasts I want, oh

```
   C
3. What ever happened to T.S. and Robert

   And what is this frost on my soul?
        A                          D
   And what ever happened to setting things straight?
        F            G         C      G/B   F
```

Chorus

```
C              G/B  Am
Who took our dreams away?

F                G            C
Who broke our trumpets in half?

F           G        C  G/B Am
Why do I feel like a waning whine

F           G       A
Suddenly close to a laugh?
```

```
   C
4. And what ever happened to Dickie and desperate

        A                          D
   And all of the dreams of our youth?

        F        G           C      G/B F
   And what ever happened to me and to you?
```

Chorus

```
C              G/B Am
Who took our eyes away?

F             G            C
Why did the dream have to end?

F          G          C  G/B Am
Why do I feel like I'm waking up

F            G             A
Robbed of my old dreaming friend?

F          G          C  G/B Am
Why do I feel like I'm waking up

      F            G             A
Oh, robbed of my old dreaming friend?

      F            G             A
Oh, robbed of my old dreaming friend
```

#1
INTERNATIONAL BESTSELLER
JOHN
IRVING
A PRAYER
FOR OWEN
MEANY

SECOND CHANCES
THE LINER NOTES

This album is a little miracle in three acts. It begins in Chicago. Voiceover: To paraphrase Dickens, whether I shall turn out to be the hero of my own life, these pages must tell. But we can cut to the chase. I do not turn out to be the hero. The heros here are Jeff Jacobs, Lu Steed, Ben Wisch and Eugene Ruffolo.

Act. I. In Chicago, in a neat little studio on Halsted, Jeff Jacobs, composer and keyboardist, pursues a little side business, producing commercials, helping artists and songwriters turn out first rate demos and other musical tasks. Jeff is the keyboard player in Foreigner, having been with the band for more than 15 years and he played with Billy Joel for five years on the "Storm Front" and "River of Dreams" albums and tours. Those are only a few of his credits. In 2004, Jeff placed an advertisment in Performing Songwriter Magazine, and advertised his services in making "killer" demos. When I saw that ad, it was a revelation to me—I thought of all of my poor little songs with their ripped pants and runny noses and longing eyes, led around by a songwriter whose singing and playing chops were not enough to feed the hungry. I was stunned to think that my songs might get a second chance in the hands of a true pro. Keyboard player for Foreigner, Billy Joel—and he will make demos? Could it be true?

Well, it was. That little ad led to a grand adventure. At first, we took some songs from my debut album, "Choices and Chances" (it went double foil!), and sent them off to Chicago for finishing school. "The Love That Lasts" left Atlanta in jeans and a tee shirt, and came back in white linen, with the voice of Josie Aiello. And one led to another. I am still floored every time I listen to Jeff Jacobs and Cheryl Wilson's duet of "If I Can Love Enough." To hear these songs brought to life by great artists was like really hearing them for the first time. To accomplish this feat, Jeff brought an avalanche of talent, not only producing, but playing keyboards, piano, guitar, drums and sometimes even singing.

As each song went off and came back, I began to see the seeds for this album. Songs that never made it to the "Choices and Chances" album began clamoring for a trip to Chicago. So I flipped through various songs I had recorded over the years at Songbird Studio with David Romine, and started sending them off to Jeff. These were some of the most amazing surprises. Songs like "Homemade Song" and "I Wanted Everything" that I wrote and recorded, but did not like my version, boarded the internet for a flight to Chicago and came back as movie stars. Indeed, I was so blown away by Jon Allmett's version of Homemade Song that I entered it

in the 2004–05 Unisong International Song Contest and it took Second Place in the Pop Ballad category out of more than 900 entries worldwide. Talk about a second chance. From the cutting room floor to a ticker tape parade.

And that song led to the launching of my website—www.legalguitarist.com. The good folks at Unisong asked me for my web address, and I told them I was a lawyer and only a dabbling songwriter, and I certainly had no website. But I had to launch one so that Homemade Song could take its little victory lap—and cdbaby.com has a service called hostbaby—and in no time, we were in business. Choices and Chances which was distributed through cdbaby and iTunes and other services was now getting some competition (and indeed being put to shame) by new songs that came flying out of Chicago on brand new wings. My old songs were having such fun, I started writing new ones—like "Everything Gold" and "One Heckuva Little Girl." Greg Ferguson sings the former and Jon Allmett the latter—amazing performances. The curtain closes on Act I with the release of All Blue To Me (available on cdbaby and iTunes)—Jeff Jacob's debut album, which we co-wrote. For accidental collaborators, we were turning out some surprising stuff.

Act II. Atlanta. Enter Lu Steed. Lu is a renowned Atlanta artist, a thin reed of burning energy, innocence retained, filled with a joy and a sense of humor far bigger than her little paintbrush of a body. She is a versatile artist who has painted every thing from trucks to still lifes to portraits—her canvases are studies in enthusiastic observation. Lu happens to be married to my law partner, Bob Steed, and I have tracked her for years like a bounty hunter with the idea of letting me and my guitar step up on to one of her canvases. After a decade, Lu warmed up to the idea—especially when I said that the result would become the cover for my planned album. And then she got into the project big time. Lu approaches painting like detective work, and she wanted to see my songwriting scribblings, lyric sheets—she was intent on climbing into my head before painting it. Ultimately, she painted the study you see on the cover, and caught me good in a moment of serious thought (I was thinking "what if my law partners see this?"). And the backdrop of the painting is a huge version of my lyric and chord sheet for "Marie".

When I went to her home, I saw that canvas, and the painted version of the "Marie" lyrics. I had written that song in a little flight

of imagination (there is no Marie, there is only Helen) in 2003. The song is hard to sing so I never recorded it. It had no chance of being on this album. There was no plans for it whatsoever. But Lu Steed liked the lyric and she painted it on the canvas for all to see. And since that was to be the cover for this album, something had to be done. Marie was saying—can you believe you must come back for me? What to do? Curtain.

Act III. New York City. Bailey Building and Loan Studio. In 1992, I stumbled on what is perhaps my favorite album of all time—David Wilcox's "Home Again." (It ranks up there with great albums like "JT" and "Fool for Every Season" and "Room for Squares"). It was produced by famed producer, Ben Wisch. When I saw Jeff Jacob's advertisement in 2004, it was not lost on me that right above it was an ad for Ben Wisch's services as a producer. I knew that Ben had produced David Wilcox's albums, as well as many others, including Marc Cohn's debut with the fantastic single "Walking in Memphis." In 2004, I decided I needed to scrub up my stuff before I could ever look for a chance to work with Ben Wisch.

But by 2006, we had this little problem of Marie and this painting. Jeff had put some fantastic tracks in the can. I seized on a wild idea. Maybe Ben might take a listen to what we had worked on so far, maybe give some production ideas—and what the hell, maybe he can take on Marie. I went to Ben's website—and we need a big white spotlight and violins here—and looked at some recent albums he had produced. And one artist for whom he had produced or co-produced three albums was Eugene Ruffolo. Strike up the magic moment violins. I listened to some track snippets of Eugene that Ben had on his site, and I was knocked out. Pure voice with heart. Clean guitar chops. Unique and talented, with the influences of James Taylor like the slightest hint of just the right color.

So I went to the Ruffolo site, listened some more, ordered all three of his albums (cdbaby), and took a week to go through them all. It was like stumbling on David Wilcox's albums in 1992—the greatest joy for a lover of songs is to hear beautiful songs performed well—and here they were, track after track—"Fool for Every Season", "Sweet Southern Eyes", "Holding on To Faith", "Irreplaceable"—one right after another.

So I get up my nerve. I do a rough recording of Marie. I send it to Jeff. Jeff whips out his own version—and suddenly, Marie seems to be coming to life. I close my eyes, fold my arms and jump off the cliff—I write to Ben Wisch—Hello, you don't know me I know but I was wondering if by any chance you might like to take a flyer and produce a song called Marie—and oh, by the way, no big deal, but I was just wondering, if, somehow, by any chance, well—do you think you might interest Eugene Ruffolo in doing this? Deep breath. I think a day and a half passed. And then—did I read that right? Ben Wisch just said yes.

And so the co-production part of our journey began. Ben and Eugene sent me a rough draft and then a finished version of "Marie." I still cannot believe it. And four more songs followed. "Wherever You Are." And then new songs freshly written and sent right

away to New York. "Massapequa." "A Second Chance" (written after finishing John Irving's latest novel, Until I Find You—with a nod to Amsterdam, where many scenes are set and where there are a legion of Ruffolo fans—see eugeneruffolo.nl). "Deeper" (my entry in a John Mayer contest, where he wrote the lyrics and challenged folks to write music to it). (I sent my version of the song to Mr. Mayer—I wish the deadline had been postponed so I could have sent what Ben and Eugene turned out.) In the process, Ben, Eugene and I became friends and correspondents. And their work is nothing short of amazing.

This album ends where it began—in Jeff Jacobs' studio in Chicago. One cold winter day in December 2005, I went to the studio to hear an artist sing "Who Took Our Eyes Away". As fate would have it, the planned singer did not show. I was in a bit of a rush for a meeting on one of my cases with one of Chicago's great law firms. But as long as I was there, and Jeff had a nice track—well, Jeff sat at his control board, and handed me the mic. "You sing it," he said. And so I did. It was my own second chance.

Jeff and Ben and Eugene took a little act of faith and made me a believer—I think it's true now. I really am a songwriter after all.

I want to thank the heroes. I also want to thank all the musicians who lent their talents to this project—Lucy Kaplansky, Alan Zahn, Cameron Wisch and all the others I list in the song credits. In a way, this album reminds of a house where the whole community turns out and lends a hand and raises the walls and builds a house. It would never be built without them. Whenever I think of all these talented souls making their way to a studio to give their very best to songs of a perfect stranger, I am moved.

I want to thank Jenny Garland for the wonderful way this album is laid out and put together. I want to thank Helen for letting me love her and loving all the broken parts of me. I thank my daughters for the gifts of themselves and the gifts of their children. I have come alive in bits and pieces and little McKenzie, Madison, Zoe and Zach open doors I have never seen and doors I passed by once and have been lucky enough for a second chance to go back. I want to thank everyone who had the faith where I could see it in their shining eyes—the Urrutias, the Schrolls, the Barrancos, the McGintys, big and little, new and old. And I want to thank my mother for the gift of loving music and my first guitar and tape recorder. And I know I owe my sisters and my brothers one thing or another. And all of my friends in the dark days.

And lastly, I would like to thank whoever is reading this and listening to these songs. A song never lives until you listen and let it move you. It does me more than a little good to think of these songs being played in quiet rooms wherever you are.

Doc

EDDIE'S
"Writing-singing straight from their
emotional heart & soul, about emotions,
sorrows, hopes and joys, in life, love,
dreams, choices and chances shortly said
about feelings that keep our minds 24/24
wordlessly busy, by these heartists
mother-of-pearled in 4-minutes gems."
Lia

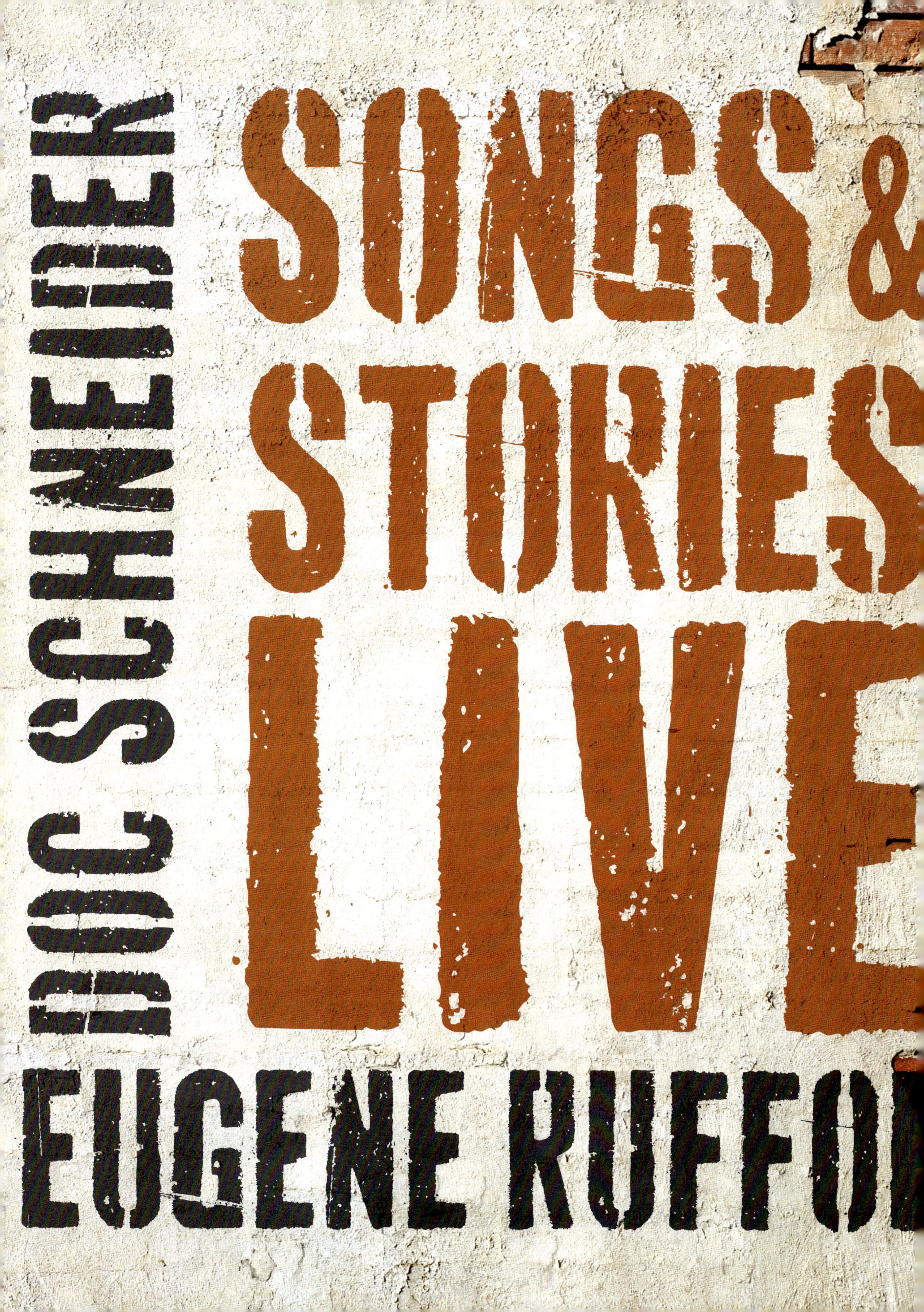
DOC SCHNEIDER
SONGS &
STORIES
LIVE
EUGENE RUFFO

Nantucket Island (The First Day of September)

Words and Music by Doc Schneider

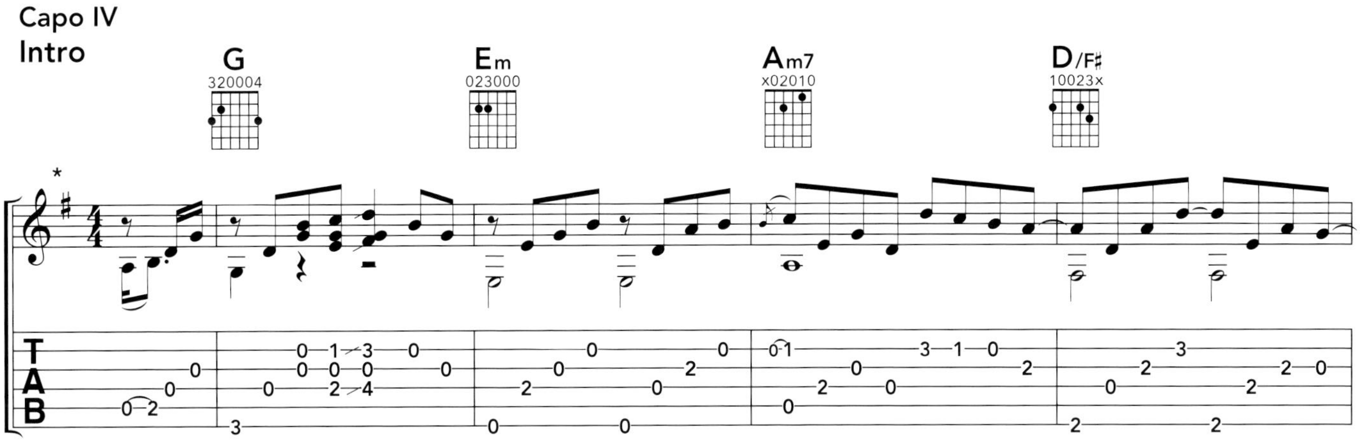

* Vocal written at concert pitch (key of B). Guitar notation, tab, and chords written respective to capoed guitar (key of G).

Em Csus2 D/F♯ Csus2 D/F♯ Bm7 Em
It shines so bright in the blue For as long as stars shine there'll be Nan-tuck-et Is - land And
To Coda 1 To Coda 2 To Coda 3
Csus2 G/B Am11 D/F♯ Gadd9
I'll be stand - ing here next to you
Verse
Gadd9 D/F♯ Em C D/F♯
2. Sure the road that brought us here Some-times kept us far a - part
Gadd9 D/F♯ Em Am7 Am7/G D/F♯
But un-der-neath those se - parate nights We held on - to one heart And we
D.S. al Coda 1
Csus2 D Em7 Am7 Am7/G D/F♯
sailed a - cross this bay And we made it to this day So here we are
Coda 1
Bridge 1
Gadd9 D/F♯ Em A7 D G Csus2 D
(you) The days we will re - mem - ber cling-ing to the flame

Intro

G Am7 D/F♯ Gadd9

Gadd9 D/F♯ Em
1. Heart to heart beneath the Milky Way

Am7 Am7/G D/F♯
Tonight these stars hear every word we say

Chorus

Gadd9 E/F♯
Here we are on Nantucket Island

Em Csus2 D/F♯
It shines so bright in the blue

Csus2 D/F♯ Bm7 Em
For as long as stars shine, there'll be Nantucket Island

Csus2 G/B Am11 D/F♯ Gadd9
And I'll__ be_ standing here next to you

Gadd9 D/F♯ Em
2. Sure, the road that brought us here

C D/F♯
Sometimes kept us far apart

Gadd9 D/F♯ Em
But underneath those separate nights

Am7 Am7/G D/F♯
We held onto one heart

Csus2 D Em7
And we sailed across this bay

Am7 Am7/G D/F♯
And we made it to this day

Repeat Chorus

Bridge 1

D/F♯ Em A7 D G Csus2 D
The days we will remember clinging to the flame

Em A7 D G Csus2 Fsus2
The first day of September will always call our names

Csus2 D Em7
And we'll sail across this place

Bm7 C/D
And we'll never sail away

Repeat Chorus

Bridge 2

Csus2 D Bm7 Em7
Here's our families, there's our friends

Fmaj9 D
They are an ocean, they are an ocean

Repeat Chorus

Intro

G Am7 D/F♯ Gadd9

Gadd9 D/F♯ Em(add9)
3. Heart to heart beneath the Milky Way

Am7 Am7/G D/F♯
Tonight these stars hear every word we say

Gadd9
Here we are

SONGS & STORIES LIVE

THE LINER NOTES

This album is the result of some unstoppable chemistry. I do not know who started writing the equation, or who figured out how to add what to what to produce wonder in our lives, but I know some ingredients who stepped in mid-equation and who produced great joy.

It reminds me of a girl with a bicycle on her shirt who I never got over and never will. Accidental chemistry. The best kind. The most powerful. Who knows how far back in the formula to look to begin? The Ardennes? The Battle of the Bulge? The Hills of Sicily? A little girl in Oyster Bay? Some family in France? A little village in Germany? A little house in Dothan? I don't know. I focus on the present formula—I know the recipe for that. One part—Lia. A perfectly beauiful girl from Belgium who loves songs and poems that speak to her heart. One part—Eugene. Surely a soul put on this earth to sing, to play, to write, to find bumblers and make them shine. One part—Helen. With the love and patience to indulge her knucklehead boyfriend and husband. One part—families of all of these that are so essential to the chemistry. One part—Jenny. Who makes our chemistry look good in shrink wrap. One part—Heather, Kristin, McKenzie, Madison, Zach, and Zoe—more than a dash of

each—who make you want to do better. One part—assorted angels—Margaret, Ben (UWisch it Was You), Jeff, Shalom, David, James, Paul, Thomas Stearns, Swingers of Birches, the Mighty Lightship, Alex and all of the beautiful Urrutias, Ardythe Mary, Christopher, Tony, Robert Thomas, Griffin Boyette Bell, Sid, Shea, Gladys, Fuzz, Lu, Bob, Father Bill, Judge Bill, Francis Albert, Sam and Serge, Guy Savoy, Dolly and the Boys, Eddie Owen, Dwight, Brenda, Kevin, Debra, Ken, Sue, Rich, Shana, MJD and JAP, Rich Reynolds, and too many other angels to name. You know who you are (Jeni Jobe—must I go on?).

So one afternoon, at Eddie's Attic in Atlanta, April 18, 2009, all the azaleas say hello, you find the right equipment, the right moment, you shake it up, you add in everything—and you throw in your heart. And here is the result. Thank you to Eugene Ruffolo. That is not enough, but you know what I mean. Thank you to Lia and Alex Kinnet. To Lem and Amit.

And to everyone that made one Saturday afternoon into a bit of unstoppable chemistry—the kind you hold in your hands, plug into your CD player or computer and carry it with you. If I get my way, we will be back every April until the chemistry runs out. And, unless I miss my bet, it never will.

Doc

SONGS IN
THE GARDEN

Songs 1974 -2006

Coming Home Again
Blue Eyes and Saturday Night
Dandelion Wine
Shovel That Snow
I Wish I Were A Goldfish
Get A Guitar (Rush Street in Winter)
42nd Street Hooker
Wooden Walls
Helen, Wear Your Tee Shirt
Brown Eyed Lady
Walk With Me Today
Too Far To Know
Raven
Golden Yellow, Better Blue
You Got Your Way (To Fade Away)
December Again
Sailor's Dream
At The End of The Day When You're Sleepy
The Sculptor
Nightingale
Steve Must Be Getting Married
Who Took Our Eyes Away
The Love That Lasts
Helen's Villanelle
These Were My Friends
Now and Then
In Her Hands
How It Looks To You
The Lucky One
Choices and Chances
Bitter Brew
Wherever You Are
I Wanted Everything
If You Must Leave Me Now
If I Can Love Enough
We're Still Standing Here
Nothing Quite Like You
Homemade Song
The Power In Your Hands
I'll Take You Back
Turn The World Around (One Light)
Thirty Nine Years
With A Longing To Say It
A Life of Love
Journey of The Heart
The Legal Guitarist
Rises Over You
Just Then
Song for the Morning
Hint of Heaven
Deeper
Best Year of My Life
The Power of One
Come to My House
You Send Your Angels
Katy, We're Ready
New Beginning
On This Graduation Day
Look What This Brings
Storkland Jingle
One Nashville Night
Wedding in June
Hold On To Love
Hey McKenzie
One Heckuva Little Girl
Headed Where My Future Meets My Past
Everything Gold
Happy Ever After
Waterville USA
Number One Fan
Driving With Voices
Under The Skies of Lisbon
Sometimes I Dream Too Much
Across The Southern District
Massapequa
Turn Me Back Around
Quiet Place
Let The Morning Show The Way
Christmas Eyes
Marie

A Quiet Place

Words and Music by Doc Schneider

Tuning: D A D G A D (D, A, D marked ˇ)

Intro

Chorus
2
A7 D Gmaj9
Give us a qui - et place to turn to when the morn-ing light shines
T
A
B
Em A7
through Give us hands to car-ry bless-ings from the deep
And through the green
F♯m Bm7
of all these a - cres there's a ri - ver that can take us Take us in
To Coda
Em A7 D Gmaj9 D Gmaj9
and show us all there is to keep
Bridge
C6 Bm7 F♯m Bm7 Em
Lis-ten to the mu - sic sing-ing in these streams
Heav - en must have found

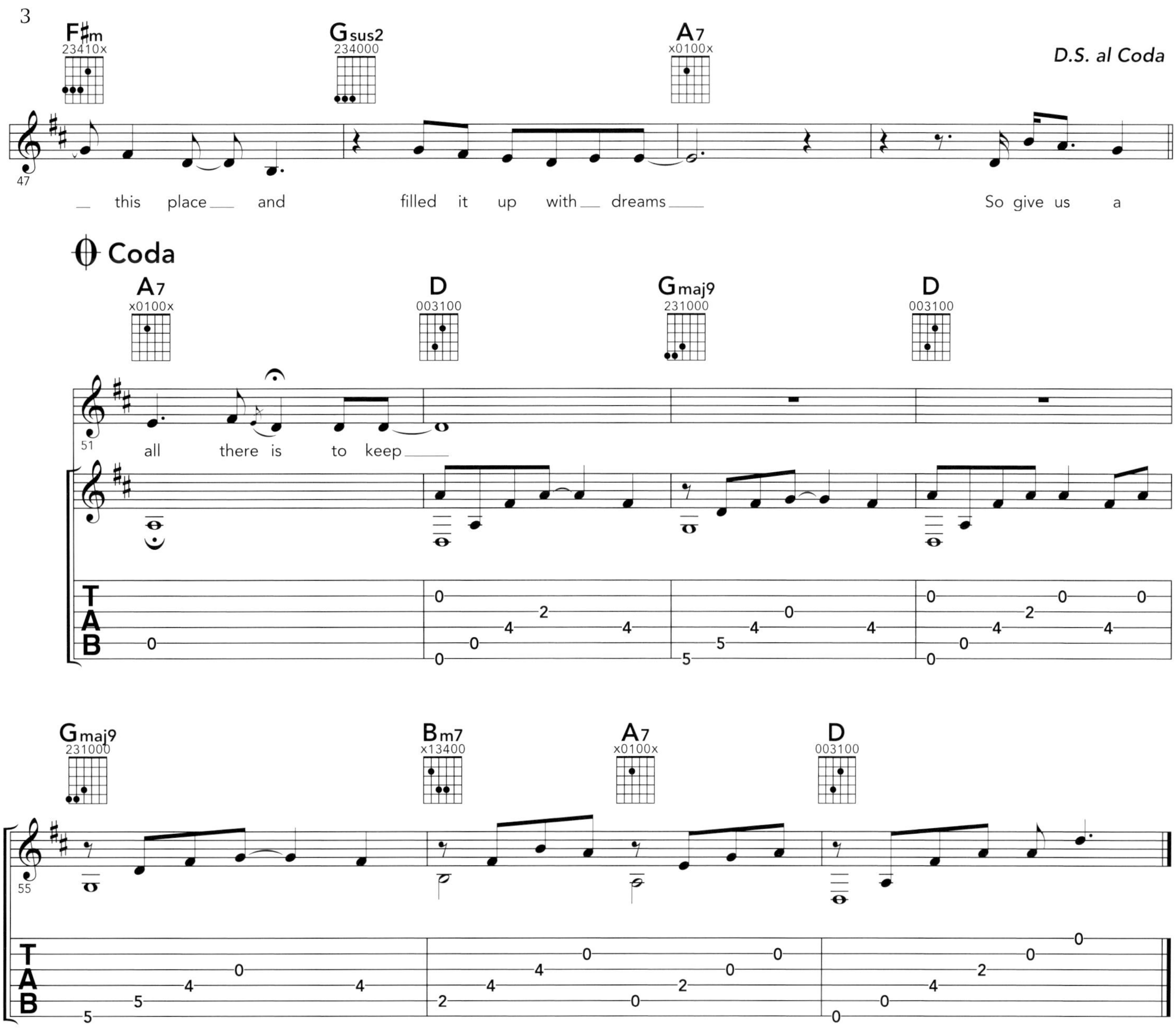

Intro

D Gmaj9 D Gmaj9
Bm7 A7 D

Bm7 A7 D C6 Em A7
1. When we see the light, we are moved to name it

F♯m Bm7 Em F♯m A7
Find a way to save it, shape it into clay

Bm7 A7 D C6 Em A7
Canvas or the anvil, pick your place to start

F♯m Bm7 Em F♯m A7
Hold it like a candle shining from your heart

Chorus

D
Give us a quiet place to turn to

Gmaj9
When the morning light shines through

Em A7
Give us hands to carry blessings from the deep

F♯m
And through the green of all these acres

Bm7
There's a river that can take us

Em A7 D Gmaj9 D Gmaj9
Take us in and show us all there is to keep

```
   Bm7        A7         D        C6                      Em   A7
2. Down below these mountains, the weave shed in these woods

   F♯m               Bm7  Em     F♯m     A7
   Waterfalls and wetlands, nature's neighborhood

   Bm7    A7   D      C6              Em   A7
   Everything in balance gently swinging through

   F♯m             Bm7     Em      F♯m  A7
   Feel the rush of freedom washing over you
```

Repeat Chorus

Bridge

```
C7              Bm7 F♯m              Bm7
Listen to the music singing in these streams

Em                  F♯m                Gsus2          A7
Heaven must have found this place and filled it up with dreams
```

Repeat Chorus

Bm7 A7 D

STATE

A Sailor's Dream

Words and Music by Doc Schneider

G Am G Am G
1.
God I'm sure I'll have a sai - lor's dream to - night
2. Got a pic
2, 3.
Bridge
Am C D Fmaj7 Am C D Am C
I look a - round me the eyes that sur - round me tell me I've been here be - fore
The girls from old New - port the boys
D Fmaj7 Am C D Am C D Fmaj7
from the best port are drink - ing and sing - ing once more
And the girl from the pin - up is hold - ing me tight And I
Chorus
Am G Am G Am G Am
think I'll have a sail - or's dream to - night
God I'm sure I'll have a sail - or's dream to - night oh
1.
G
D.S.
(take Second Endings)
3. Well my
2.
G Am C D Fmaj7 Am C
(oh) Yeah ooh
D Fmaj7 Am C D Fmaj7 Am G Am
yeah

3

Intro

G Am G Am
G

Bm G
1. Got a handful of sand that I stole from the Barbary Coast

Bm C D
Got some old red wine that I haven't opened quite yet

Am C Em Fmaj7
And pinned up to my porthole, a girl from the hometown

Chorus

Am G Am G
And I think I'll have a sailor's dream tonight, oh

Am G Am G
God, I'm sure I'll have a sailor's dream tonight

Bm G
2. Got a picture of you I stole from a highschool prom

Bm C D
Got an old dead rose that ain't lost its scent quite yet

Am C Em Fmaj7
And pinned up to my porthole, a girl from the hometown

Repeat Chorus

Bridge

Am C
I look around me

D Fmaj7 Am C D
The eyes that surround me tell me I've been here before

Am C
The girls from old Newport,

D Fmaj7 Am C D
The boys from the best port are drinking and singing once more

Am C D Fmaj7
And the girl from the pin-up is holding me tight

Repeat Chorus

Bm G
3. Well, my sands are all gone and my floor looks like Barbary Coast

Bm C D
If my wine ain't gone then I know that it is almost

Am C Em Fmaj7
And pinned up to my porthole, the girl from the hometown

Repeat Chorus

Repeat Bridge

Repeat Chorus

Am C D Fmaj7 Am C D Fmaj7
Yeah,______ ooh___________________ yeah

Am C D Fmaj7 Am G Am

Christmas Eyes

Words and Music by Doc Schneider

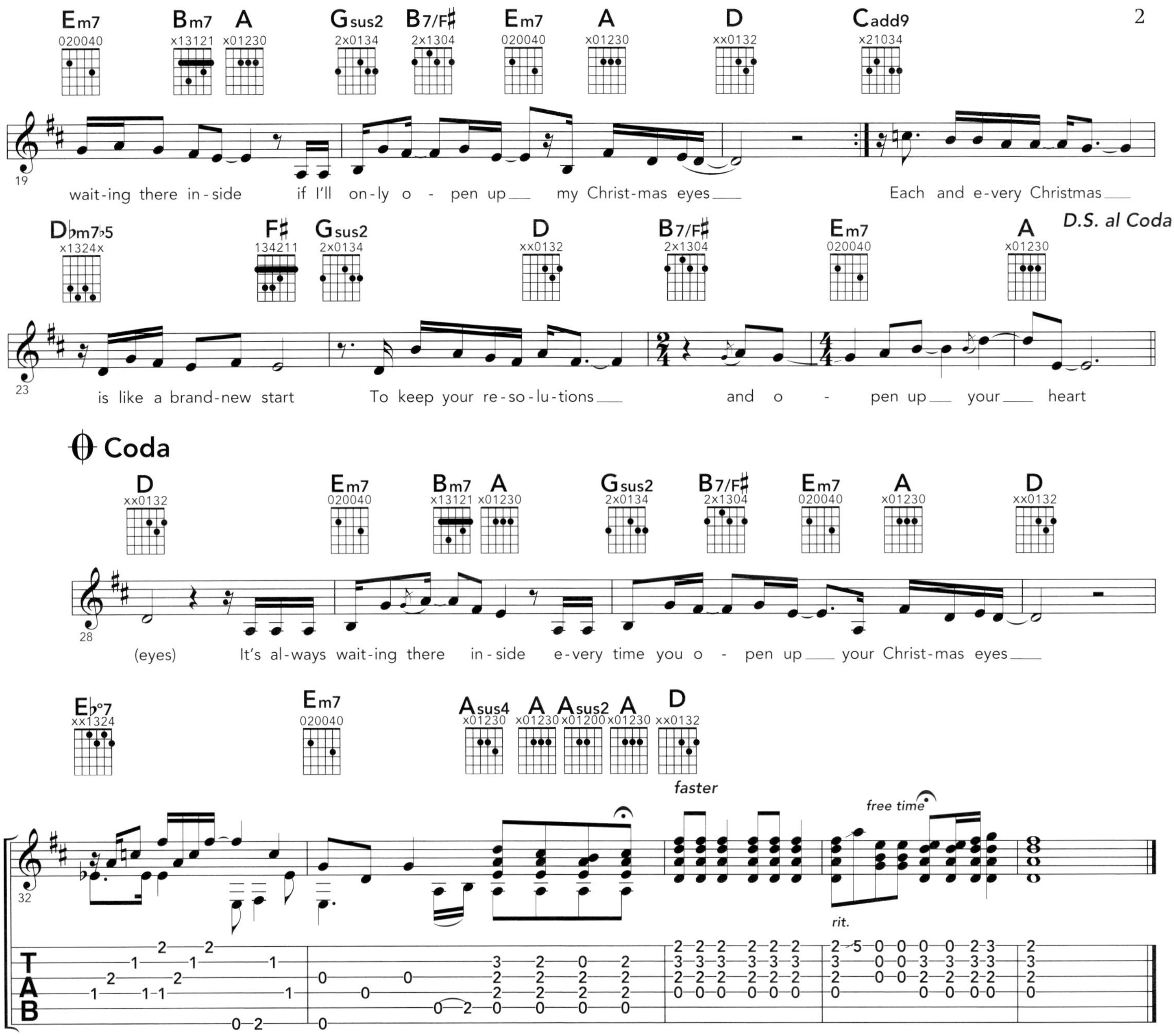

Intro

D

1. D Bm7 Em7 Asus4 A
Whenever fruitcake weather comes around this time of year

D Bm7 Em7 A7sus4 A7 A7sus2
I feel a little better and the clouds all disappear

A7 Bm7 A Gsus2 Bm7 A Gsus2
Like sliding down a ski slope through freshly falling snow

D D/F♯ Em7 A7sus4 D
There go all my troubles, how I love to see them go

Chorus

Em7 A7sus4 D
And whenever Christmas comes, I see everything

Em7 A7sus4 D
Like I have a pair of Christmas eyes

Gsus2 A Bm7
And I remember love is not a fleeting thing

Em7 Bm7 A
It's always waiting there inside

Gsus2 B7/F♯ Em7 A D
If I'll only open up my Christmas eyes

D Bm7 Em7 Asus4 A A7sus2 A
2. When I was a child, how I loved that Christmas thrill

D Bm7 Em7 A7sus4 A7
Couldn't hide my smile, and even now I love it still

Bm7 A Gsus2 Bm7 A Gsus2
Stockings on the mantle, lights up on the tree

D E♭°7 Em7 A7sus4 D
Look at all those presents maybe one of them's for me

Repeat Chorus

Bridge

Cadd9 D♭m7♭5 F♯
Each and every Christmas is like a brand-new start

Gsus2 D B7/F♯ Em7 A
To keep your resolutions and open up your heart

Chorus

Em7 A7sus4 D
And every time you do, you'll see everything

Em7 A7sus4 D
Like you have a pair of Christmas eyes

Gsus2 A Bm7
Just remember love is not a fleeting thing

Em7 Bm7 A
It's always waiting there inside

Gsus2 B7/F♯ Em7 A D
Every time you open up your Christmas eyes

Em7 Bm7 A
It's always waiting there inside

Gsus2 B7/F♯ Em7 A D
Every time you open up your Christmas eyes

E♭°7 Em7 Asus4 A Asus2 A D

Original Chords

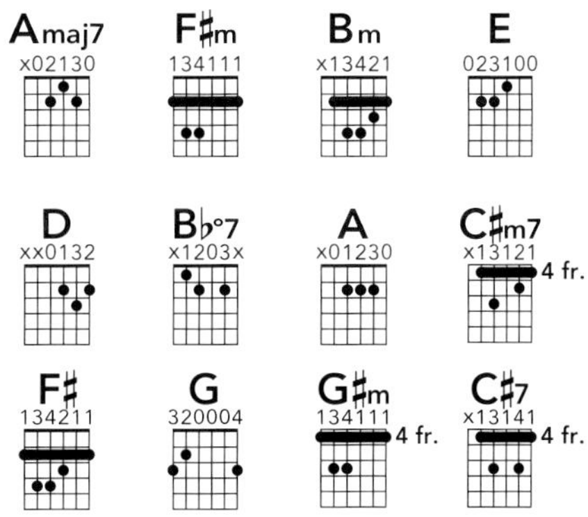

Amaj7 F♯m Bm E
1. Whenever fruitcake weather comes around this time of year

Amaj7 F♯m Bm E
I feel a whole lot better and the clouds all disappear

F♯m E D F♯m E D
Like sliding down a ski slope through freshly falling snow

A B♭°7 Bm E A
There go all my troubles, how I love to see them go

Chorus

Bm E A
And whenever Christmas comes, I see everything

Bm E A
It seems I have a pair of Christmas eyes

D E F♯m
And I remember love is not a fleeting thing

Bm F♯m E
It's always waiting there inside

D C♯m7 F♯ Bm E A
If I'll only open up my Christmas eyes

Amaj7 F♯m Bm E
2. When I was a child, how I loved that Christmas thrill

Amaj7 F♯m Bm E
Couldn't hide my smile, and even now I love it still

F♯m E D F♯m E D
Stockings on the mantle, lights up on the tree

A B♭°7 Bm E E
Look at all those presents maybe one of them's for me

Repeat Chorus

Bridge

G G♯m C♯7
Each and every Christmas is like a brand-new start

D A B♭°7 Bm E
To keep your resolutions and open up your heart

Chorus

Bm E A
And every time you do, you'll see everything

Bm E A
Like you have a pair of Christmas eyes

D E F♯m
Just remember love is not a fleeting thing

Bm F♯m E
It's always waiting there inside

D C♯m7 F♯ Bm E A
Every time you open up your Christmas eyes

Bm F♯m E
It's always waiting there inside

D C♯m7 F♯ Bm E A
Every time you open up your Christmas eyes

B♭°7 Bm E A

Come to My House

Words and Music by Doc Schneider

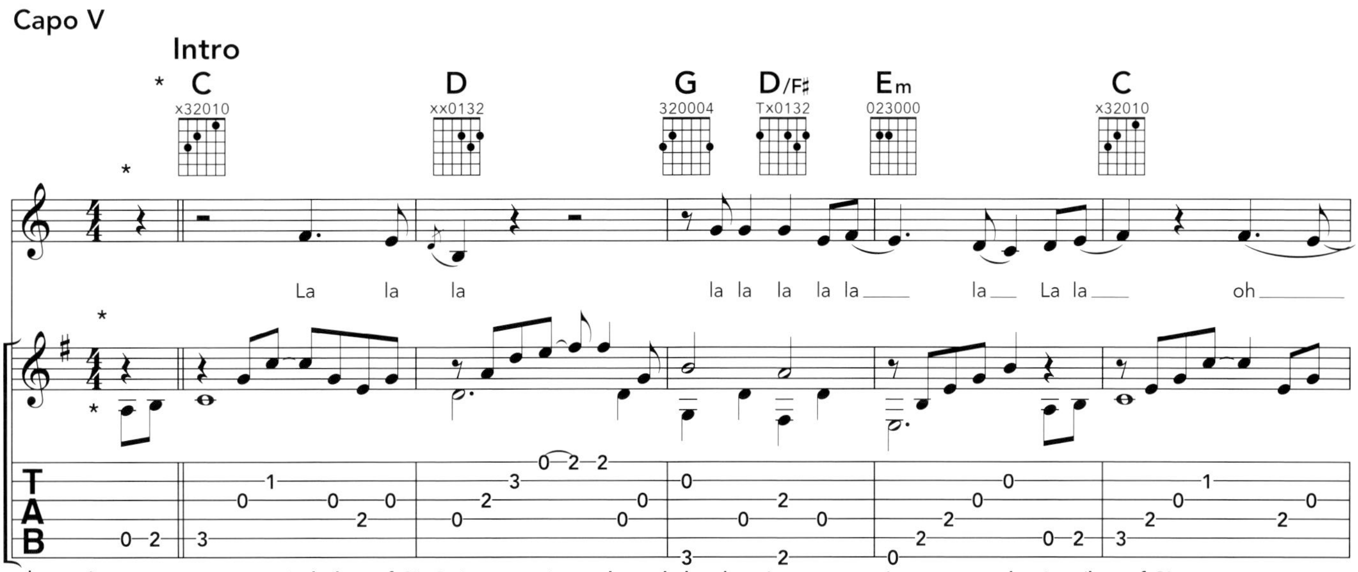

* Vocal written at concert pitch (key of C). Guitar notation, tab, and chords written respective to capoed guitar (key of G).

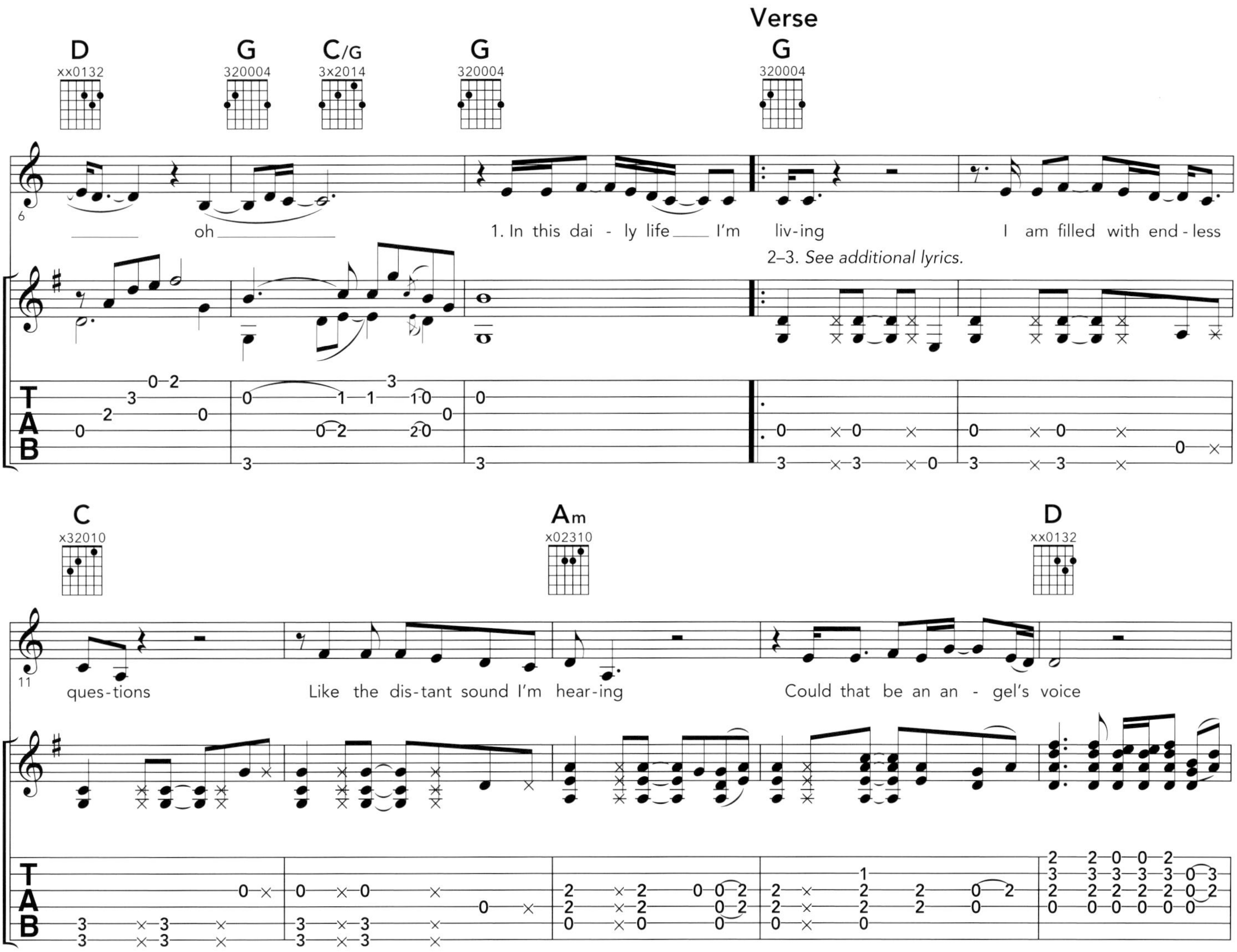

G
C
There's a hun - dred signs a - round me Just to see the hand of heav - en
Am
D
And be - lieve the doors will o - pen If I'll on - ly make this choice I will
Chorus
G D/F♯ Em C D G D/F♯
live my life with the Lord And I will find His way be - tween the sha - dows In my heart for - e - ver a - dore
Em C D C D G C D G
Like the light that shines in e - very win - dow And when I've trav - elled far In my house it's
A C D G D/F♯ Em
hard for me to see He will say come to my house You can come to my house He will
TAB

3
1, 2.
C x32010 D xx0132 G 320004 C/G 3x2014 G 320004
41
say come to my house with me 2. I will hold these hands a
G 320004 C x32010 D xx0132 G 320004 D/F♯ Tx0132 Em 023000
45
He will say come to my house you can come to my house He will
C x32010 D xx0132 G 320004 C/G 3x2014 G 320004
50
say come to my house with me

Intro

C   D G   D/F♯ Em
La la la, la la la la la la

C   D   G   C/G   G
La la, oh, oh

G
1. In this daily life I'm living

C
I am filled with endless questions

Am
Like the distant sound I'm hearing

D
Could that be an angel's voice?

G
There's a hundred signs around me

C
Just to see the hand of heaven

Am
And believe the doors will open

D
If I'll only make this choice

Chorus

G   D/F♯   Em
I will live my life with the Lord

C   D
And I will find His way between the shadows

G   D/F♯   Em
In my heart, forever adore

C   D
Like the light that shines in every window

C   D   G   C
And when I've travelled far

D   G   A
In my house, it's hard for me to see

C   D
He will say "come to my house,

G   D/F♯   Em
You can come to my house"

C   D   G C/G G
He will say "come to my house with me"

G
2. I will hold these hands around me

C
And I will let this spirit flow

Am
And the place that they have found me

D
That's a place where I will go

G
In my search for all the answers

C
There was not much I could show

Am
Now when everything eludes me

D
There is one thing I still know

Repeat Chorus

G
3. It was a child born to Mary

C
On a dark December night

Am
And in that stable ordinary

D
Such extraordinary light

G
And that light is shining clearly

C
And I can see His outstretched hand

Am
But it is love that makes me take it

D
And that helps me understand

Repeat Chorus

C   D
He will say "come to my house,

G   D/F♯   Em
You can come to my house"

C   D   G C/G G
He will say "come to my house with me"

NORWAY

Here It Is Christmas

Words and Music by Doc Schneider

* Vocal written at concert pitch (key of E). Guitar notation, tab, and chords written respective to capoed guitar (key of D).

** Multiple gtrs. arr. for one.

Chorus
This is Christ-mas time Here it is Christ-mas here it's com-ing round one more time You're feel-ing half
as old and may-be twice as wise Here it is Christ-mas you can feel your heart be-gin
To Coda
to rise and you're sure-ly glad it's Christ-mas time
Bridge
Lit-tle girls keep-ing qui-et all this si-lent night Boys warmed by fires made of
can-dle-light Choirs of an-gels sing "Oh ho-ly night
D.S. al Coda
They know that Christ-mas has come a-round a-gain whoa

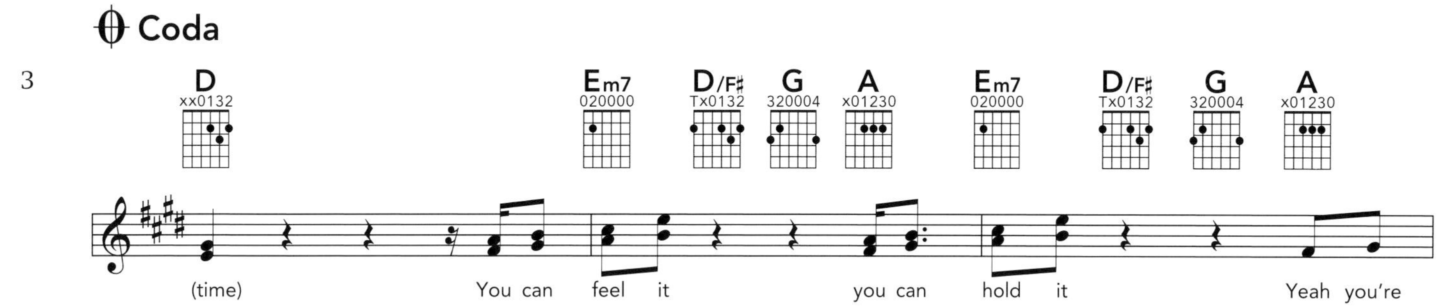

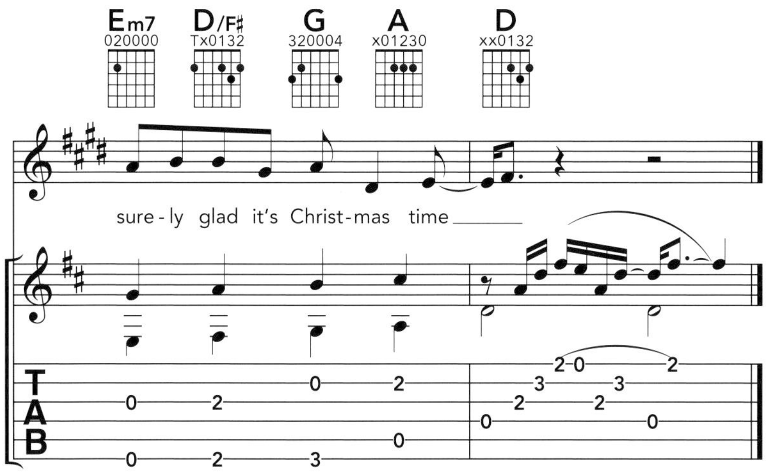

Intro

D

D Bm7 G A7sus4 A7
1. Every house is framed in lights

F♯m7 Bm7 F♯m7 G
Every fence is glazed in white

Em7 A7sus4 A7 F♯m7 B7sus4 B7
And all the world is new and bright

Em7 D/F♯ G Asus4 A
This is Christmas time

D Bm7 G A7sus4 A7
2. Every dream is turning white

F♯m7 Bm7 F♯m7 G
Everybody thinks they might

Em7 A7sus4 A7 F♯m7 B7sus4 B7
Every heart's a shining light

Em7 D/F♯ G Asus4 A
This is Christmas time

Chorus

D Bm7
Here it is Christmas, here it's coming round one more time

G6 A7sus4 A7
You're feeling half as old and maybe twice as wise

F♯m7 Bm7 Em7 D/F♯ G D/F♯
Here it is Christmas, you can feel your heart begin to rise

Em7 D/F♯ G A D
And you're surely glad it's Christmas time

D Bm7 G A7sus4 A7
3. Everyone can spare a dime

F♯m7 Bm7 F♯m7 G
Every kitchen smells like thyme

Em7 A7sus4 A7 F♯m7 B7sus4 B7
Every sentence seems to rhyme

Em7 D/F♯ G Asus4 A
This is Christmas time

Repeat Chorus

Bridge

Bm7 Bm7
Little girls keeping quiet all this silent night

G D/F♯ Em7 A7sus4 A7
Boys warmed by fires made of candlelight

F♯m7 Bm7 F♯m7 G
Choirs of angels sing "Oh, holy night"

Em7 Bm7 Em7 A7sus4 A7
They know that Christmas has come around again, whoa
.

D Bm7 G A7sus4 A7
4. Peace on earth, good will to men

F♯m7 Bm7 F♯m7 G
Love is on the rise again

Em7 A7sus4 A7 F♯m7 B7sus4 B7
I feel just like I did back then

Em7 D/F♯ G Asus4 A
This is Christmas time

Repeat Chorus

Em7 D/F♯ G A Em7 D/F♯ G
You can feel it, you can hold it

A Em7 D/F♯ G A D
Yeah, you're surely glad it's Christmas time

Original Chords (no capo)

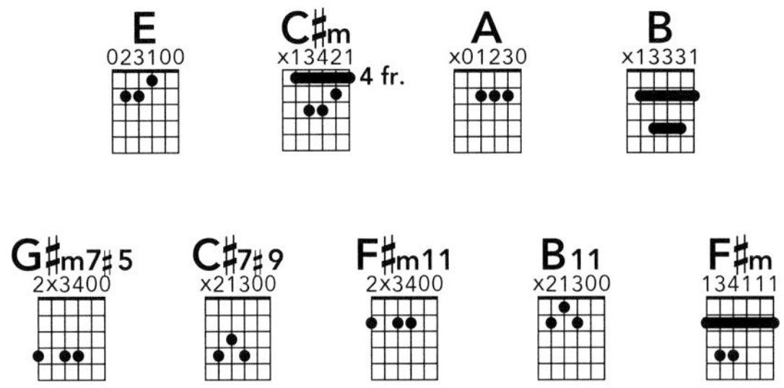

Intro

E

E   C♯m   A   B
1. Every house is framed in lights

G♯m7♯5 C♯7♯9   G♯m7♯5   A
Every fence is glazed in white

F♯m11   B11   G♯m7♯5   C♯7♯9
And all the world is new and bright

F♯m11 G♯m7♯5 A   B
This is Christmas time

E   C♯m   A   B
2. Every dream is turning white

G♯m7♯5 C♯7♯9 G♯m7♯5   A
Everybody thinks they might

F♯m11 B11   G♯m7♯5   C♯7♯9
Every heart's a shining light

F♯m11 G♯m7♯5 A   B
This is Christmas time

Chorus

E   C♯m
Here it is Christmas, here it's coming round one more time

A   B
You're feeling half as old and maybe twice as wise

C♯m   F♯m   C♯m   A   E
Here it is Christmas, you can feel your heart begin to rise

F♯m11 G♯m7♯5   A   B   E
And you're surely glad it's Christmas time

E   C♯m A   B
3. Everyone can spare a dime

G♯m7♯5 C♯7♯9 G♯m7♯5   A
Every kitchen smells like thyme

F♯m11   B11   G♯m7♯5   C♯7♯9
Every sentence seems to rhyme

F♯m11 G♯m7♯5 A   B
This is Christmas time

Repeat Chorus

Bridge

C♯m   G♯m7♯5
Little girls keeping quiet all this silent night

A   C♯m   A   B
Boys warmed by fires made of candlelight

G♯m7♯5   C♯7♯9   G♯m7♯5   A
Choirs of angels sing "Oh, holy night"

F♯m11   G♯m7♯5   A   B
They know that Christmas has come around again, whoa

E   C♯m   A   B
4. Peace on earth, good will to men

G♯m7♯5 C♯7♯9   G♯m7♯5 A
Love is on the rise again

F♯m11   B11 G♯m7♯5   C♯7♯9
I feel just like I did back then

F♯m11 G♯m7♯5 A   B
This is Christmas time

Repeat Chorus

F♯m11 G♯m7♯5 A   F♯m11 G♯m7♯5 A
You can feel it,   you can hold it

F♯m11 G♯m7♯5   A   B   E
And you're surely glad it's Christmas time

I'm Still Here

Words and Music by Doc Schneider

G6 Dadd9/F♯ Bm11 A/C♯
makes me strong - er the way they say it should And though the win - ter comes to our neigh-bor-
Dsus2 Bm11 Esus4 E
Chorus
Dsus2
- hood I can't get my heart to hard - en You've been gone so long You tell me you don't know
A/C♯ Bm11 Esus4 E
the way to go back home You say that you for - get But how can that be
Dsus2 A/C♯ Bm11
so When you go back in time You're gon - na find that I'm just a block past Chel - sea

To Coda
1.
Esus4 E Bm11 Esus4 E A E/G♯
Mar - ket Right there turn there I'm still here
G6 Dadd9/F♯
2.
Bridge
E/G♯ G6 Dadd9/F♯
We say good-bye the way you do
F° F♯m Dsus2 A/C♯
Bra-zil-ian kiss - es and sum-mer dew Some - day I'll be o - ver you But it
D.S. al Coda
Bm11 Esus4 E
just won't be to - day You've been gone so
Coda
A
here

Intro

A **E/G♯** **G6** **Dadd9/F♯**
Bm11 **A/C♯** **Dsus2** **Bm11** **Esus4** **E**

A **E/G♯**
1. In the aftermath of our love affair
G6 **Dadd9/F♯**
Where the flags half mast stand everywhere
Bm11 **A/C♯** **Dsus2**
I have worn a path where you left me here
Bm11 **Esus4** **E**
In these rooms that were our garden

A **E/G♯**
2. And the years on years have done no good
G6 **Dadd9/F♯**
Nothing makes me stronger the way they say it should
Bm11 **A/C♯** **Dsus2**
And though the winter comes to our neighborhood
Bm11 **Esus4**
I can't get my heart to harden

Chorus
E **Dsus2**
You've been gone so long
A/C♯
You tell me you don't know
Bm11
The way to go back home
Esus4
You say that you forget
E **Dsus2**
But how can that be so?
A/C♯
When you go back in time
Bm11
You're gonna find that I'm…
Esus4 **E**
Just a block past Chelsea Market
Bm11 **Esus4** **E**
Right there, turn there, I'm still here
A **E/G♯** **G6** **Dadd9/F♯**

A **E/G♯**
3. There you are in the doorway now
G6 **Dadd9/F♯**
Unhinge me with each kiss somehow
Bm11 **A/C♯** **Dsus2**
And it breaks my heart how you look around
Bm11 **Esus4** **E**
I never ended what we started

A **E/G♯**
4. Let me lend you this, let me lend you that
G6 **Dadd9/F♯**
This is how it works, sure, you can bring it back
Bm11 **A/C♯** **Dsus2**
I pretend to be so matter of fact
Bm11 **Esus4**
We are the breeze and the broken hearted

5

Repeat Chorus

```
             Bm11    Esus4  E           A    E/G♯
…Right there, turn there, I'm still here
```

Bridge

```
G6                           Dadd9/F♯
We say goodbye the way you do

F°              F♯m
Brazilian kisses and summer dew

Dsus2           A/C♯
Someday I'll be over you

    Bm11              Esus4   E
But it just won't be today
```

Repeat Chorus

```
             Bm11    Esus4  E         A    E/G♯
…Right there, turn there, I'm still here

        G6(9)  Dadd9/F♯          Bm11   A/C♯   Dsus2
I'm still here, reliving every year

                   Bm11    Esus4
Reliving every year

E          A5
I'm still here
```

Original Guitar Chords (Capo VII)

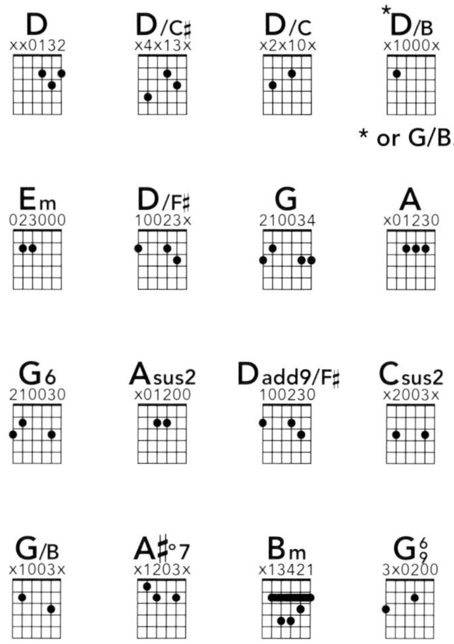

Guitar Intro

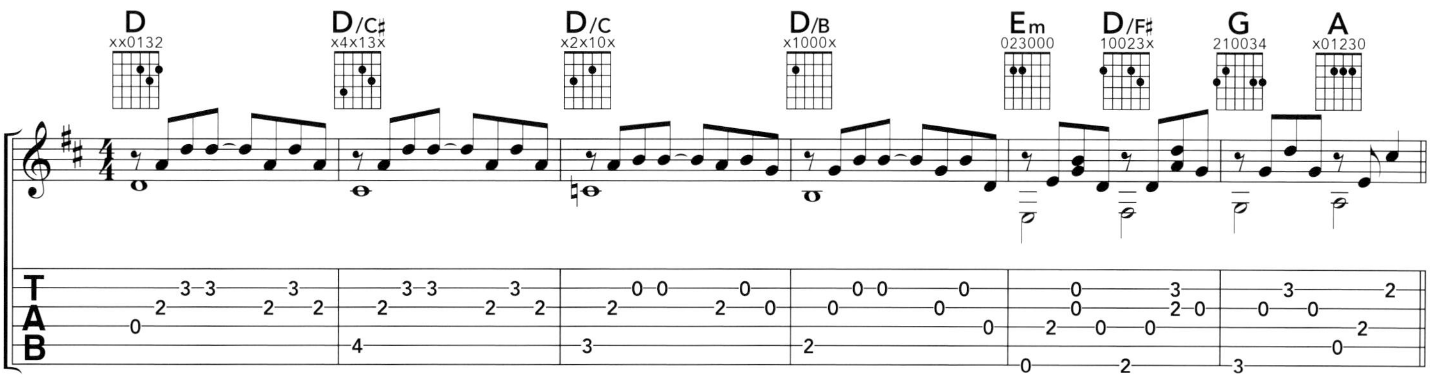

Intro

D D/C♯ D/C D/B
Em D/F♯ G Em A

D D/C♯
1. In the aftermath of our love affair
D/C D/B
Where the flags half mast stand everywhere
Em D/F♯ G6
I have worn a path where you left me here
Em Asus2
In these rooms that were our garden

D D/C♯
2. Now the years on years have done no good
D/C D/B
Nothing makes me stronger the way they say it should
Em D/F♯ G6
And though the winter comes to our neighborhood
Em Asus2
I can't get my heart to harden

Chorus

G
You've been gone so long
Dadd9/F♯
You tell me you don't know
Em
The way to go back home
Asus2
You say that you forget
G
But how can that be so?
Dadd9/F♯
When you go back in time
Em
You're gonna find that I'm…
Asus2
Just a block past Chelsea Market
Em Asus2
Right there, turn there, I'm still here
D D/C♯ D/C D/B

D D/C♯
3. There you are in the doorway now
D/C D/B
Unhinge me with each kiss somehow
Em D/F♯ G6
And it breaks my heart how you look around
Em Asus2
I never ended what we started

D D/C♯
4. Let me lend you this, let me lend you that
D/C D/B
This is how it works, sure, you can bring it back
Em D/F♯ G6
I pretend to be so matter of fact
Em Asus2
We are the breeze and the broken hearted

Repeat Chorus
Em Asus2 D D/C♯
…Right there, turn there, I'm still here

Bridge
Csus2 G/B
We say goodbye the way you do
A♯°7 Bm
Brazilian kisses, summer dew
G Dadd9/F♯
Someday I'll be over you
Em Asus2
But it just won't be today

Repeat Chorus
Em Asus2 G6(9) Dadd9/F♯
…Right there, turn there, I'm still here
G6(9) Dadd9/F♯
Baby, I'm still here
G6(9) Dadd9/F♯
I'm living every year
Em Asus2 D D/C♯ D/C
And I'm still here
Em D/F♯ G Asus2 D
(spoken:) I'm still here

Sing Some Bluegrass, Goodnight Fellows

Words and Music by Doc Schneider

as recorded by:

A x01230 D xx0132 A x01230
Fel-lows all good - night Sing some blue-grass good - night Fel-lows sing some
To Coda 2
G 320004 D xx0132 A x01230 D xx0132
blue-grass good - night Fel-lows Good-night Fel-lows sing some blue - grass good - night
Coda 1
Bridge
F♯m 134111 G 320004 D xx0132
Blu - er than this blue-grass you've been so true blue to me and tru - er than a bounce
A x01230 F♯m 134111 G 320004
pass and a jump-shot from the key Blu-er than this blue-grass you've been so true blue to me
D xx0132 A x01230 D xx0132
D.S.S. al Coda 2
and tru - er than a bounce pass and a jump - shot from the key Could you
Coda 2
A x01230 D xx0132
Good-night Fel - lows sing some blue - grass good - night

3 *Intro*

D

D

1. Here in San Francisco, where we will leave our hearts

A

I better tell these Fellows how the whole thing starts

D G

So crank me up some bluegrass and let me tap my foot

D A D

Settle down the Fellows and let's make them all stay put

D

2. Down in Alabama, where we laid our scene

A

I saw your tiny face through your window screen

D G

Then here we start our story, then there begins all things

D A D

Opelika glory and this boy from Union Springs

Fiddle Solo (over Verse progression)

D

3. Well, I sensed the day I met you that I better not be late

A

I sort of learned the hard way when I showed up for a date

D G

Your father and your brother met me steaming at the door

D A D

I think they both had shotguns, but I never could be sure

D

4. You were Smith and I was Princeton, and we made a perfect pair

A

Everybody told us we're the wedding of the year

D G

I wish they'd played some bluegrass if it's okay now to level

D A D

'Cause blue's my favorite music and Blue's my favorite Devil

Chorus

A

Could you guess the day you met me,

G D

I would love to say Krzyzewski?

A

I can't spell it but I sure can say it right!

D

Like a couplet penned by Milton,

G D

One named Morgan, one named Chilton,

A D

And it's time to tell these Fellows all goodnight

A

Sing some bluegrass, goodnight Fellows

G D

Sing some bluegrass, goodnight Fellows

A D

Goodnight Fellows, sing some bluegrass, goodnight

Mandolin/Banjo Solo (over Verse progression)

D

5. In a garden full of lawyers, came upon our child of God

A

What a joy to have our daughter, how we worked, but all played hard

D G

Lester Flatt and Earl Scruggs playing, there's a bit of Bill Monroe

D A D

A little law, a little music, and we watched our Ashley grow

D

6. I became her soccer coach, I reigned for sixteen years

A

And when those Jets stopped flying, well, I cried a trail of tears

D G

And when our daughter flew away to do a world of good

D A D

I bought a madras sport coat 'cause I just felt like I should

Repeat Chorus

Fiddle Solo (over Verse progression)

D

7. Now just like I predicted, you're a legend in the law

A

But I'm the one who loves you and who walks you through that door

D G

And I know you love the College but it fills me with remorse

D A D

Every time that they compare you with a hermit and a horse

D

8. We traveled for the College, seems like twice around the sun,

A

But I hung out with the spouses and I found it's twice as fun

D G

Thank heaven it's October, we can finally kick this bucket

D A D

Pack your bag up, Madam President, we're heading for Nantucket

```
        D
9.  I never thought I'd love a President, but darlin' I do now

                                                  A
    I never thought I'd get my hips replaced, but I got 'em fixed somehow

        D                          G
    I never thought I'd love this College quite the way I do

        D                              A           D
    I never thought I'd love a Fellow, but I sure as hell love you
```

Bridge

```
F♯m                              G          D
Bluer than this bluegrass, you've been so true blue to me

                                                    A
And truer than a bounce pass and a jumpshot from the key

F♯m                              G          D
Bluer than this bluegrass, you've been so true blue to me

                                      A            D
And truer than a bounce pass and a jumpshot from the key
```

Repeat Chorus

```
                                 A           D
Goodnight Fellows, sing some bluegrass, goodnight
```

This Is Love

Words and Music by Doc Schneider

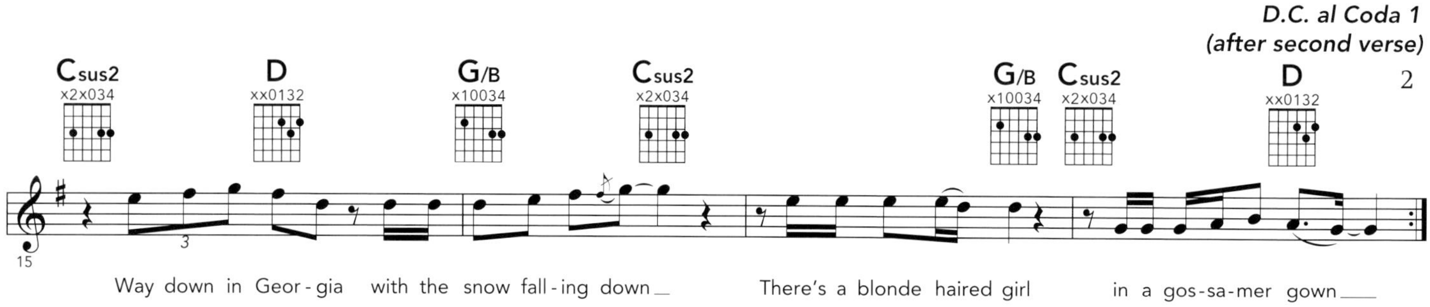

Coda 1

Bridge

Coda 2

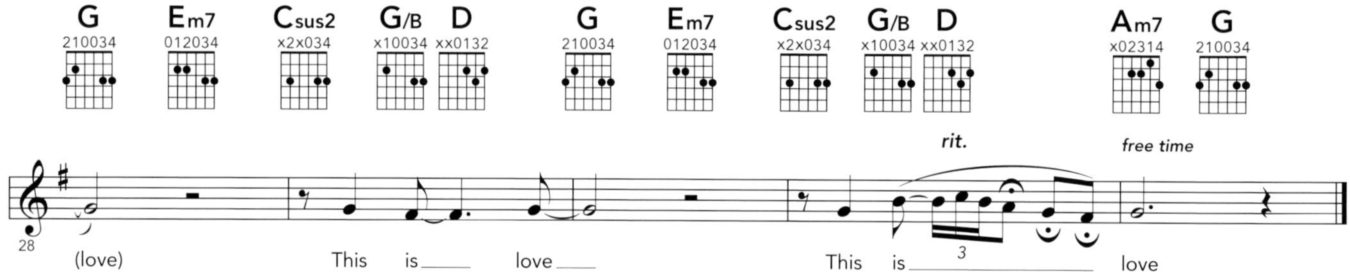

Chorus

G D Em7 G
You ask me what love is, this is love

Csus2 G/B Csus2 D
You found the heart that you were meant to be part of

G D Em7 G
You ask me what love is, this is love

Csus2 G/B Csus2 D
Like heaven planned it long ago and high above

Csus2 G/B D G
This___ is__ love

Em7 Csus2 G D
1. Up in Kentucky the roses will run

Em7 Csus2 G D
Where a boy will search this world for the one

Csus2 D G/B Csus2
Way down in Georgia with the snow falling down

G/B Csus2 D
There's a blonde haired girl in a gossamer gown

Repeat Chorus

3

Em7 Csus2 G D
2. You made this journey with little hearts of your hearts

Em7 Csus2 G D
Wove them together, a quilt of all your sweetest parts

Csus2 D G/B Csus2
Put your head on his shoulder, let her be the one

G/B Csus2 D
The green's getting golder and the sweet mint juleps run

Repeat Chorus

Bridge

Bm Csus2
Time is an ocean

G Csus2
And here's your shining shore

Em7 Bm7
Let your eyes take your pictures

Csus2 D
And hang them on October's door

Chorus

Csus2 G/B D G Em7
…This___ is__ love

Csus2 G/B D G
This___ is__ love

Csus2 G/B D Am7 G
This___ is__ love

Original Chords (Capo III)

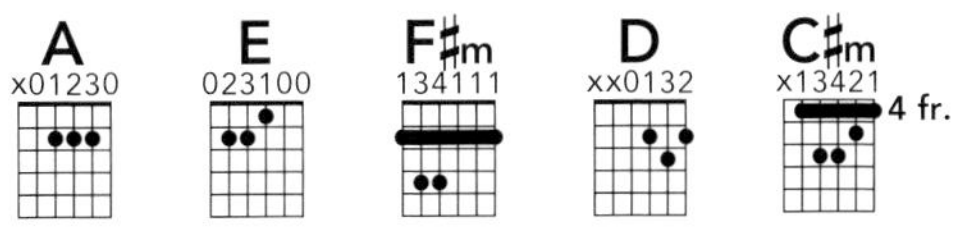

Chorus

A E F♯m A
You ask me what love is, this is love

D C♯m D E
You found the heart that you were meant to be part of

A E F♯m A
You ask me what love is, this is love

D C♯m D E
Like heaven planned it long ago and high above

D E A
This is love

F♯m D A E
1. Up in Kentucky the roses will run

F♯m D A E
Where a boy will search this world for the one

D E C♯m D
Way down in Georgia with the snow falling down

C♯m D E
There's a blonde haired girl in a gossamer gown

Repeat Chorus

F♯m D A E
2. You made this journey with little hearts of your hearts

F♯m D A E
Wove them together, a quilt of all your sweetest parts

D E C♯m D
Put your head on his shoulder, let her be the one

C♯m D E
The green's getting golder and the sweet mint juleps run

Repeat Chorus

Bridge

C♯m D
Now time is an ocean

A D
And here's your shining shore

F♯m C♯m
Let your eyes take your pictures

D E
And hang them on October's door

Chorus

D E A F♯m
…This is love

D E A F♯m
This is love

D E A
This is love

You Can Go Back Home Again (Michelangelo)

Words and Music by Doc Schneider

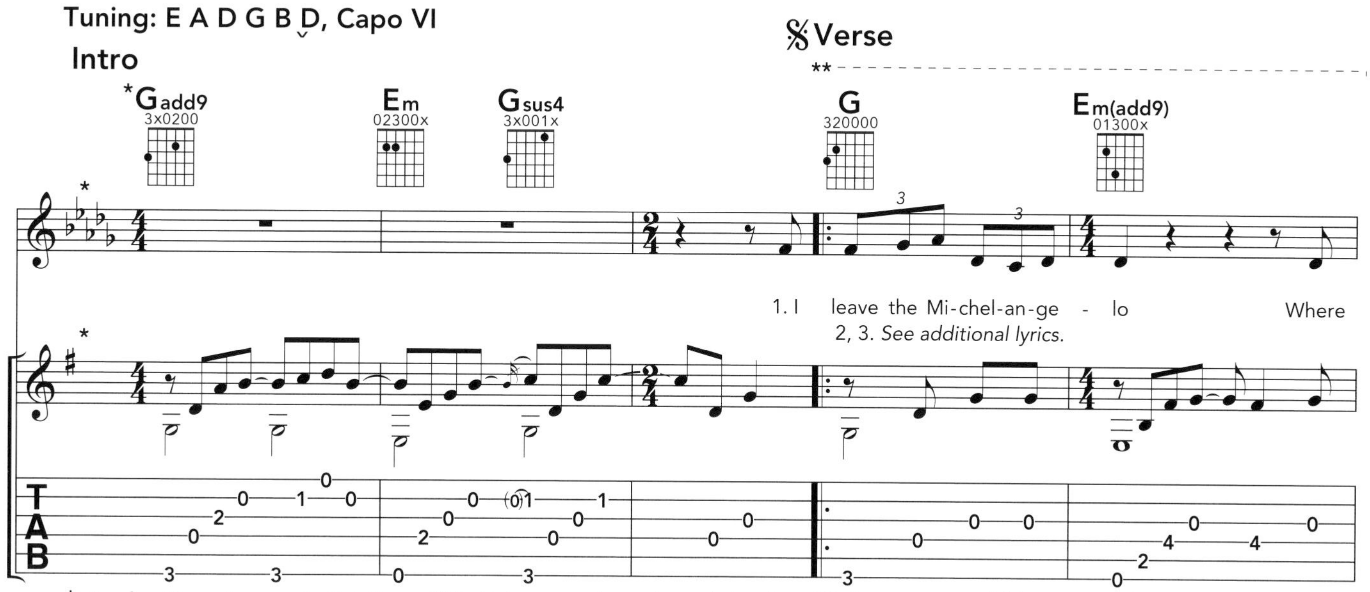

* Vocal written at concert pitch (key of D♭). Guitar notation, tab, and chords written respective to capoed guitar (key of G).

** One measure of 4/4 on second verse (not a measure of 2/4 and a measure of 4/4).

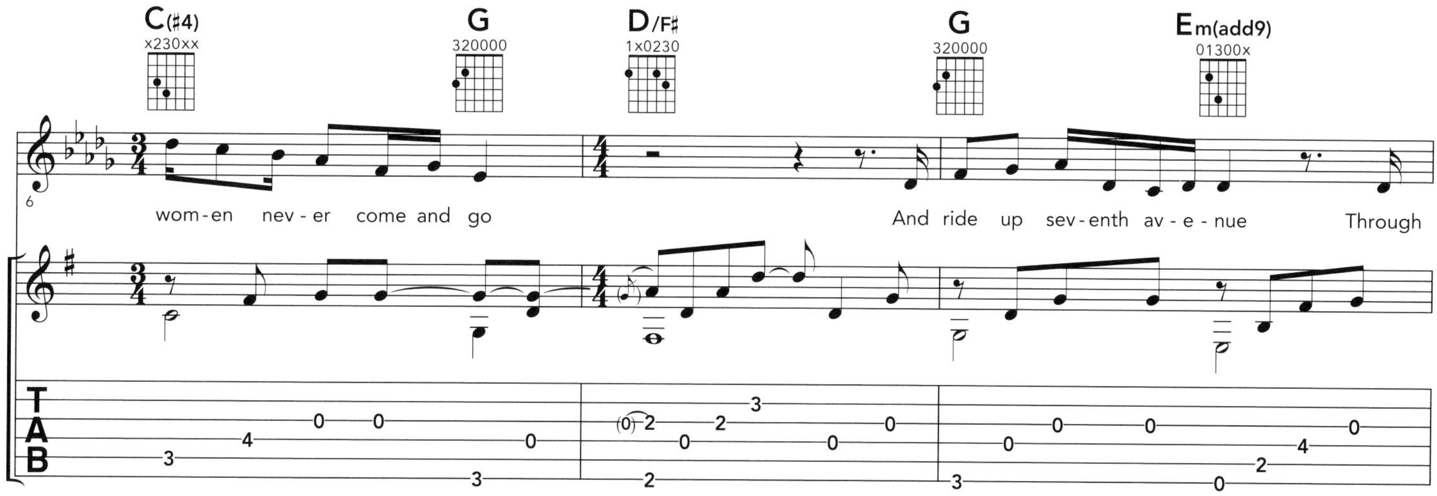

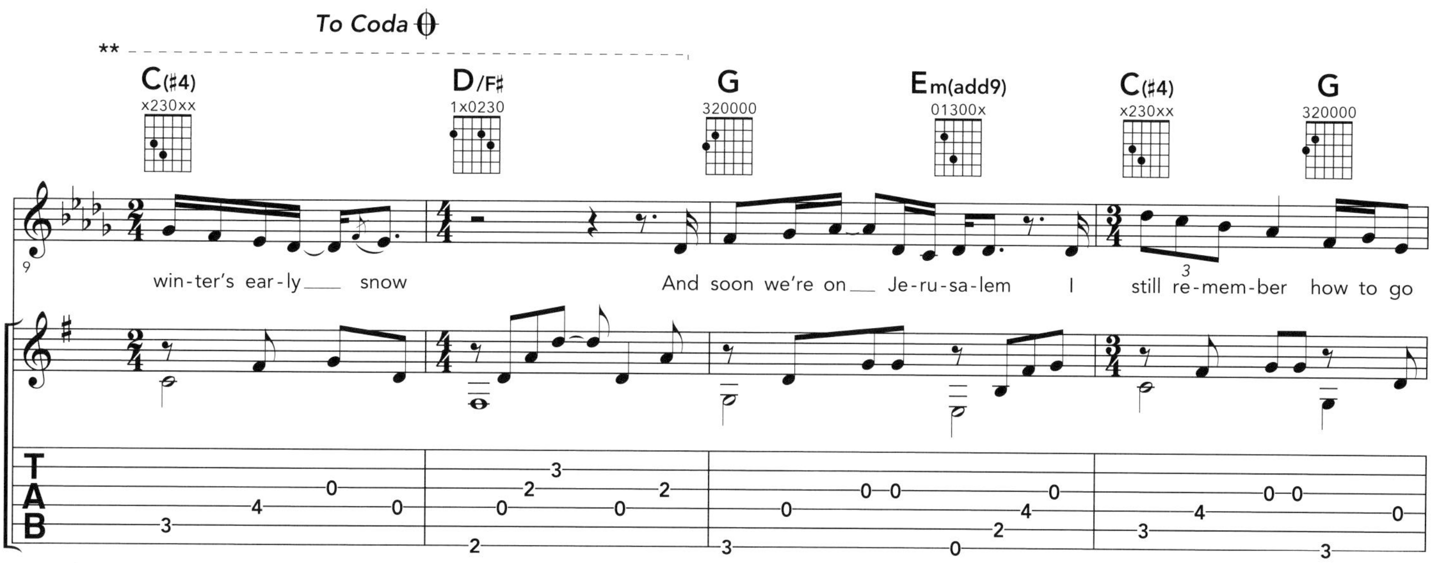

* One measure of 4/4 on second verse (not a measure of 2/4 and a measure of 4/4).

2
D/F♯ G Em(add9) C(♯4) D/F♯
I tell my driv - er what I know And where to turn for home And the
PreChorus
Em7 Csus2 G D/F♯
na-ked trees on ev-ery street They're in a dream that calls me So I go
Chorus
Cadd9 G Dadd4/A Em9
back to say I'm sor - ry For the things I did-n't do I ride my
Cadd9 G Dadd4/A Em9
bike back down that high-way In my end - less search for you And if I
Cadd9 G/B D/F♯ Cadd9 D/F♯
find you there where I left you Then Then I will know You can go back home a-gain
1. Gadd9 Em Gsus4
2. Gadd9
2. I
And

Bridge
3
Cadd9 x32010
Gadd9 3x0200
Dadd4 x32010
Em7 023000
Cadd9 x32010
how man-y years did I turn a-way How man-y years did I wait___ And how man-y tears did you shed
Gadd9 3x0200
D/F♯ 1x0230
w/ ad-lib vocals.
Cadd9 x32010
G 320000
for me___ When you said it's nev-er too late___ ooh___
D/F♯ 1x0230
Em9 013000
Cadd9 x32010
G 320000
D/F♯ 1x0230
D.S. al Coda
3. We
Coda
D/F♯ 1x0230
Em9 013000
Cadd9 x32010
G 320000
D/F♯ 1x0230
(heart) a-gain___ The way I found my heart__ a-gain
Gadd9 3x0200
Em7 023000
Cadd9 x32010
G 320000
D/F♯ 1x0230
Gadd9 3x0200
Mm_______
T
A
B

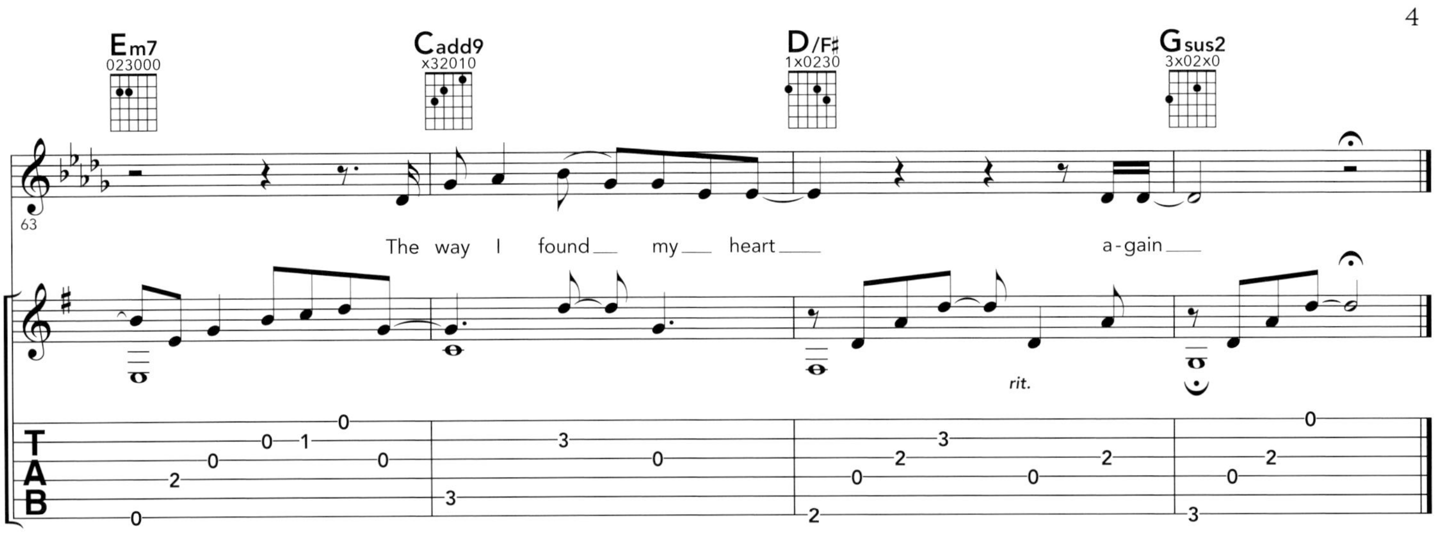

Intro

Gadd9 Em Gsus4

G Em(add9)
1. I leave the Michelangelo
C(♯4) G D/F♯
Where women never come and go
G Em(add9)
And ride up seventh avenue
C(♯4) D/F♯
Through winter's early snow
G Em(add9)
And soon we're on Jerusalem
C(♯4) G D/F♯
I still remember how to go
G Em(add9)
I tell my driver what I know
C(♯4) D/F♯
And where to turn for home

PreChorus

Em7 Csus2
And the naked trees on every street
G D/F♯
They're in a dream that calls me

Chorus

Cadd9 G
So I go back to say I'm sorry
Dadd4/A Em9
For the things I didn't do
Cadd9 G
I ride my bike back down that highway
Dadd4/A Em9
In my endless search for you
Cadd9 G/B
And if I find you there where I left you there
D/F♯
Then I will know
Cadd9 D/F♯ Gadd9
You can go back home again

Em Gsus4

G Em(add9)
2. I ride past all those Christmas lights
C(♯4) G D/F♯
Strung across those hopeful nights
G Em(add9)
And feel like I might make it right
C(♯4) D/F♯
Before it's time to go
G Em(add9)
The children's voices sing to me
C(♯4) G D/F♯
It feels just like they set me free
G Em(add9)
And once again I hear the sound
C(♯4) D/F♯
That I was meant to know

Repeat PreChorus
Repeat Chorus

Bridge

Cadd9 Gadd9
And how many years did I turn away?
Dadd4 Em7
How many years did I wait?
Cadd9 Gadd9
And how many tears did you shed for me
D/F♯
When you said it's never too late, ooh

Cadd9 G D/F♯ Em9 Cadd9 G D/F♯
(ad-lib vocals)

G Em(add9)
3. We make our way through Central Park
C(♯4) G D/F♯
And watch the moonlight kiss the dark
G Em(add9)
And in the morning I will tell
C(♯4) D/F♯
The way I found my heart again

Em9 Cadd9 G

D/F♯
The way I found my heart again

G Em7 Cadd9 Gadd9

D/F♯ Gadd9 Em7
Mm
Cadd9 D/F♯ Gsus2
The way I found my heart again

You're the Song

Words and Music by Doc Schneider

G F G
28
Where we go we'll go together
You'll always be my favorite song
Wagon Wheel
Chorus
F G C Gadd9/B Am F
Touch of Grey I will give Those songs some play But you're the song that I'll be
G C F G C Gadd9/B Am
singing every day You're the song you're the song You're the song you're the song You're the song
F G C
that I'll be singing every day
1.
2.
2. Oh
Guitar Solo
Half Time Feel
C/E F G/B C C/E F G/B C
Oh
C/E F G/B C Dsus4 D F
yeah

3 Bridge
F G Em F G Em
And e-very time I see you you al-ways knock me off my feet
End Half Time Feel
F G C G/B Am F G
My M. B. A. tells me to say You are the sweet-est bal - ance sheet So
Slower triplet feel
C Am Em C Am Em
come on pret-ty ba-by let me seal the deal No one e - ver made me feel the way you make me feel
F G C G/B Am F
Turns out once up-on a time is real-ly some-thing real I got a coach and six for us Let's
G
D.S. al Fine
rock the wag-on whell Let's rock the wag - on wheel

Intro

C

C
1. You are the song that time was writing

F
You are the words I want to say

G
There in the light where you are shining

F G
That's where I'll always want to stay

C
2. I give my heart to you forever

F
Forever we'll be going strong

G
Where we go we'll go together

F G
You'll always be my favorite song

Chorus

F G
Wagon Wheel, Touch of Grey

C Gadd9/B Am
I will give those songs some play

F G C
But you're the song that I'll be singing every day

F G
You're the song, you're the song

C Gadd9/B Am
You're the song, you're the song

F G C
You're the song that I'll be singing every day

C
3. This is a vision I'll remember

F
I'll always see you standing there

G
I will remember each November

F G
I'll always be your easy chair

C
4. They said wherever I would find you

F
Pressed all in organdy you'd be

G
Turns out that I was right beside you

F G
Destined to find you, Emily

Repeat Chorus

Guitar Solo

C/E F G/B C C/E F G/B C

C/E F G/B C Dsus4 D F

Oh, yeah

Bridge

F G Em
And every time I see you

F G Em
You always knock me off my feet

F G C G/B Am
My M.B.A. tells me to say

F G
You are the sweetest balance sheet

C Am Em
So come on pretty baby let me seal the deal

C Am Em
No one ever made me feel the way you make me feel

F G C G/B Am
Turns out once upon a time is really something real

F
I got a coach and six for us, let's rock the wagon wheel

G
Let's rock the wagon wheel

C
5. You are the song that time was writing

You are the words I want to say

Heather and the Funky Bunch
Go Overboard!
Niagara Falls 2012
Doc

Niagara Falls --1967

Capo II

1.

Gadd9 (300200)

Leaving Long Island for a new frontier

Cadd D (x30030) D/F#

Wonder of the world was waiting way up there

Gadd9

Driving for forever on a hot summer day

CaddD D/F#

Funny how the memory never went away

Chorus

C D/F#

Niagara Falls

Am Am/G

the way it felt to me

Em A

was like me falling free

C D/F# G

the year Niagara Falls was calling me

2.

Later on the river on the Maid of the Mist

Tried to hold the moment in the palm of my fist

I watched those walls of water, felt those tears on my face,

I was just a boy but I remember that place

Bridge

Cadd D G/B (x20030)

Water fall down,

Em D/F#

Let me feel your spray,

Cadd D G/B

Water fall down,

Em D/F#

wash my sins away.

3.

Picture of my daughter and that river still there,

Waterfalls behind her and the wind in her hair,

Remembering the wonder of that water go by,

Always keep that memory in the back of my eye

Doc Schneider (copyright 2012)

(Inspired By Heather's and Shawn's 2012 Trip)

Scenes from Beach Haven
and the Schroll Family Beach Trip
Doc

Highway 30A

        Amaj
I may come from Alabama
        F#m
with no banjo on my knee,
        G
I may come on down from Georgia,
          E
I might come from Tennessee,
            D   C#m
I might ride on in from Texas,
   C#m   D
or from nearby Lousianne,
  G
but wherever I come from
      E
I have found the promised land.

Chorus
                   F#m
For when I ride the road through Heaven,
C#m
30A is on the sign,
  D   A
just a slice of paradise,
 G   E
put here by design,
           F#m
I need to soak up all this beauty,
          C#m
let my troubles fly away,
           F#m –E -- D --- F#m
yes, and oh, you beautiful beaches,
     D   A   (Amaj)
and Highway 30A.

When I travel down this highway,
It's like a calm comes over me,
I know God's been to South Walton
painted all this scenery,
so I say Good Morning Grayton Beach,
Hello Seaside too,
Watercolor, Water Sound,
let me lay my eyes on you,
D   C#m
and Alys, Seacrest, Rosemary Beach,
C#m   D
such a sight to see,
 G
I marvel how this highway
  E
can set my spirit free.

(Chorus)

I might come in here in the Summer,
I might come here in the Spring,
I might come here in the Winter,
just to hear the singers sing,
I might eat in every restaurant,
and drink in every bar,
and fall asleep on beaches,
and wink at every star.

Bridge
F#m
Sure, my dream is just to stay here,
C#m
like all you natives do,
D   C#m
and if I am a good boy,
      Bm   E
I'm gonna grow up just like you.

(Chorus)
Doc Schneider (© 2013)
Written For 30A Songwriters Festival
Intro – Amaj (Arpeggio)
Alternate Intro – F#m-C#m-D-A-G-E

Song of Rescue (2015)

When the sixteen boats have passed you by,
With their longing and their striving,
When the voice of God is lost on high,
And the fire fights reviving,
Then in the darkness, stand up strong,
And listen for your calling,
You were made to hear a newborn song,
Just as the night was falling.

And in the dark night of the soul,
You can sing this song of rescue,
What makes you empty makes you whole,
Come and sing this song of rescue,
Song of Rescue, this will be your Song of Rescue,
Let it find you and it will find you
and it will be your Song of Rescue.

Everyman is everyman
And no man has the answers,
But make the choice to take a chance,
And be the one who dances,
In the darkness you can hear
The sound of distant humming,
You can always hear the angels clear,
Every time love is coming

And it's something like love, something like love,
Something like love will lift you up, yes,
Something like love, something like love,
Something like love comes shining through
To rescue you

Turning Grey [Standard -- Capo V] (2012)

[G]There is a sentence I've been writing since the age of seventeen,
[Em] but the faith it takes to write it left me somewhere in between,
[C] I have told you I would find it, and I have [G] promised [D/F#]you the [Em]page,
[C] I know there's no way to unwind it, I know its time to act my age -

In my [G] end is [D/F#] my [Em]beginning,
that's what the [C] Queen of [G] Hearts would [D]say,
turn your [G] losing [D/F#] into [Em] winning,
throw your [C] used up [G] parts [D] away,
I hate to [C] say what I've been [D/F#] doing
is riding [G] down my [D/F#] road to [Em] ruin,
[C] but I will find a better [D] way
[C] even [D] though I'm turning [G] grey.

Jenny and Matilda miss the man I used to be,
and I am so bewildered by the broken part of me,
I can wake up every morning and come looking for the sun,
but every night I still remember how it feels to come undone.

[Chorus]

[Em]And I can choose to [C] die [D/F#] here,
[G] or I can choose to [Em] live,
it only [C] takes a little courage
to walk across this [D/F#] bridge.

I won't be haunted by the vision of how you'll remember us,
I am certain you'll remember just exactly how it was,
but I have sworn to make it bettter, to make it how it should have been,
I'm gonna get up off the deck and be your hero once again --

A CASE OF JONI

Both sides then were new to me
I put up a parking lot,
I only saw the part you see
when you don't know what you've got

And if I had a river now
out frozen in the sun
I'd teach my feet to walk on that water
where she was brave enough to run

Yeah, I fell late
far too late for Joni
far too late
far too late to fall
ah, but just a case
is all it takes
and you can watch me fall
I can't stay on my feet at all.

Night ride home is what I need
if you are passing through
and all I want may never be
and I can't paint it blue

But I might sing this simple song
and send it out to you
I'll teach my heart to be a gypsy dancer
And make myself brand new.

Yeah, I fell late
far too late for Joni
far too late
far too late to fall
ah, but just a case
is all it takes
and you can watch me fall
I can't stay on my feet at all.

And if I'm filled with longing
it really does no harm
for when you fall inside a song
it's like a false alarm

Yeah, I fell late
far too late for Joni
far too late
far too late to fall
ah, but just a case
is all it takes
and you can watch me fall
I can't stay on my feet at all.

Doc Schneider

Chords

Intro, Verse, Bridge Forms

C x3005x
G/B x2003x
Am x0xx1x – or x12xx13x
F x8xx10x
Em x7xx8x
Dm x5xx6x

(Standard Forms in First Part of Chorus)

C-G/B-Am-Am/G-F-Em-G/B

(Second Part of Chorus –Verse Forms)

Dm-C-G/B, C-G/B-Am (1st) –Am(12th)
F –Em-G/B, (G), Dm-C-G/B-(G)-C

Intro and Outro
C-G/B, F-Em, Am(12)-Dm,C-G/B, G/B-C(Regular)

ALL ACROSS THE SOUTHERN DISTRICT

Gadd2 D/F#
They say the Southern District
Em7 Bm
has the sweetest spots of all -
G D/F#
Augusta in the Springtime,
Em7 A
Savannah in the Fall,
G A
Dublin down to Brunswick
D /C# G
soon you'll find those Golden Isles
Em D/F# G
and all across the Southern District
Em7 A
look how heaven smiles --

CHORUS

G A
I found my home in Georgia
D /C# G
she opened every door for me
Em7 A
from the Carolina border
D /C# G
to Sea Island's shining sea --
G A
Southern District towns, they call me
D /C# G
I like to visit every one
Em7 A
For when you find your home in Georgia
G A Bm
you are Georgia's native son.
G A D
you are Georgia's native son.

Across the Southern District

from the marshes to the squares,

every place enchants you,

city lights and county fairs

(Remember) the Tick Tock in Swainsboro

Down in Waycross, coconut pie

and Statesboro's old Trellis Garden

is on my mind tonight --

(CHORUS)

Bridge

Em7
Take me home
D
on those rivers
G A
let those rivers roll --
Em7 D
Ocmulgee and Oconee
G A
run for the Altamaha
Em7 D
Ogeechee and Savannah
G A
under a blanket of stars --

CHORUS

They take me home to Georgia -- etc

Bridge Lyrics Suggested by Griffin B. Bell

Long Island Sound

I grew up on Long Island
always longing to be free,
full of longing every morning
in the inner dome of me,
I could hear it cross the surface
of the vast Long Island Sound
just. the voice of someone calling
on every street, in every town.

I would go down on the shoreline,
feel the stones beneath my feet,
and that longing would be with me,
to meet the faces I would meet,
I would look out on the water,
of the vast Long Island sound,
every wave was full of longing,
and only I could hear the sound.

Once I came here to these beaches,
just to lay the whole thing down,
and as far as the eye reaches,
I could see Long Island Sound,
and I tried to pour my sorrow
out like ashes on the sea
but there was no way to empty out
the longing inside me

It was the chance that came to save me,
when the longing came around,
and filled me with the courage
to listen to the sound,
to follow where my heart went,
and go where I was bound,
and find a song that's lives up
to my own Long Island sound

Long Island Sound (2012)

I grew up on Long Island
always longing to be free
full of longing every morning
in the inner dome of me
I could hear it cross the surface
of the vast Long Island Sound
just the voice of someone calling
on every street, in every town

It was the chance that came to save me
when my longing came around
it filled me up with the courage
just to listen to the sound
to follow where my heart leads
to go where I am bound
to find a song that lives up
to my Long Island sound.

I would go down to the shoreline
feel these stones beneath my feet
and that longing would be with me
to meet the faces I would meet,
I would look out on the water
of the vast Long Island Sound
every wave was full of longing
and only I could hear the sound.

Once I came here to these beaches
just to lay the whole thing down
and as far as the eye reaches
I could see Long Island Sound
and I tried to pour my sorrow
out like ashes on the sea
but there was no way to empty out
the longing inside me

And when I heard them singing
in a distant town
I packed up my belongings
and I sailed across the Sound

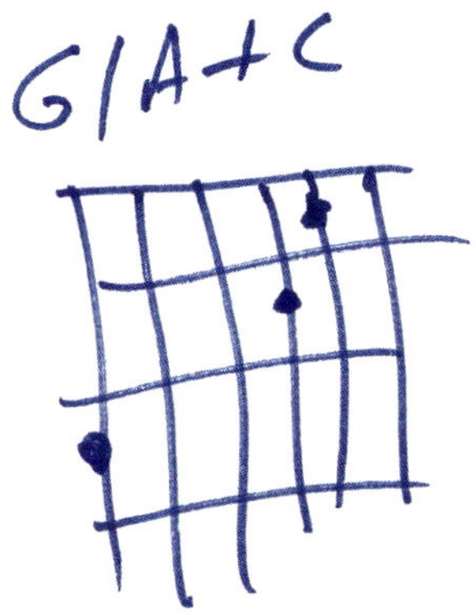

Don't You Do It

C
Maybe you're lost just a little
 Am
maybe it's more than a little
 F(9)
as hard as it is,
 G
you just have to fight it

 C
maybe you're stuck in the middle
 Am
locked up inside of this riddle,
 F(9)
it's not yours alone,
 G
you don't have to hide it

CHORUS
 C   Em
I don't know the answers,
 F   C -- G
and I don't know the way,
 C   Em
but I can stand beside you,
 F   Am
and hunt for the light of day,
 F
and help you through it,
 G
but whatever you do,
                  C
don't you do it.

Whatever you fear or remember

whatever might make you surrender

it's okay to cry

it's okay to show it

We all march inside of the mystery

it's part of the heart of our history

but we'll be alright

and somehow you know it

I don't know the answers

and I don't know the way

but I can stand beside you

and hunt for the light of day

and help you through it

but whatever you do,

don't you do it.

 Em
'Cause when you take all your hope away
 Am
it's not just your own you take
 Csus/Bb
it's all of the hearts you'll break
 Csus/A
it's all of the hearts you'll break

(Chorus)

Doc Schneider (December 13-14, 2008)(In Memory of My Friend, George Covington)

Tuning: CGDGBD (Distant Water Chords)
C: 002010
Em: 445000
F(9): 557000
G: 779000
Am: 99(10)000
Csus/Bb: x3331x
Csus/A: x2301x

Les Deux
BEHIND THE
CURTAIN.

HELEN, WEAR YOUR TEE SHIRT TONIGHT

Words and Music by
RICHARD A. SCHNEIDER © 1976

D C Bm C

1. All the time thinking if I say I love you – will it all fall down?
2. All the time knowing that there have been others – that have told you so

D C Bm C

And all the time knowing that it doesn't matter – I can leave this town;
And all the time knowing that you didn't want it – and you let them go;

Bm C D G

Break out of this town, and leave you behind. – But you're in my mind.
The way I'm going to go, and leave you tonight – But that isn't right.

C Bm C D

You come so close sometimes to letting me unload, and
Now this guitar and me ain't the best you're gonna see

C Bm C D

You come so close sometimes to letting me explode. (CHORUS)
Some fine singer will come along and show you what it meant to me (CHORUS)

F(Bar) G(Bar) F(Bar) G(Bar)

(CHORUS) Oh, Helen, wear your tee shirt tonight – when I leave you, when we ride around

F(Bar) G(Bar) F(Bar) G(Bar) D

And if we are laughing and telling our stories; I'll keep the rising feeling down

(Last verse Repeat) I'll keep the rising feelings down

RESTAURANT-BAR
La Closerie des

HELEN'S VILLANELLE

You hold me in a pair of gentle eyes
so like a swimmer in a summer pool
I break the surface shimmer ~~and~~ AS I rise.

Once shadowed in the shelter of my lies
the growing warm outgrew the slowing cool
you hold me in a pair of gentle eyes.

The melting wall around my ice disguise
so quickly molds a davenport from stool
I break the surface shimmer and I rise.

My heart's a wall so like a wall, denies
a stranger the dominion it can rule
Yet hold me in a pair of gentle eyes.

A peddler loves the ragged wares he plies
yet hold me till I turn from that full fool
and break the surface shimmer as I rise.

My stubborn heart, your burning love defies
and turns to fire warm the icy cool
You hold me in a pair of gentle eyes
I break the surface shimmer ~~and~~ AS I rise.

Now after fifteen years,
I find this poem behind a door
And I find my heart remains where it was before, —
And a love can always grow
as we continue on
what we began
a villanelle ago.

R.A. Schneider
April 26, 1977
an excercise in verse for Helen
because I love her.

Choicest Chances

The ~~Choices That We~~ Make

Capo IV or V

Fast paced.

G
When I was younger I knew Dickie,
Bm
but Dickie wasn't me —
C G Bm D
Dickie was a prisoner when I was running free.
C
In my house, we were not what we were,
G Bm C
We were what we could be —
G Bm C
And I could be any story I could spin,
G
till the truth caught up with me.

G
My father was a diplomat,
Bm
but a banker by his trade.
C G Bm D
To leave the Foreign Service was the saddest choice he made,
C G Bm G
And he never could forget it (and it haunted him each day —)
G Bm C
till that heart that he inherited so young
G
Just took his life away

CHORUS

C G
Oh the choices that we make — (Mmmm)
Am D
Oh, the ~~clear~~ voices that we hear
G G
Sometimes chances slip away,
C D G
Sometimes choices are not clear.

Sometimes, chances came my way,
And all my choices brought me here

I chose to be a lawyer,
I'm still a lawyer now,
G Bm D
though I ~~may~~ know I may not end my days that way somehow
C G Bm C
Like my Dad before me, I am not what I am,
G G Bm C
And I can be any story I can tell,
G
If I ~~could~~ can just convince myself.

Written w/ No Capo
Capo II sounds better

Single Note intro ↙ Notes on 5th String
A/ B/ C#/ B/ A/ Em7 A D

ALL THAT I NEED IN JUNE

CHORUS

Em7 A
NOTHING TO DO,
F#m Bm
NOTHING TO SAY.
Em7 A
BEING WITH YOU,
F#m Bm
ON THIS JUNE DAY.

Em7 A
NOTHING BUT ME,
F#m Bm
NOTHING BUT YOU —
Em7 A D
ALL THAT I NEED IN JUNE.

Em7 D A G F#m Gmaj7 Bm Fmaj7 D add F#

G F#m
THE NIGHTIME SMOULDERS,
Em7 A
AND THE SHINE ON YOUR SHOULDERS
D G A
GLISTENS LIKE A MEADOW IN THE MOON.
G F#m
AND IN THIS BED,
Gmaj7 Fmaj7 G
AND IN THIS ROOM —
Em7 F#m A
IS WHERE I'LL STAY IN JUNE.

G6 F#7

CHORUS

G6 F#7
Gmaj7 Fmaj7
NEVER APART,
Bm G
THERE IN MY HEART —
Em7 A D
ALL THAT I NEED IN JUNE

G6 F#7
Gmaj7 Fmaj7
SUCH A SWEET SONG,
Bm G
COULDN'T BE WRONG —
Em7 A D/F# G
ALL THAT I NEED IN JUNE —
Em A D
ALL THAT I NEED IN JUNE.

© Richard A. Schneider (June 13, 1992 – For Helen's Birthday June 14)

No Capo

Storkland Jingle

```
C
Your baby's on the way,
 F (Bar)                                 G (Bar)
You're looking forward to the day
 C                              F
when you can tell the world
                  G
the baby's name —
           F                     G7
And we're looking forward too
                        C      G7?      Am
we wish the very best to you
          F                               G7
Let Storkland help you shape
                     C
your happy time!
```

RA Schneider
© 1981

~~First Light~~ Wherever You Are

I close my eyes, ~~on~~ to this December night,
in this cold air, ~~then~~ turn my face up to the light,
I feel your lips, ~~from twenty~~ thrown down years ago,
I feel my pain, melting like this falling snow...

I feel my feet, rising from the ground,
this busy street, hardly makes a sound
I hear my voice, promising forever,
and though we left, this moment left me never...

Does ~~this~~ that first light reach you tonight where you are?
Shining hopeful and bright like that winter star,
all the distance I've gone doesn't seem so far,
I can still feel that heat...
I can still see that star.

So Wherever you are,
look in the sky tonight
You are never so far
and you cannot find that light
~~so~~ and when it grows dark
it shines where you are
Even from this distance
I can still see that star

CHORUS

On this very night,
~~on hearts the world around~~
there are eyes upon this light,
as and feet are rising from the ground
~~you can almost hear the sound~~
I am imagining the sound,

I lost your face, some[…]
and of your eyes, the colo[…]
But on this night, the falling sno[…]
And in this light, all the rest […]

CHORUS

It is the hope that I remem[…]
It is the life that I ~~felt~~ remember breaking clear,
It was your hand I felt within my hand,
a burning warm burning down this frozen land...

THE LITTLE MERMAID

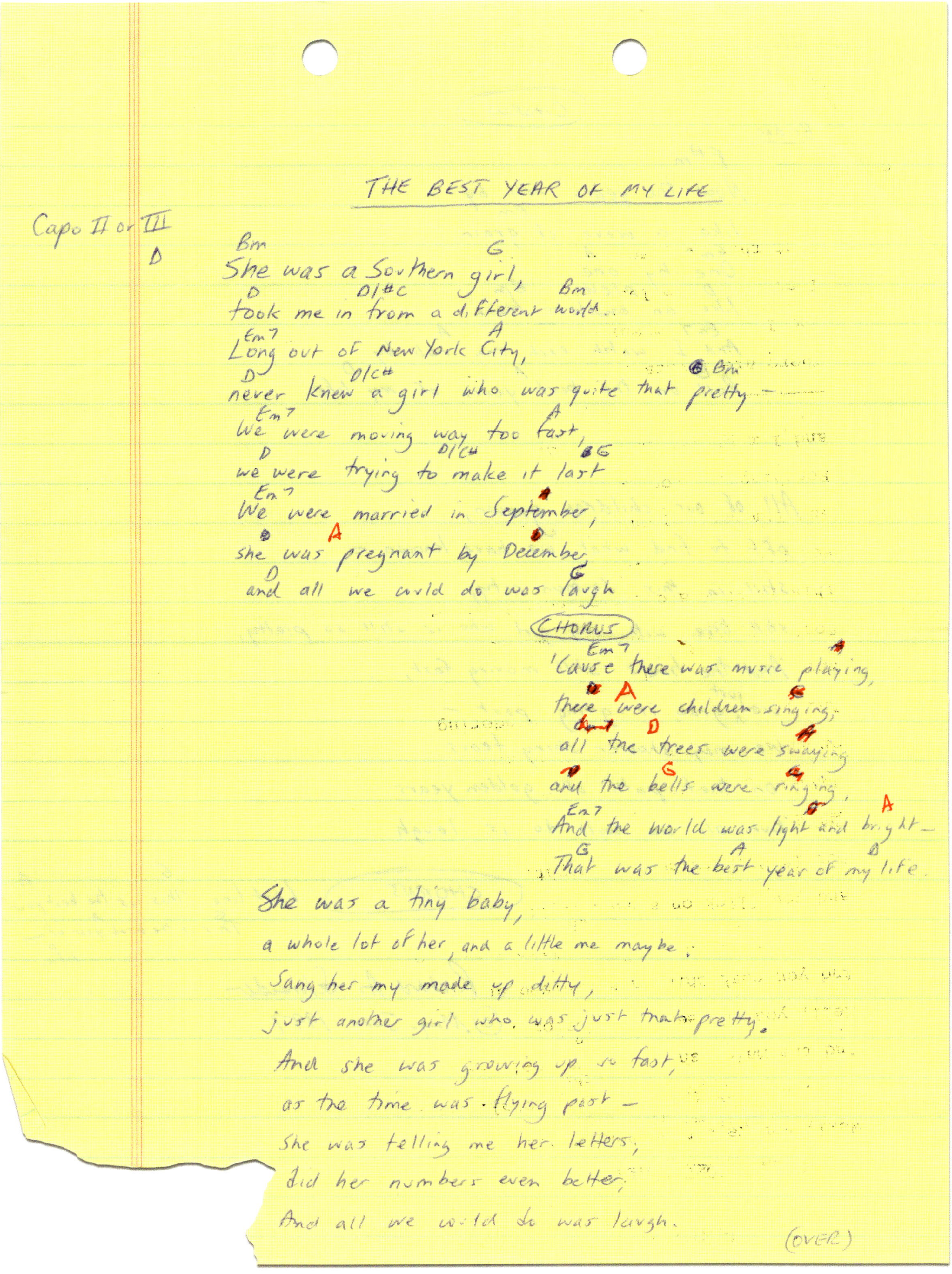

THE BEST YEAR OF MY LIFE

Capo II or III

Bm G
She was a Southern girl,
D D/C# Bm
took me in from a different world.
Em7 A
Long out of New York City,
D D/C# Bm
never knew a girl who was quite that pretty —
Em7 A
We were moving way too fast,
D D/C# G
we were trying to make it last
Em7 A
We were married in September,
D A D
she was pregnant by December,
D G
and all we could do was laugh

CHORUS

Em7 A
'Cause there was music playing,
D A G
there were children singing,
Em7 D A
all the trees were swaying
D G A
and the bells were ringing,
Em7 A
And the world was light and bright —
G A D
That was the best year of my life.

She was a tiny baby,
a whole lot of her, and a little me maybe.
Sang her my made up ditty,
just another girl who was just that pretty.
And she was growing up so fast,
as the time was flying past —
She was telling me her letters,
did her numbers even better,
And all we could do was laugh.

(OVER)

COME TO MY HOUSE

© 1997 R.A. Schneider

CAPO IV, V or VI
(VI on Tape)

Notes ↑ on 5th string

Intro

Ⓐ Ⓑ Ⓒ C D
~~Ah—ah—ah~~ oh-oh, ah
G D/F# Em
La-la-la-la-la-a
Ⓐ Ⓑ Ⓒ C D G
Ah-a-a, ah-a-a, oh-oh

1

In this daily life I'm living, (G, C)
I am filled with endless questions,
like that distant sound I'm hearing— (Am)
Could that be an angel's voice? (D)

There's a hundred signs around me, (G)
Just to see the hand of heaven, (C)
and believe that doors will open (Am)
If I only make this choice. (D)

(CHORUS)

I will live my life with the Lord, (G, D/F#, Em)
I will find his way between the shadows. (C, D)
In my heart forever adored, (G, D/F#, Em)
like a light that shines in all my windows. (C, D)
And when I've traveled far, (C, D/F#, G, C)
and my house is hard for me to see— (C, D/F#, G, A)
He will say "Come to my house— (Ⓐ Ⓑ Ⓒ C, D)
You can come to my house," (G, D/F#, Em)
He will say "Come to my house with Me." (Ⓐ Ⓑ Ⓒ C, D, G)

2

I will hold these hands around me,
I will let the spirit flow—
And the place that they have found me,
is the place where I will go.

In my search for all the answers,
there was not much I could show,
Now, when everything eludes me
There is one thing I still know.

→ CHORUS

3

There was a child born to Mary,
on a dark December night.
And from that stable ordinary,
such extrordinary light.

Now that light is shining clearly,
I can see his outstretched hand,
It is love that makes me take it,
And that helps me understand.

CHORUS + CLOSE

- il popolo del blues

reviews

Doc Schneider & Eugene Ruffolo - Songs & Stories
(Homemade Songs. Inc.)
www.cdbaby.com / cd / schneiderruffolo

Doc Schneider is a lawyer by day and night , and a songwriter in between . Eugene Ruffolo at ia good songwriter with an amazing voice . Together They give us an intimate afternoon of songs and stories documented by a double live cd .

In the past we have spoken already of Doc Schneider , a lawyer and songwriter with a passion that can write great ballads worthy of the best James Taylor shows how excellent Second Chances 2007. We find him paired with Eugene Ruffolo good , good talent and excellent songwriter and guitarist from the beautiful voice , a double live album recorded in April last year to Altlanta to ' Atlanta 's Eddie 's Attic . Schneider and Ruffolo interpret the songs of both duets with great elegance and class , often exchanging songs. Ruffolo gives a very intense moments before with the new "World Minus One "and then with the beautiful and touching "A Rose for Pierrette ", dedicated to his father that he met his mother during the Second World War. Magnificent is then made of "The Hills Of Sicily " , written by Artie Traum that goes together with the composition of Schneider , or " Massapequa "," Everything Gold " and " Marie " contained in Second Chance. Do not miss some nice covers like "Shower The People "by James Taylor and the beautiful performance of "Dream Again "by David Wilcox . Listening is very pleasant and is palpable throughout the artistic talent of these two songwriters, whose songs reflected by living all their love for music and poetry. A little gem that should not be reserved only for professionals, but which deserves more consideration on a large scale.

Salvatore Esposito

FolkWorld CD Reviews

Eugene Ruffolo & Doc Schneider "Songs & stories live"

Label: Own label; 2009

Two men with a guitar, as self released live album, I have to admit that I was a bit sceptic when I first put my eyes on the album. I think I see dozens CD's of guitarists both solo and in duo each year and only a few know to surprise me. Thankfully this is such an album. Ruffolo I know from his great lead vocals on the song *Win back your love* which you can find on one of my all time Dutch American folk albums *Elsewhere bound* by the Very Girls and the Watchman. Ruffolo has a warm, beautiful voice that calms me down and which I love to listen to. He knows how to sing his sings and really makes me want to hear what he is singing about. Sometimes with a good sense of humor, other moments more serious or a small love song, he always now to convince me. The good thing about this album is that he is joined by Doc Schneider which was totally unknown to me. His fine backings and lead vocals show a bit more shyness, but sound natural and convincing. On this album the singers match, the guitars match and the atmosphere is good. Thirty four songs (it's a 2-cd set) is a bit much to listen to on one evening. But I like to choose one of them and just listen a few and catch this good, positive vibe these two albums have. An album that makes me curious to hear more from both artists both solo and together.
www.eugeneruffolo.com, www.legalguitarist.com
Eelco Schilder

FOR FANS OF:
Beck – *Sea Change*
Thievery Corporation – *The Cosmic Game*
Zero 7 – *The Garden*

The Alternate Routes
Good and Reckless and True
[Vanguard]

A spontaneous trip to Mohegan Sun casino funded this Connecticut band's demo CD, but that roll-the-dice approach doesn't apply to their debut album. Instead they present 11 well-written tunes whose tight ensemble playing is often reminiscent of Mr. Petty's Heartbreakers. Singer Tim Warren's soaring vocal on the spacious "Aftermath" is an exhilarating moment, and the band shines on the pounding "Going Home With You," a lustful tale sung by a guy whom a woman has just anointed Mr. Right Now after Mr. Right has stood her up one too many times. Warren and co-writer/guitarist Eric Donnelly display a knack for colorful imagery with lyrics like "*11:30 every time / Two buttons loose, now you realize / I see the eyes that your momma gave you / I see the mess that your daddy made you.*" Elsewhere, Donnelly's frantic slide solo on "Are You Lonely?" serves notice that they can bash with the best of them, while their softer side comes out in the piano ballad "The Black and the White," a poignant drinking tune where Warren decides to "*let a Jim shot of whiskey take a good man back to his yesterdays.*" The elements come together in the majestic "Time Is a Runaway," which has "romantic movie soundtrack" written all over it. While the Alternate Routes aren't stretching the envelope, their unfailingly melodic and soulful touch makes this an enviable debut. —*BC*

FOR FANS OF:
The Damnwells – *Air Stereo*
Gomez – *How We Operate*
Snow Patrol – *Eyes Open*

Aqualung
Memory Man
[Columbia]

Though any act billing itself as "Aqualung" is begging to become the butt of bad jokes involving Jethro Tull tribute bands, the music made by Matt Hales and his mix of family and friends sounds dead serious. The group's new album is so bold in its attempt at beauty, so seemingly unconcerned with critics who may deem it dull and pretentious, one hopes the disc finds an audience.

Memory Man comes across as the record U2 or Coldplay could produce if someone hit them over the head with a pan and made them forget how to write radio-friendly hooks. To say there are 11 songs here would be somewhat misleading because Hales appears less concerned with showcasing each individual track and more intent on orchestrating layered noise. Even when he sings, his words serve not as narration but as tools to craft an overall feeling. Aqualung's music—tranquil despite its complexity—is bound to put some people to sleep. That doesn't mean, however, that the resulting naps won't be packed with soothing dreams. —*DS*

FOR FANS OF:
Animal Collective – *Feels*
The Beach Boys – *Surf's Up*
Coldplay – *X&Y*

Harry Connick, Jr.
Oh, My NOLA
[Columbia]

As its name implies, Harry Connick, Jr.'s *Oh, My NOLA* is an elegy to hurricane-battered New Orleans. But instead of tearful odes or angry laments, Connick—whose father served as the city's district attorney for nearly 30 years—pays

They've also included a straight-up country ballad ("Old Ways Die Slow"), complete with a honky tonk and a cheating heart. But we're still calling these Hearts rock perfection.

Dennis Crommett
The Evening Sorrow

Featured Download: "Green Depression Glass"
denniscrommett.com

Jangly guitars and softly layered vocals are the signature sound of Massachusetts-based artist Dennis Crommett, who successfully bounces from the somberness of Elliott Smith to the merriment of the Monkees.

"Some Kind of Friend" kicks the album off with a peppy brushes-on-snare beat while Crommett admonishes a former friend. "*You think it's cool to meet in a cool place, like sitting in cafes, sipping so fast,*" he sings, softening the lyrics with his sighing tenor. Other highlights include the luxurious cello sounds on "Larkspur," the country twang and pedal steel of "Oranges and Reds" and the enigmatic "Green Depression Glass." "*In from the sea the glass gets smoother and rounder / In with the tide your memory floats in my head,*" Crommett sings over a mellow groove. *The Evening Sorrow* will alternately sooth and surprise, but it won't disappoint.

Emilia Dahlin
God Machine

Featured Download: "God Machine"
emiliadahlin.com

Ever think to yourself, "I wish I could curl up and listen to a sweet-voiced girl with smart songs backed by accordion, ukulele, sabar and kashishi"? No? Well, you should check this out anyway. The Portland, Maine–based Emilia Dahlin has just released *God Machine*, and she's turned folk music on its ear by making it spin and groove.

Highlights include the melancholy "Home to Grey" ("*Islands don't forget me, I fear you'll drift away ... the dormancy of winter is shortening the day*"), and the deliciously blasphemous title track ("*Mary rakes her nails across the floor ... to make a messiah, girl you gotta writhe*"). Overall, a sparkling, spunky record that we highly recommend.

Bronwen Exter
Elevator Ride

Featured Download: "Float"
myspace.com/bronwenexter

OK, picture this: Lou Reed and Astrud Gilberto have a baby. She's raised by the band Mazzy Star until the age of 16, when she falls in love with James Bond and runs away to Argentina. Got it? The soundtrack for this story is the music of New York resident Bronwen Exter. Hypnotizing you with her husky, half-whispered vocals, she'll thrill you with the mixture of samba, tango and NYC cool, and entice you with lyrics about dreams, pain and roads from the moon to the sun.

To the instrumental foundation of bass, drums and guitar, Exter adds organ, piano, trumpet and saxophone. The work of songwriter and producer (and one-time *PS* DIY artist) Jonathan Spottiswoode is evident in the offbeat yet refined sound. From the refreshingly eccentric lyrics to the creative arrangements, *Elevator Ride* will be a trip your ears will want to take again and again.

Ted Russell Kamp
Divisadero

Download: "The Last Time I Let You Down"
tedrussellkamp.com

Divisadero, the fourth release from Ted Russell Kamp, is classic country. A simple up-tempo drumbeat sets the mood for "Swinging Doors," as subdued electric guitars

WHEREVER YOU ARE

4 string pick pattern

I close my eyes to this December night,
In this cold air, I turn my face up to the light,
I feel your lips floating down from years ago,
I feel my pain melting like this falling snow.

I feel my feet rising from the ground,
this busy street hardly makes a sound,
I hear my voice promising forever,
And though we left, this moment left me never . . . .

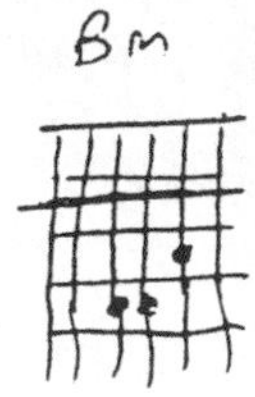

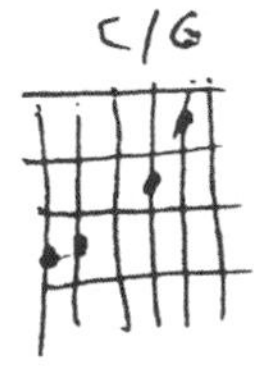

STRUM

Wherever you are,
Look in the sky tonight.
You are never so far,
that you cannot find that light.
When it grows dark,
it shines where you are . . .
Even from this distance,
I can still see that star
from wherever you are.

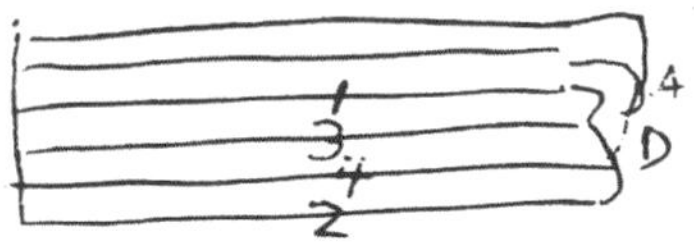

4 String

I lost your face somewhere long ago,
And of your eyes, the color now is all I know.
But in this Night, this falling snow can bring you back,
And in this light, all the rest just fades to black.

It is the hope that I remember here,
It is the life that I remember breaking clear,
It was your hand I felt within my hand,
a burning warm burning down this frozen land.

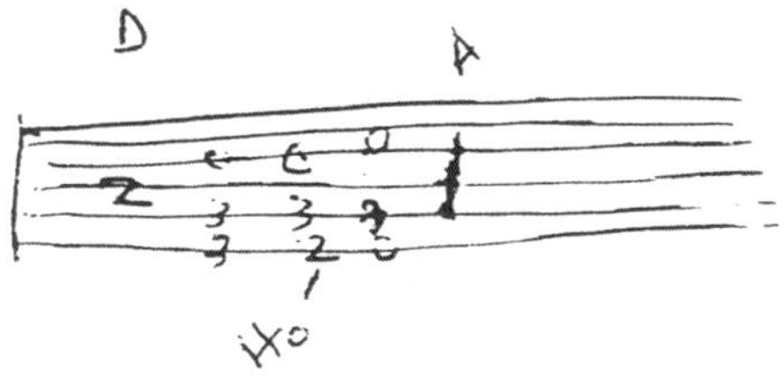

Wherever you are,
Look in the sky tonight.
You are never so far,
that you cannot find that light.
When it grows dark,
it shines where you are,
Even from this distance,
I can still see that star,
from wherever you are

On this very night,
I am imagining the sound,
there are eyes upon the light,
and feet are rising from the ground.

Intro Riff

D /A Bm | Bm G |
A A | D

Wherever you are,
Look in the sky tonight.
You are never so far,
that you cannot find that light,
When it grows dark,
it shines where you are,
Even from this distance,
I can still see that star . . . .
Wherever you are,
Wherever you are,
Wherever you are.

Richard A. Schneider

UNISONG
2004 SECOND PLACE
The founders of UNISONG are proud to congratulate
RICHARD A. SCHNEIDER
for winning second place with the song
"HOMEMADE SONG"
in the Pop Ballad
of the 2004 UNISONG Int
Your song was c
out of over 4,500 entri
DAVID STARK
SCOTT

UNISONG INTERNATIONAL SONG CONTEST
(213) 673-4067
5198 ARLINGTON AVE PMB 513
RIVERSIDE, CA 92504
934
Date 4-20-05
Pay to the Order of Richard A. Schneider
$ 500.00
Five-Hundred and 00/100 Dollars
Bank of America
Warner Center
5959 Canoga Ave
Woodland Hills CA
818.994.8200
For 2nd PL Pop Ballad - 2004

A LIFE OF LOVE

To the top of a tower,
with the sun shining bright,
she rose with her arms raised,
unafraid of the height.

With her children below her,
gazing up at the sight,
of their mother above them,
in a gown made of light.

Then when the wind blew,
she floated away,
in a fountain of bluebirds,
as the years flew away.

First, she was a mother,
then she was a wife,
then she was a college girl,
preparing her life.

And there were her parents,
while she was at play,
for she was an only child,
with love to give away.

And love comes in,
and love goes out . . . that way.

And love comes in,
and love goes out . . . that way.

There is a legacy of love that she has laid behind her,
There is a value in each soul that she has seen,
There is a goodness that brings brightness to the darkest heart,
There is no end to what a life of love can start.

So I stand by this tower,
fill my heart up this day,
For she holds the rarest flower
of love to give away.

And love comes in,
and love goes out . . .that way.

And love comes in,
and love goes out . . .that way.

Richard A. Schneider

HOW IT LOOKS TO YOU

Kicking at sticks again,
walking alone.
Waiting here on your wings,
to carry me home.
For you are my morning sun
and my shining light,
and you need to lead the way tonight.

CHORUS
If I stand where you stand,
would this patch of brown land
turn into a field of green?
If I see what you see,
could I look back at me
and see me just how I am seen?
Would these songs that I sing
really sound sweet and true,
the way you say they do?
If I leave me behind,
would the world that I find
look the way that the world looks to you --
how it looks to you?

Never been satisfied,
always been starry-eyed.
Having you by my side,
is helping me through.
For you are my steady ship
in oceans of waves -
and we need to sail away today.

REPEAT CHORUS

Some dreams are beacons,
that help you weather the rough,
but some dreams are devils
that say there's never enough.
I say enough is enough.

Don't need a hundred ears
to make it sound real.
Don't need a thousand hands
to say that I feel.
For I'm in the land of light
where rainbows arise -
Just help me open up my eyes.

REPEAT CHORUS

Richard A. Schneider
© November 1993

C#m7 Bm A G
Your voice was like a river
E D E/G# D/F# A G
rolling out across the land,
F#m Em7 C#m7 Bm
and sometimes I could hear you
A G
calling for my hand
B A
calling for my hand.

E D
Just to take me past
C#m7 Bm
the bars and walls
A G B A
that locked me up inside
E D
And then at last
C#m7 Bm
I'd see it all
A G B A
if only for one night -

Chorus Part I
A G E D B A E D
Oh, but I did not believe that dream
C#m7 Bm A G B A
I never thought I'd ever find my way,
C#m7 Bm A G
when it seemed too late,
E D B A
you opened up the gate
A G
and set me free 7th fret
F#m7 (9th Fret) Em C#m7 (4th) Bm D C
I can't believe that you came back for me --

Part II
E D
Marie,
C#m7 Bm I have loved you forever
we can ~~be children~~ forever,

A G
Marie,
E D C#m7 Bm
we can walk out together,
F#m7(9thFret) Em7 (7th fret)
Marie,
C#m7 Bm D C E D
I can't believe you came back for me.

"Marie"

Play in D
Till Last
Chorus & Modulate
Up To E
Closing walk to E
Bm G D A-B
Now the words I finally get to
Then
Chorus in
E

And so the wheel is turning
that turns this world around
and all the stars are burning
that once fell to the ground
that once fell to the ground

Here beneath the sky
you begin to dance
where I dreamed you danced before
Only you and I
in an old romance
what else are chances for?

Oh, and now I do believe that dream
I never thought I 'd ever find my way
When it seemed too late
you opened up the gate
and set me free -
I can't believe that you came back for me

Marie, I have loved you
we can ~~be children~~ forever,
Marie,
we can walk out together,
Marie,
I can't believe you came back for me.

9th

Last: I'm so glad you came back for me

Bridge C#m7 Bm F#m (9th fret) Em 7th fret A G B A
I've got a pocketful of songs that I can sing you
E D C#m7 Bm B A
I have this heart that I never gave away
C#m7 Bm A G Bm C#m7 B A
I have a head full of dreams that I can bring you
C#m7 Here's Bm A G E D A B C#m7 D B
~~I have~~ these words that I finally get to say
or C-D

Chorus -Part II

Modulate to Chorus in E

Schneider
11/03

Nantucket Island (The First Day of September)

Intro

Heart to heart beneath the Milky Way

tonight these stars hear every word we say

(Chorus)

Here we are

on Nantucket Island,

it shines so bright in the blue,

for as long as stars shine,

there'll be Nantucket Island

and I'll be standing here

next to you.

Sure, the road that brought us here

sometimes kept us far apart

but underneath those separate nights

we held on to one heart -

and we sailed across this bay

and we made it to this day

So here we are . . . (Chorus)

The days we will remember

clinging to the flame

the first day of September

will always call our name

and we will sail across this bay

and we will never sail away

So here we are . . . .

Now there's our families

and there's our friends

they are an ocean

they are an ocean

So hear we are . . .

Outro

Heart to heart beneath the Milky Way

tonight these stars hear every word we say

For the Wedding of Cameron Davis and Robert Glass on Nantucket

September 1, 2007

Miller, Kristin

From: Schneider, Doc [DSchneider@KSLAW.com] **Sent:** Sat 1/29/05 3:12 PM
To: Miller, Kristin
Cc:
Subject: FW: You got Lyrics popping out of me --here is a tearjerker
Attachments:

-----Original Message-----
From: Schneider, Doc
Sent: Wed 1/26/2005 5:07 PM
To: 'JJKEYJAM@aol.com'
Cc:
Subject: You got Lyrics popping out of me --here is a tearjerker

1.
Massapequa
you're my home
but you ain't home to me
I can look down your tree-lined streets
but lonely's all I see
I know it's not your fault
but I blame you just the same
And that is why my heart still breaks
every time I say your name

Chorus
Massapequa
I was your native child
and like the ones who named you
I needed to run wild
Massapequa
was it you or was it me
who locked away that child
and threw away the key?

2.
Massapequa
I forgive you
but I can't forgive myself
for leaving without saving them
just to save myself
There are days I can't remember
there in every picture frame
which is why my heart still breaks
every time I say your name

3.
Massapequa
I come home
and pretend you're home to me
I try to find my memories
and some way to set me free
I watch the ones who love you
and I wish I felt the same
'cause I know your other hearts don't break
every time they say your name

http://islay.agnesscott.edu/exchange/ksmiller/Inbox/FW:%20You%20got%20Lyrics%20po... 1/29/2005

Massapequa **(Doc Schneider)**

```
Chords are A/B, C#m, Bm, D, F#m, E, Esus,G, A

A/B is 002200
Esus is 022200
F#m is 244222


Intro

A/B-C#m-Bm -Esus-E-Esus -E


A/B
Massapequa
           C#m
you're my home
     Bm              Esus-E
but you're not home to me
A/B                               C#m
I can walk down your tree-lined streets
 Bm                 E
but sad is all I'll see
      F#m      G           A
and I know its not your fault
    C#m                    D
but I blame you just the same
        Esus                E
which is why my heart still breaks
Bm        E             A
every time I say your name

CHORUS

 G                                  A
And have I waited long enough to tell you,
F#m   F#m         G
      Massapequa?
         A
Massapequa?
C#m  D     Esus-E
Oh  oh oh oh
C#m D     E
oh oh oh oh



Massapequa

please forgive me

if I don't forgive myself

for leaving on my own
```

Schneider, Doc

From: Schneider, Doc
Sent: Wednesday, March 24, 2004 5:08 PM
To: Schneider, Doc
Subject: Lyrics To This Heart

-----Original Message-----
From: Schneider, Doc
Sent: Wednesday, March 24, 2004 5:08 PM
To: Schneider, Doc
Subject: RE: Reminder of Friday deadline

-----Original Message-----
From: Schneider, Doc
Sent: Wednesday, March 24, 2004 9:50 AM
To: Schneider, Doc
Subject: Re: Reminder of Friday deadline

With this heart screaming in my chest
When this life I love the best
Lies slipping through my fingertips
All the words that I would say
Every song that I would sing
Lies unspoken on my frozen lips

Chorus

Oh, oh, they'll say
He brought it on himself
Oh, oh, they'll say
He would not watch his health
But this heart loved you anyway
And they can't take that away

When the world was first in bloom
When we sang another tune
When a new love waited to be found
With the sun upon your face
In another time and place
When I did not know this screaming sound

Chorus

This heart was handed down to me
This heart has traveled far
This heart will be the end of me
For you are just what you are

Lay your head upon my chest
Say I need a little rest
Place your finger on my frightened lips
Maybe stay a little while
Let me see another smile
Trace your tender with my fingertips

Chorus

1

poems
in
the
cupboard

AFTER THE LANDING

From the reef, their battered bodies pounding,
I dragged the boys in with fishnets and sang
of Garbo's breasts and cats and kids. Soft things.
I loaded my rifle and spilled children
of others Gods. I was no poet.
I dreamed about long white cross rows. And drank
in deep dark bars, where the dog tags rattle.
I asked for scotch and pushed my mind around.

I will turn myself in for desertion.

February 26, 1976
Annapolis

THE BOY WHO WOULD FLY

With his arms held straight out
from his wafer thing fuselage,
his jet engine buzzing in his throat,
he ran under the fig trees,
banking into a left turn and then a right,
zigging and sagging, always buzzing
as footballs zipped
over his fingertipped wings,
running that way, round and round,
until one day,
he took off.

Now they watch him coming,
squinting into the sun
shielding their eyes with their hands.
In the moment he lands,
the thin profile of the wings
looks like the arms of a boy
dipping down for the down and out,
his stethoscope swinging from his neck,
like a visitor from the sky.
He makes his rounds
and little feet run after him
as he turns his tiny plane on the runway
arms straight out—
he takes off.

At the Dawn of Flight
Atlanta

FROM THE BENCH

for Jim Van Langen

Look at me: with my caged eyes. My stick
is neatly angled across my knees. Words
will never master it. The damned thing laughs
when I whisper my anguish. I wonder what
the young girls think of my stenciled number.
Dressed for battle looking grandly ready,
I am Homer watching Hector sitting still.

But you: drenched in shining swift legged power
Running, weaving, moving—a stick that snaps
is your arm—moves whenever you move. Eyes
that know precisely where to fly and when…
the flash, the sound explodes!
The up-thrown arms surround this bright new hero
built from the base by God. The beauty of power.
Look now: even the net bends deep and bows.

I braced my stick to break the rules
to break you in your stride
to plant my stick across your chest
to try to change the tide.
I drew the dark accusing eyes
that tracked down mine on fire
and then my trespass struck me hard
and burned me down inside.

When we're the color of the clouds
that we once played beneath,
I'll tell the rising how you ran
and of my firm belief.
The stick I drew to take my chance
could never stop the thrill
no stick I drew could stop you then
and no stick ever will –
For I am ever Homer watching Hector standing still.

March 19, 1976
Annapolis

MESMERIZED TRANSCRIBED

In perfect, chiseled profile, she sits
with speechless lips, with legs of polished stone,
this work of art that tends the work of man.

Her hands are like the wings of birds that rise
and fall as voices rise and fall, and ride
the rush of words in silent shapes and sounds.

Around her beams the light of dreams that rise
and fall like sighs inside these legal minds.
And silent eyes at tables dark with blue
that strain to hold their lawful point of view
now wander back, now drawn and drawn again.

The march of human business stands surprised
and by this sight this world is mesmerized.

July 1998
Miami

THE UNSHAKEABLE CADENCE OF THE LOVE SONG

In my own voice,
I have heard the telltale timbre –
the words strung on a line
like pebbles and pearls,
the sound of surrender,
of resignation, of realization.
I heard it once
and more than once,
the click of the pebble and the pearl.
And, in truth, I could not shake the sound,
the rhythm and the rhyme,
the hold of something infinitely gentle
infinitely suffering, infinitely true,
whispering words that repeated,
advanced and retreated
in my own ears
like my own voice.

December 2, 1999
Atlanta

AFTER THE ICE STORM

It came as rain
dripping down a branch,
snaking down a trunk,
clinging to a jagged edge.

It came as chance,
spinning down a sighing branch,
sliding down the frozen bark,
gliding through the winter dark,
freezing into icy paths,
glittering like frosted glass.

In the crackling morning,
the confectioner's trees shivered,
streaming white tears under the gray sky,
seeming human there,
glazed in accidental beauty,
bending
and breaking
under the weight
of their own nature.

January–March 2000
Atlanta

24 SEPTEMBERS

This field that rolls behind us and ahead,
rolls in golden accidental beauty—
dappled there by twenty-four Septembers,
springing from the dreams of one December,
with blades of light that ride the tides unseen,
wave upon wave of rolling gold and green.

In the winter that one summer gave us,
it took hold there, undaunted by the cold—
in the wrong season against all reason
growing warm green while winter storms swept through
till green became our lasting point of view.

I said accidental. I mean like grace
and days that take you over on their own.
Like children born in the wrong season
against all reason who ache your heart with love.

Take my hand. Let's feel these gold blades of green
nestle like love around our grateful feet.

September 3, 2001
Atlanta

IN MEMORY OF WILLIAM C. HENDRICKS, III

I see death holds you
like a handful of fireflies
held by a child some dark summer evening -
the way the blonde light leaps out
fluorescent
soft as powder
streaming between those helpless fingers
radiating across the silent night.
There are not any hands
that could ever contain that light.

Your hands too I well remember
orchestrating your phrases
keeping cadence in your renaissance minutes,
bringing the point up, down, gently, now louder—
pausing only to pull each cuff back into place
all the while leading with those hands
that could cradle a clarinet
or a jury
or an elegant cigar
with sheer delight and equal grace.

When they ask me
whose light is shining in the distant darkness,
I will tell them
it is the midnight oil of a lawyer's lawyer.
It is your luminous mark of day
upon the face of night.
There are not any hands
that could ever contain that light.

November 12, 2001
Atlanta

ON READING MILLAY'S SONNETS

Her knowing eyes wait at an open door
till they sweep you up in her endless gaze.
Take a peek, take a sip, take a bit more.
See fearless love you feared, and nights and days
you never had yourself. Her sonnet form
and bonnet hair, drawing words and lovers,
a lovely vessel in a savage storm
of phrases and couplets, sheets and covers.
And now she bursts into the room, deathless,
arms full of sheets, sheets full of words. Take them,
these poems as warm and red and breathless,
as the life it gave and took to make them.
What soul is this that finds a way to keep
her love awake while she has gone to sleep.

November 7, 2002
Atlanta

A CANDLE

In such a bleak house,
there must be someone with a candle.
Rejoice that fate has left us here
on the hierarchy.
That we are not down on our haunches
blood dripping from our mouths
and spears looking for food
that we have wishes and imaginations.
Even if I am moments before hitting a brick wall
I enjoyed being with you
below the salt
laughing with the innocent children
I loved the feeling of loving and being loved
I loved the sounds of the songs and the poems
the way the truth of them felt on my chest
I do not need to go on forever to go on at all.
I peer in amazement, not dimly.
And when my arteries revolt and pain engulfs me
come and bring me this candle
I won't be able to see it, but you will.

March 27, 2004
Atlanta

A POEM FOR KIT REILLY

The nature you loved loved you too
and took you back too soon,
and as was your nature and your kindness,
we lie in the leaf bed of your life
and remember—

We remember all of your winters and your summers
the soles of your tiny feet under your first February
before they grew harder than you ever were
hiking the Nepali Coast.
When we knew we held in our hands
a light as soft as powder
and a heart with no doors or walls.

Now even the stars remind us of you
reflected in the shining eyes of children
under the skies of Santa Cruz
taking lessons in modest amazement
from a young man in love with the universe.

We hear your Spanish laughter
in the Guatemala straw market,
we feel the warmth of your smile
on some new face in Kauai
or waiting in a station
as you hiked the world
in your ministry of wonder
as if you knew the measure of your time.

And now we give you back
to the rustling leaves,
to the blinking stars
to the causes you cherished,
to the stories and tales
you wrote and left unwritten,
to the music that gave you wings
to the nature you loved
that loved you too
and gave us you forever.

June 25, 2003
New Orleans

LOVE POEMS

With both eyes over my shoulder
looking back where I can see things clearly
I write the love poems I remember
that I could not write when love was there.
There are no pockets for pens or paper then
though you might speak a poem,
and I often thought you did,
a poem is meant to be written first
before it is whispered.
And love is meant to be whispered first
before it is written.

July 2004
Atlanta

THE WHISPERED NAMES

In the hallways of our high school
hearts still stand still when love comes through
the way yours did in your days here.
The hallways still hold your handprints
the first time your locker opened wide
the little scrap of looseleaf paper
you wrote your dreams on one by one
in the minutes and the hours
while we waited for the world to turn
and welcome us. When that day came
we rose from here, we flew from here
these hallways that remember you.

And now, after your dreams, your life
these hallways still remember you
even when your time arrived too soon
with no appointment, one by one
the world remembered all your dreams
tonight someone will whisper your name
and wish you were here
and you will be.

August 11, 2004

THE BOY WHOSE EYE WENT OUT

When he let his mind whisper to him
the one thing it always said
the one thing he and his mind knew for certain
they had their eyes open
they saw how things were
they could look up to the heavens
and see nothing there
even when they were flying through it
they still looked up.
Of course, there is nothing there
his mind would whisper.

Like a window shade
falling from its window at night
his eye fell into the bottom of his eye
he knew it in the morning
when he began seeing half of everything
there was his brother but his brother's wife was
one screen over
or so he reasoned for he could not see her
and his reason was used to supplying his vision
but then his mind whispered
something's wrong.

Your retina is detached as you are
and his mind whispered—
did he really say "as you are"
and then they went in and began working
trying to rehang his window shade.
His mind whispered I think they let in painters
who painted the window black
when they needed shade men
and for weeks he sat
one eye on the world
peering at the rest through reason.

He told them very simply
I look and there is nothing there
There is something there they said
you just cannot see it
they laid him back to let the workers in
when his mind whispered
the window's open a bit
I see a blade of light
is there a cord? Pull the cord
let the shade up. Let me see again.

Soon they were flying again
both arms straight out
both eyes wide open
with the light pouring in
till his mind whispered
we are flying blind
against every fiber of my being
after all the anger and frustration
to have both my eyes
and to be flying blind
straight across the universe
into nothing anyone can see.

February 24, 2005
Atlanta

ON THE GOOD LIFE OF DOLLY BARRANCO

In the little white pockets of her heart,
she kept her months and years like photographs,
till they tumbled all around her laughing
till there were too many days and faces
till again she let fall the tears of grace
till they ran down the lines of her smile.
Half a century ago, they wondered
how her tiny soul could climb the mountain
till one night they saw her flame rise before her
and four little licks of light like kite tails
flying in her wake till the night gave in.
And in her months and years, she ran circles
round the mountain till her family spread out
the way lilies of the field bring white light
to every dark patch till everyone knew
they loved her little fierce fire of faith.
And now, after daughter, wife, and mother,
after grandmother and great grandmother,
after all the months and years and masses
she climbs once more up the morning and turns
to blow a kiss to her field of flowers
and heads once more towards heaven to come home.

August 2005
Atlanta

TESTAMENT ONCE MORE

From their judicial chambers,
on the wings of courage and hope,
through day and night and day again,
they journeyed to America
to stand with their brothers and sisters in the law
on the edge of an open world,
to prove in the passing of a single week
that one could throw open a window
in Ukraine or in America
and breathe the same air.
And coming back,
walking through the streets of Ukraine,
coming in or out of their judicial chambers,
these five judges, this one doctor
would show again and again to the children
the rule of law and the promise of the future
and stand under the sky
where Schevchenko dreamed
to tell them:
we have seen the face of freedom
and it is ours.

November 3, 2005
Atlanta

THE LAKE THAT DROWNED ITS CITY

I flew over the tear-stained, mortified Pontchartrain
the lake that drowned its city.
Its vast undulating surface glinting in the sun
hiding its sorrow and its shame.
Swelling with pride after beating the hurricane,
it rose to peek at the big easy bowl of a city
and felt a tickle of fear
like a knife blade cutting through a diver's leg
below the water, the water masking everything
until the lake began to hemorrhage
bleeding through the levees.
The great lake tried to will itself to stop
but still it poured out and spilled into the city.
On Canal Street, they cried in the waters of Ponchatrain,
On St. Charles, streetcars stood naked and betrayed,
and in the parishes, the blood of the lake was everywhere.
In the Quarter, water rose and filled the trumpets,
and beneath every street light
and in the houses and the walls floating in the streets
there was no hope
there was no hope at all.

I went down to the water
and laid my hands on the lake
as it rose and fell in soft and silent sobbing.
I cried too.

April 2006
New Orleans

AUGUST 29, 2015 (KATRINA TURNS TEN)

Ten years later, this morning,
the sun rises up over Pontchartrain,
long ago forgiven, always remembering
what no one forgets.
This morning Pontchartrain is a movie screen,
and across the wide expanse of its shining face,
runs the miracle of Katrina receding
and New Orleans returning
and the eyes and faces and hearts and souls
of those who fought the battle.
The light chop of the lake in this light
looks like tears of joy
running down the face of Pontchartrain
the way the good times roll.

August 29, 2015
Atlanta

OUR LAST NINE: BROOKHAVEN, THE OLD COURSE

The fairways of Brookhaven have browned out
like the coarse, sunburnt stubble of the beards
on the faces of rugged men riding
in search of water and the green gone by.

Thus on its knees, we come to slay it now,
this course that never gave us any ground
we come to play and lay our memories down
to pay respects and play our final round.

The stubble of these browning fields will go
some rolling wave of green will turn them new
we will return and we will swing in time
and somewhere in that brand new time and place

this old course will come back to us like grace.

November 2007
Atlanta

ON REMEMBERING GRIFFIN BELL

This morning, your doctor heard the last beats
of your lion heart, of your eagle wings,
and listened to the brand new sound of things,
as your soul takes flight, as the past retreats.

Now we begin remembering for real,
as we believed remembering would feel,
wading through waters, pondering a choice,
listening for the rumble of your voice.

In your eyes smiling over your fingertips,
in the jagged cliffs of your penmanship,
as if you never left, never would at all,
I shall find you forever down the hall.

January 5, 2009
Atlanta

OF WHAT YOU HAVE WOVEN

Spinning oatmeal into chocolate you began,
your odyssey through the shoals of the South,
through plains and fields and streams that slowly ran,
determined eyes above determined mouth.

And so you wove your legend in your time,
this tapestry of friends within the law,
what you have woven rises above rhyme,
like lilacs ever blooming by the door.

Or lightships bravely riding savage shoals,
the way they hold their beacon lights aloft,
while inside weaving baskets weaving souls,
and from the crashing waves comes something soft.

Like Nantucket itself, beauty and truth,
a hook of land above swirling water,
the power of empowered dreams of youth,
the resolve of Alabama's daughter.

With your boat now safely on the shoreline,
and aglow in the bonfire of your friends,
now with your glass freshly filled with new wine,
tell stories from our book that never ends.

Words and wine are not enough to last you,
now take this friendship basket in your hands,
woven well with love enough to tell you,
You are our mighty lightship on the land.

November 2009
Atlanta

PORTRAIT OF THE ARTIST ON THE DUST JACKET

As I catch myself smiling,
I turn back to the dust jacket photo
and look into your black and white eyes.

I nod as if we had hold of the same metaphor,
or the same private semaphore.

I sing your serenade. I vote you in
as the Mayor of Schoolsville. And I turn back
over and over; we smile and nod
as if we have been winking friends forever,
because we have been winking friends forever,
all I do now is wink.

Even when we get down to the business
of the poems of others,
exposing themselves everywhere,
and here I am handing you one
like a leaflet for a ballet
that nobody watches.
Artless, airless—still, I wink.

December 2009
Atlanta (For Billy Collins)

Epigraph

I can almost see you now,
holding the poem,
waiting just one more polite moment
before you let it fall from the table
letting it waft down like a sigh
to the floor
by the little hole in the floorboard
where the mouse waits with a match.

FOR THE TUSKEGEE AIRMEN

Just as the unstoppable light of morning
lifts the dark curtain of a misbegotten night,
so the brave hearts of these men and women
rising up in the palm of America
in Tuskegee, Alabama
lifted the yoke of a broken world
and became the beginning of a brand new day.

From Moton Field, the Tuskegee Airmen,
the pilots, the navigators, the bombardiers,
the specialists, the machinists, the nurses,
the 99th, the 100th, the 301st, the 302nd, the 332nd,
they took a deep breath and took to the air
and rained down thunder and lightning on a world gone mad,
with red tails breaking through the mean-spirited clouds
that lead human hearts astray from what is right and just.

And now, decades and decades on,
we stand before our better angels from Tuskegee,
who took flight against all odds so that finally
we did overcome.

Doc Schneider
October 4, 2012

A POEM FOR ED MOSS

In the pockets of your life,
you carried all of Miami
like a handful of colorful, blown glass candies
that you gave away as treasures
to those who met the measure of your heart.
I hold mine in my hand right now and remember.

When I first found you, you were high above the glistening bay,
presiding over your lawyer's desk, wielding a fountain pen
plucked from a zippered case brimming with half a dozen others,
in an office that was all legal and nautical and aeronautical.
You walked me through the photographs that flanked you
your mother and your father and your sister,
your sons and your grandchildren, and in between them here and there,
you were everywhere, a man of the world
a star of the silver screen in black and white and color,
at the prow of Old Smuggler, at end of a perfect swing at La Gorce,
fighting a fish in the glinting sun, big square hands on the reel,
stepping into the cockpit of a plane or wearing a straw hat drink in hand
arm around a friend, lawyer and lion, larger than life.

You were a fisher of men and women,
you glided the boat of your friendship into our lives and lifted us out of the sea,
you took your friends to heart and took them home,
you nourished them at your bar and at your table
and filled them with so much laughter and affection
that they never left, they will never leave.
You let us inside your story, you let us see everything,
the loves of your life, the joy of your sons,
the success of your practice, the admiration of your peers,
the graceful way you walked with your father at the end of his life,
the courageous way you walked to the end of your own.

I hold the gift you gave me in the palm of my hand,
and stand in an ocean of eyes who do the same.
I know your code, your calling card, your highest praise,
"He is a friend," you would say— and that said it all for you.
It says it all for me too.

March 6, 2015
Miami

LIL MISS AAVAH

You were the infinitesimal petal
of a heavenly flower, tiny tumble,
little flutter of a precious soul.
We wrapped you in all the pieces of ourselves,
feeding you teardrops and scant slivers of wishes,
we banished our disbelief and threw open the windows
to let the hope in.

and tiny by tiny, wee by wee,
the whole flower of you arrived,
stood up, straightened your pink striped hat,
and set off to garden on the shoreline
wondrous innocent scooping the grains of sand.

Tuck this poem in your pocket, child,
whisper these words to your world,
Never forget what your family remembers
for you are their miracle girl.

July 2015
Atlanta

ANY SPRING BEFORE YOU

You kept the green gold
longer than it lasted
any spring before you
with the blue water of your eyes
you touched everything you touched
and left it shining.
Some song of songs sings as you go
and the first tips of green
in your next field of gold
tilt toward the sun and wait for you.

A TOAST TO BOB STEED

If I had a jacket
the color of a Cosmopolitan,
I would wear it for that Bowdon boy
who was such a metropolitan
and a patron of the arts
and a father and a prankster
and a lover and a brother
and a lawyer and a writer
and the fisher king of hearts.

But I don't have that jacket
so I raise this glass instead
and steal a laugh or two
repeating everything he said.
The provenance of clever
is not lost upon the crowd
and that's how I will raise a toast
to the man who lived out loud.

June 21, 2016
Atlanta

LITTLE
TALL TALES

CUPCAKES

A BIRTHDAY MEMORY

If you are between the moon and New York City, you usually can catch a cab up FDR drive, slide over the RFK bridge, hit the Long Island Expressway, shoot down Meadowbrook Parkway, pick up the Southern State, get off at Exit 31 Linden Street, and in about another mile or so, you can sail up Linden to Carmen Road, take a left past Our Lady of Lourdes Catholic Church and just after you cross back over the parkway, you will see on your left a non-descript collection of modern day Long Island condominiums in the post-War Long Island town of Massapequa Park.

If your memory comes with rewind, if you hit the back button about 50 years, the condos will fall away and in time a low lying brickish structure will emerge bearing the name Parkway Oaks Elementary School. And if your memory and imagination is so well-equipped that they can make 1950's era public schools out of 2010 condo outgrowths, well, then, you will be able to imagine me, in perpetual downsize motion, as I morph from evolved gorilla, broad-backed, Pickwick girthed, more pepper than salt laurels on a bald head, into a little dark-haired impish peanut of a soul, as thin as a string-bean, as dream driven and as ever gazing at the green light as the man the little soul would become in the fullness of time.

I do not know when Parkway Oaks lost its job as a school and turned over title to the condo developers, but it is pretty clear that the school never turned to me for a good recommendation. I have nothing good to say about Parkway Oaks. Even though the school song is forever ingrained in my mind because its author was the school music teacher—Miss Conneally—and she taught piano to my sister—and they would always end their piano practice sessions with that horrifyingly grating alma mater.

Parkway Oaks and I did not get along. And it is not because of Parkway Oaks. It was because of me. I might have been a little peanut of a soul but I was a troublesome one. I lived under an iron hand at home. As rigid as the ruling class of Parkway Oaks might be, they were not nearly as strong as the iron hand that pulled the strings during non-school hours.

School for me was a chance to go wild—and go wild I did. I was not in the least Pavlovian about it. Going wild was met with an immediate call home—and although the iron hand delivered iron for each romp, I never tired of pushing the envelope and breaking every rule I thought I could get away with. Looking back, I broke a lot of rules, and never got away with any of them. But I kept at it. I was a defiant little kid.

What I remember most sadly now is that my teachers seemed to have no affection for me. My overwhelming sense is that they saw no promise in me, just trouble. And they watched me like a hawk. I felt that way about the whole world. All Mr. Murdstones, no Peggotties anywhere to be found, no Betsy Trotwood. It is a perpetual mystery to me how I emerged so optimistic, and I like to think it could not have been half as bad as I remember. There must have been something good, although I will be damned if I can remember what it was.

As a child, I lived a life of crime. As some dark shadow of original sin, I was prone to an uncontrollable longing for candy corn, Suzy-Qs, cupcakes, ice cream, pizza, Wetson's hamburgers and shakes. I was forever a stocky man trapped in my Slim Jim boyhood body of a street urchin from Bombay.

While we lived a more than comfortable middle class life and while sugarplums of all sorts descended at Easter and Christmas, it was a long dry spell in between in a family which did not believe in catering to a boyish sweet tooth, especially not mine. Instead of accepting my lot in life and holding in check my unquenchable appetites, I devised all manner of schemes and techniques for acquiring what I considered to be the rightful fruits of youth. Thus, given 50 cents to take rugs to the coin- operated laundry, I figured out how to stuff all of the rugs in a single machine, choking it to death, so that I could salvage a quarter for a shopping spree: 10 cents for a hamburger; 6 cents for a box of candy.

When I did not have the coin of the realm, I turned to the tricks of Fagin, pick pocketing from the shelves of unsuspecting stores my rightful treasures. And that is only the beginning of my rap sheet. Given that history, what I am about to tell you about what happened when I turned seven is not surprising at all.

As I recall, I was in second grade with Mrs. Gibson, who in the silvery frame of memory was something like Mrs. Gulch. She did not like me at all. She was forever ringing the phone off the hook at my house to report to my mother what sin I committed that day. Sometimes, old Mrs. Gulch would tell me when she had called my mother, and other times she wouldn't. On days that I knew she had called, I would ride the bus home, dreading the punishment that was surely to come. And come it did. But on days when she did not tell me she had called, I would ride home dreaming of petty thefts, only to come through the door and confront punishment I did not expect. What surprises me now is that I never gave in. I took my punishment—

regardless of how fierce—and I went back the next day to Mrs. G's class and kicked up dust unabashed.

Mrs. Gibson had a little birthday tradition of having the birthday child bring a birthday treat for the whole class, which would be shared at the end of the day. In March 1961, my birthday came rolling around and I told my mother that I would have to bring something for the 20 or so students in my class. My mother was superb at celebrating events like birthdays and she was not going to let her little troublemaker down. She set about to make something for the whole class that they would really enjoy. I remember watching her as she made twenty absolutely perfect chocolate iced cupcakes.

After she finished making them, she went into her kitchen cabinets and emerged with two round tins with lids on them. She removed the lids and in a miraculous example of careful planning, placed 10 cupcakes each into those two tins. I tried to keep my emotions in check as I watched each cupcake take its place in the tin. My mother carefully shimmied each one into place and then put the lids on. She put the tins into the refrigerator so they would be cold and fresh when I took them to school in the morning.

I woke up on March 10 that year to Happy Birthdays from my brother and sister and my mother. My father had slipped back between the moon and New York City long before I awoke, sliding in his Dodge Dart in the early dawn towards Wall Street. My mother said that we would have cake and presents that night, and she got me ready for school. As I left the house to walk to the corner bus stop, she gave me those two tins, one on top of the other.

When I got to Parkway Oaks, I walked down the long linoleum halls, carrying my precious cargo of two tins, like an altar boy bringing gifts to the altar. I entered the classroom, got to my desk in the back row, and loaded the tins into the little cubbyhole under my desk. And so the day began.

For an inconsolable half hour, it seemed to me that I was sitting atop Aladdin's lamp—all my dreams came true inside those two colorful tins. I began to think bad thoughts. I tried to suppress them. They overcame me.

As I remember now, it was about 30 minutes after school began that I carefully, criminally, using all my gifts of stealth, slipped one of those tins out from beneath my desk and on to my lap beneath my desk. My original hardly sinful plan was just to eat cupcake No. 1—the one for me.

With my tiny burglar's fingers, I silently, painstakingly worked the cover off the tin, slowly, methodically held the lid in place, while my other hand plucked one of the iced marvels from the company of its companions. Carefully, I replaced the cover, unwrapped the cupcake, and through a series of furtive movements, hidden behind math books and Dick and Jane readers, popped an entire cupcake into my mouth, and devoured it in quick, tight-lipped maneuvers from the rapturous first taste to the sensual swallow.

Ms. G was clueless. She droned on and on in her high-pitched wail studded with numbers and letters and places and things, as I pulled off the heist of the century right in front of her eyes.

It was my intention to only eat MY cupcake.

Somehow, the darkness got a hold of me, and on 17 more occasions that day, I repeated my sleight of hand, popped a cake, closed the lid, wait a bit, repeat. I knew disaster loomed ahead but I could not stop myself.

As I filled beyond belief with cupcakes, I began conceiving wild plans of how I would extricate myself from this situation. Could I claim to need to throw up and dash to the door wildly and hide out in the woods for a week? My mind whirled through a thousand ideas -- until my frightened reverie was interrupted.

"And now, boys and girls, we have come to the end of our day, and it is time to celebrate little Dickie's birthday today," oozed Mrs. Gibson.

The usual cheer went up, as children rose from their desks and gathered round Ms. G's desk.

"Come on up here, Dickie, " said Mrs. Gulch, " and bring what you brought."

I knew enough to leave the container that was totally empty behind in my desk. I grabbed the one that still had some heft. I could not recall how many were left—my movements were so fast, so furtive, I confused myself.

I came up to the desk, and Mrs. Gibson noticed the glum look on my face. She took the canister and opened it. There in that shiny space sat two lonely cupcakes. Two. Out of 20, all that were left were two.

"What is this?" Mrs. Gibson squealed, the flush of red anger coming up in her face.

"I told my mother it would never be enough, " I said. That was one of the lies I cooked up as a possible escape scenario.

Some do-gooder chimed in:

"Dickie ate them all—he ate our cupcakes," he screamed.

Mrs. Gibson dismissed the class, while holding fast to my arm.

"We are going to call your mother, young man, " she said.

Listening to that phone call nearly killed me. I heard my mother's disbelief and then abject apology coming through the earpiece, down across Mrs. Gibson's hateful face, and right down in front of me like an indictment.

Outside, when I waited for the bus, I thought about walking over to the shopping center and seeing if I could catch a bus somewhere far away. I knew I could make it. I was brave. God knows, I wasn't hungry.

But I did not do it. I went home and took my medicine. And yes, there was no birthday cake and no presents. And we did not sing me happy birthday.

I just went to bed with a sore backside, read a little bit of my Hardy Boys, pulled the cover up to my neck, thought about what I had done— and I laughed. I knew even then that I would never forget that day and I didn't.

I have since eaten all the cupcakes—so to speak several times—one day, I am going to be nothing but a good boy. But that day has not yet come.

Doc Schneider
March 2010

THE RED HOT PAPER CLIP

In June 1978, I was in my last year of serving in the U.S. Navy Reserves as a hospital corpsman—which is the Navy and Marine's version of a medic. A year earlier, I had resigned as the Deputy Brigade Commander of the Class of 1979 at the United States Naval Academy—much to the Superintendent's disbelief.

The Admiral's revenge was to send me to a Marine Reserve Unit where my two weeks of summer duty consisted of a mock attack on the shores of North Carolina.

Our mission was to set up a MASH unit on the beach, while the fighting units attacked the shore to re- take Camp Geiger. I had just graduated from Auburn University—and I had left my wife, Helen, and our baby-to-be at her parent's home in Dothan, Alabama, while I served my country.

We decided to attack Camp Geiger by sea. I was riding in a smallish naval vessel, heading for an unloading where we would have to scramble up netting draped over the side of a huge Navy amphibious ship, to scurry up the sides of the ship, like rats climbing upward out of the sea to get on board.

In a day or so, we would ride out in duck boats from the mouth of the big ship—hell-bent to attack the coast. I remember how the mouths of those duck boats opened, and we marched out with packs on our back in full marine fatigues and helmets, rifles held high, as we jumped into the swirling surf. But that is another story. For the story told here is about a day or two before we jumped into the water.

While on the little vessel, I enjoyed the sun-kissed waves skipping in the distance, the painted blue sky—and my mind wandered to the past and the future—and left the present. My right index finger, however, did not join me in my daydreaming, and it lingered on the edge of a hatch that served as the center skylight for the pilot's cabin—from which the vessel was commanded and where the helmsman was at the wheel.

The sun-kissed water and the wind conspired at that moment to whip up a huge set of waves that began leaping up on to the deck of our small craft like playful dolphins. Water began spraying into the cabin where the vessel captain piloted the boat.

One particularly playful wave leapt up in the air and appeared to be intent on pouring itself directly into the hatch hole. One of the cabin crew saw it coming and grabbed the hatch cover to slam the hatch shut, like a submarine captain, scrambling down a ladder while pulling the hatch down above him.

All wonderful.

Except that my right index nail was on the hatch rim.

"Hey," I said bravely, and used my left hand to make an upward uncoiling gesture to signal the anxious crewman to undo the hatch so that I could remove my finger.

The wave had slithered back into the sea by then, and the hatch was lifted up. I removed my finger which was then only a hazy shade of purple at the edges. I put it in my mouth for a moment of safekeeping and comfort—and then removed it, declaring that all was well.

Our tiny vessel then came along side the gargantuan gray painted ship that rose from the surface of the ocean like some fantastic blade of Poseidon's trident. We climbed up the rope netting, a succession of souls pursing their sailor's dreams.

On board, we headed for our quarters, unpacked our packs—I had a bunk slung from the ceiling. In those days, I was as thin as a slice of paper, and I easily fit between my mattress and the bulkhead ceiling directly above my head. It was a space of about a foot and half between the mattress and the ceiling. (If I climbed into such a bunk now, one of two things would happen. The mattress would fall from the ceiling from whence it hung, or I would have become lodged in the space so tightly, that I would need to diet for two months before I could release myself.)

After checking out our assigned bunks, getting a feel for it, we went and had a meal in the ship's mess hall—eating as the trays slipped this way and that in rhythm with the waves that gently tossed the mighty ship. We swabbed a few decks, painted a few rust patches, watched a movie on the aft deck and went to sleep.

In the meantime, the color purple grew.

I occasionally held out my finger before me like a foreign object, inspecting it—gazing at the Aurora Borealis being painted on the nail from below by some tiny Michelangelo. It felt a bit uncomfortable—but I was young and brave and not about to complain.

That night, we climbed to our various perches to be rocked to sleep by our creator in the gentle cradle of the waves.

I lay dressed in white skivvies, my dog tag around my neck, and conjured up visions of Helen—who lay in the deep south in a bare-shouldered kerchief of a blouse. Beneath the blouse lay the promise of July, where she carried a little baby who was to be born two weeks later—tiny Heather Elizabeth. I dreamed of those shoulders and that baby to be.

I suppose it was about an hour or so after I climbed up into the bunk to begin dreaming that the nightmare began.

My index finger began to send out a throbbing Morse code of pain. At first, it was a beat or two, separated by long intervals.

Quiet and small at the outset, they grew louder and bigger and unbelievably painful. I tried to quell the pain with my mind. I tried to imagine those shoulders, that shirt—I tried to focus on Helen's smile and laughter.

Nothing was working. The Morse code of pain pulsed on like a scream coming from my beneath my nail and then in no time, from my whole finger, and then it seemed like someone should hack my arm off, so fierce was the pain.

I felt like my finger had the worst ten toothaches I had ever had in my life. I swung my head from side to side. I held my finger up—momentary relief, and then the code again. I draped it down—crushing pain. I put it in my mouth and felt its throbbing pulse echo through my skull. Around me, my fellow sailors-for-two-weeks-a-year breathed in perfect harmony -- as my finger consumed my life and was sure to stop my heart.

I decided to go to the head (the bathroom) to run cold or hot water over my finger. I did some sort of maneuver to get myself dislodged from my sleeping perch, hung in the air, stepping on a ladder or bunks below me to reach the deck.

I was a skinny, white-shirted, white-shorted kid, with a wife and baby- to-be in Alabama, with a finger dipped in permanent merlot that was about to kill me in the gaping maw of a naval vessel.

I got to the head, the Morse code coming in endless dashes of blinding pain, and I tried cold water and hot water. I tried to tie my tee shirt around the finger to cut off the blood supply. I looked around for morphine, heroin or a gun. I was staggered by the ravenous pain that had engulfed my finger, hand, arm and now was hungry for the rest of my body.

I decided I could not take it any longer. I was a hospital corpsman, but I did not know how to fix me or save me—but I did know that if a man went down on the battlefield with a serious wound, you slid along the ground to get by his side and inject him with morphine. I concluded that I needed to get to the medical office on the ship and jab morphine into my legs until I began to see Timothy Leary.

I staggered along the bulkheads and climbed to the deck that housed the corpsman headquarters. My finger screamed in agony. Beneath the door, a blade of light bled out into hall—was someone actually awake? I knocked with my good hand, as my other hand screamed and cried.

The door swung open and a red-bearded corpsman petty officer in full uniform greeted me. He could see right away that something was wrong as I gave him the finger. He picked up the phone and made a call. I can't tell you what he said. I could not hear over the screaming.

Within a few minutes, another corpsman petty officer appeared in the door, in full uniform, ready for action at 2:00 in the morning.

"Slammed his finger," said Red Beard.

"Uh huh, "acknowledged Corpsman 2.

"Is there something you can give me?" I asked pitifully, offering a vein.

"We'll take care of it," Red Beard said. I began to think of Eugene O'Neil and Long Days Journey into the Night—and how I would have to go into detox to get off the morphine, but I was ready to get strung out.

I watched Red Beard fumble in his draw and pull out a copper paper clip. He reached into his pocket and fished out a lighter, emblazoned with the crest of the ship we were on.

In those days, every sailor smoked. I had a lighter in my pocket—although I did not have my pockets with me. I was confused by the appearance of the paper clip and the lighter. I suspected Red Beard was going to take out a spoon and cook us up some smack. But that was fine with me. I had to stop the screaming.

Red Beard unbent the paper clip, straightened it out and held it in the flame of his Ronsin lighter. He held it there for a minute or too—and it began to glow like smelting iron—a glowing smoldering red, red yellow heat.

Red Beard gazed at me, and Corpsman No. 2 did too. I watching anxiously as the screaming mounted, the Morse code sending telegram after telegram, each with a single word—"HELP."

I sat at a table across from Red Beard, with my arm laying across the table, my right vein exposed and ready. Although I was a trained corpsman, I did not care about cleaning my site of injection with an alcohol swab—I did not care about the needle and the damage done. I needed relief.

As I readied for hallucinations, Red Beard and Corpsman No. 2 swung into unexpected action.

"Grab him," Red Beard ordered.

Corpsman No. 2 somehow got himself in front of me, and grabbed my right hand, and held it down on the table applying the full force of his body. My natural reaction was to pull away, but this big block of a guy held my hand in place, like the scene of Luca Bracci at the bar in The Godfather where they garrote him.

At this point, Red Beard grabbed the screaming finger with his left hand, and held the red hot paper clip in his right hand—and my eyes could hardly believe what happened next. Red Beard plunged the paper clip directly into the purple screaming nail on my index finger—and as quickly as he plunged it in, he pulled it out.

I gasped. My eyes popped forward in disbelief and in excruciating pain. Just when I did not think the screaming could get worse, it got worse—my whole body began screaming for what seemed like a second or so—and then the screaming ended. Like a conductor lifting a baton in front of a sea of banshees—and signaling them all in the same moment to put their lips together and stop. A great hush.

A volcanic explosion of purple and red and white and green erupted through the hole in my nail, shooting up into the air and raining down on the table of Pompeii. The pressure and pain beneath my nail was relieved in an enormously painful, enormously shocking and enormously thrilling moment.

Red Beard looked at me like a wise man from the forest looking at a young warrior who just learned a lesson that saved his life. Corpsman No. 2 released my arm and my hand.

"Holy shit," I said. It was one of the few prayers I knew by heart.

"Get some rack time," Red Beard said. He gave me four aspirins. "You won't need 'em, but have 'em. But it should be okay now."

"Thank you, man," I said. "I never even heard about this technique in corps school."

"This is what you learn at sea, college boy," Red Beard said.

I rose like Lazarus and walked out in the passageway—born again. I began to dream of shoulders and babies—and the wonder of mankind and the ways in which we have discovered solutions to save each other. I climbed the wall of bunks to my perch on the ceiling. There was no screaming; there was only the slow wave upon wave of deep breaths until sleep came to take me—alive once more.

Doc Schneider
December 2010

ACKNOWLEDGMENTS

A special thank you to Andrew Dubrock who transcribed the songs for this book. I followed Andrew's work for years in Acoustic Guitar magazine, as I played numerous songs that he transcribed so well for that wonderful publication. He is the best there is—in addition to being a profoundly gifted musician, author, and instructor—and it was one of the many miracles of my musical life that he signed on for the mission here. I appreciate his attentive and painstaking transcriptions. Thank you, Andrew.

I also want to thank Dr. Marc Jolley, Jim Burt, and Mercer University Press for their tireless work and dedication to this project. I knew the Mercer Press could make me look good. I have been riding its coattails forever. Thank you for the ride.

I want to thank all the writers and songwriters who put pen to paper and moved me—especially those who wrote and sang so well and played so memorably that I saw the fire and the rain and the distant water and I heard the dynamite in the distance. You have been my friends and that has always been the sweetest part. You gave me the moments and fragments that I have shored against my ruins.

I want to thank David Romine, Jeff Jacobs, Ben Wisch, and Eugene Ruffolo who lifted me from the river—and especially Eugene who always lets me borrow his truck.

And I want to thank my daughters, my Little Bud, my Funky Bunch, my great big family, my wonderful friends, Mercer University and King & Spalding—I know you have carried me in the palm of your hands and I am grateful.

And finally, I will end where all things began. On Stanford Drive. With Helen. All I had to do was hold on. I love you, Helen. This is not the page I promised—but it's a start.

Doc Schneider
September 3, 2016 (39 Years)

ABOUT THE AUTHOR

Doc Schneider is a Senior Partner in the international law firm of King & Spalding LLP and a Fellow of the American College of Trial Lawyers. He graduated from Mercer University's School of Law in 1981 and eventually served as Chairman of the Board of Trustees of Mercer University from 2013–15. He currently serves as the Chairman of Mercer University Press. His life began in earnest in 1976 when he met Helen Schroll in Alabama. And then came daughters Heather and Kristin and grandchildren McKenzie, Madison, Zachary, and Zoe. Doc and Helen live in Atlanta in the light of their family and friends.